GOD

THE CONTEMPORARY DISCUSSION SERIES

SEXUAL ARCHETYPES, EAST AND WEST

SEXUAL ARCHETYPES, EAST AND WEST

EDITED BY
BINA GUPTA

A NEW ERA BOOK

PARAGON HOUSE
New York

Published in the United States by
PARAGON HOUSE PUBLISHERS
2 Hammarskjöld Plaza
New York, New York 10017

A New Ecumenical Research Association Book.

Library of Congress Cataloging-in-Publication Data

Sexual Archetypes, East and West.

(God, The Contemporary Discussion Series)
"A New ERA book."
Bibliography:
Includes Index.
1. Women and religion—Congresses. 2. Sex role—Religious aspects—Congresses. 3. Archetype (Psychology)—Congresses. I. Gupta, Bina, 1947- . II. Series.
HQ1393.S49 1987 261.8'3442 86-25441
ISBN 0-913757-59-4
ISBN 0-913757-68-3 (pbk.)

In memory of my father,
the late Dharam Bhushan Bansal,
who made all things possible,
and to my daughter, Swati,
who makes all things worthwhile.

Contents

Foreword

An obvious feature of modern life is the intensified struggle of minorities and other oppressed peoples the world over for social justice, economic opportunity, and cultural equity. Such overarching goals naturally admit of many different interpretations and expressions. Overall, however, the dominant movement has been away from the marginality to which subordinate groups traditionally have been consigned and toward full participation in the mainstream of social life.

At some point in the struggle for a new place in the social order, protagonists typically begin to press their claim for a more useful past. Mythical and real heroes are discovered; a record of past injustices is placed on display; neglected sources are culled for whatever supportive documentation they supply. In the American setting, for example, the emergence of Afro-American and Native American histories affords instructive cases in point. Illustrations from countless other subcultures throughout the world might likewise be adduced. In each instance, a past is constructed from which oppressed peoples may derive a sense of collective identity and legitimacy.

The case of women, however, is somewhat different. As Gerder Lerner noted some years ago in her presidential address to the American Historical Association, women have had a historical experience dissimilar from that of men. On the one hand, women appear in all classes and ranks of society; and they share, by virtue of their connections with males, many of the values, aspirations and forms of life experienced by their male counterparts within a given class, race, culture, or ethnic group. On the other hand, like colonials, women hardly constitute a minority, despite the obvious fact that more often than not they have been treated as such. Hence, women sometimes live and function in a *separate* culture *within* the larger societal milieu. Moreover, unlike many other subordinate groups, women are divided among themselves by culture, class, race, ethnicity, and religion.

Nevertheless, it is a commonplace to observe how women always have been participants in the work of civilization-building. And if until recently women have lacked the wherewithal to reclaim their own past, that situation is now changing. Slowly but inexorably, a women's culture is being recorded, analyzed and celebrated. As new questions are raised, there is a burgeoning awareness of, and appreciation for, the role of women as co-creators of human history.

Part and parcel of the international women's movement is a critical reappraisal of all features of culture, both past and present, serving to reinforce the subordinate status assigned to women. Among the many cultural determinants of subordination must be counted the influence of religious tradition.

Even the most casual student of comparative religion cannot help being impressed by the ubiquity of female figures in the world's pantheon of deities. Long before the dawn of recorded history, the figure of the Earth Mother in one guise or another epitomized the impulse of desire and love, the spirit of fecundity, germination and fruition so necessary for human survival. She was to find multiple incarnations among the ancient Semites as Ashtoreth, Ashtar or Astarte; she was revered as Ishtar by the peoples of Mesopotamia; she was known to the Phrygians as Cybele; and worshipped by the Persians as Anaitis.

Little ingenuity is required to discern her later appearance among the Greek Olympians as Aphrodite or as the goddess Venus in Roman mythology. Many of the same attributes belonged to Isis, the all-important sister-consort to the great Egyptian god Osiris. Nerthu was the archetypal Earth Mother of the Teutons, as was Freyja, goddess of fertility. In many of the world's religions, female deities thus assume a place of prominence, whether one thinks of Kuan Yin, the goddess of mercy in Chinese Buddhism, the Shinto sun goddess, or the Hindu goddess variously represented as Durgā, Satī, Pārvatī or the malevolent Kalī.

Only within the world's three great monotheistic traditions—Judaic, Christian, and Islamic—do feminine ascriptions and characterizations of the divine appear to be lacking altogether. Discounting for a moment the medieval cult of the Virgin Mother within Orthodox and Roman Catholicism, in the West divine attributes have been exclusively masculine in character, reflective perhaps of the patriarchical cultures in which Judaism, Christianity and Islam originated.

The ploy adopted by some feminist Christians, of course, has been to expunge gender-linked references to the deity from all liturgical observances and the scriptural canon, substituting female or neutered pronouns wherever possible. Yet for many celebrants, so radical an expurgation is neither theologically persuasive nor aesthetically pleasing. The resultant artificiality, some critics claim, only serves to highlight the need for a more creative approach to the development of an adequate theology of feminine consciousness.

The chief virtue of the present collection of papers, it seems to me, lies in its potential for extending discussion in novel directions. Moving beyond now-familiar issues of cultural sex-role determination or biology, this volume will encourage its readers to think afresh the multiple connections between religious ideology and feminist awareness, between empiric male-female relationships and the images through which religious beliefs have found expression throughout history.

Above all, what is herein supplied is an opportunity to reexamine the metaphysical and ontological underpinnings upon which sexual stereotypes have been thought to depend. Each paper in its own fashion explores the dimensions of the linkage, analyzing, criticizing and highlighting the many subsidiary issues deserving closer scrutiny.

An obvious advantage of the strategy pursued is that gender-linked social patterns and roles are highlighted in cross-cultural perspective. The discussion is far-ranging, including many divergent religious and philosophical strains, and it is not limited to any particular setting or cultural situation. One may hope, therefore, in the final analysis that *Sexual Archetypes, East and West* will succeed in achieving the goal implied by its title, namely, to enrich philosophic debate over sexual archetypes and to carry the discussion in a new and more fruitful direction. At a very minimum, it is reasonable to expect that this compilation will mark a useful point of departure for such an ambitious undertaking.

CHRISTOPHER J. LUCAS
Professor, Department of Higher
and Adult Education
Director, Center for International
Programs and Studies
University of Missouri-Columbia

Preface

This volume is an outcome of the growing interest in women and, in particular, of the emergence of a concern about women and religion that has swept through academic disciplines within the humanities and the social sciences. The result is a partial reconstruction of the proceedings of a conference entitled, "Is There a Divine Intention for Male-Female Relationships?" held in Seoul, Korea, August 9–15, 1984. The conference was sponsored by the New Ecumenical Research Association (New ERA) whose aim is to promote interreligious, cross-cultural dialogue.

All the papers presented at the conference were distributed to the participants two months prior to the conference, along with prepared critiques. This left the conference time free for extended exchange on the disparate viewpoints presented. In preparing this volume, I wanted to give the reader a sense of the diversity, breadth, and scope of the topics covered. Out of the twenty papers presented, I have selected eleven, by scholars from traditions both East and West.

From time immemorial, patterns of interaction between the sexes have provided religion with its chief imagery, and this relationship in turn has had a profound effect on the way in which men and women have viewed their respective existences. The essays in this volume fill a growing need to reexamine the role of religion in shaping the cultural images of women. They raise such questions as these: To what extent, as is sometimes argued, were religions responsible for combating an earlier degradation of women? Have religions had a beneficial effect on the social status of women in modern times? It is a major goal of this volume to provide an impetus for further research on these questions.

An introductory essay attempts to supply background on the circumstances that brought a select group of scholars together to discuss the role of religion behind male-female relationships.

Although summary references to the papers themselves appear, it was not my intention to allude to each and every one of them, nor to discuss each contribution except as it illustrates the broader themes explored within the narrative.

I wish to express my gratitude to Professors Joel Brereton, Christopher Lucas, and Krishna Sivaraman for many insightful suggestions made and courtesies extended. I also wish to thank Trish Love and Sally Henrikson for the graciousness with which they carried out the many clerical tasks involved in the preparation of this manuscript. I want to acknowledge my appreciation to the Research Council of the Graduate School, University of Missouri-Columbia, for giving me a modest grant to cover the typing and xeroxing expenses of the manuscript.

BINA GUPTA

1
Introduction

This volume has grown out of the 1984 meeting of the theme group, "Is There a Divine Intention for Male-Female Relationships," of the Fourth God Conference: Contemporary Discussions, held in Seoul, Korea. This theme holds a special appeal at a time when so much attention is being paid to gender-linked roles and social patterns.

In recent years, relationships between men and women have aroused a great deal of debate and often acrimonious polemics. Participants in these exchanges have devoted a greal deal of time and energy to what is certainly an important contemporary issue. Yet, protagonists have very rarely expressed any awareness that these issues rank among the most ancient in human thought, and that different cultures have treated them in variant ways.

The present volume, *Sexual Archetypes, East and West* addresses enduring and recurrent themes in male-female relationships the world over. In any sophisticated discussion, investigation will begin with the temporal status of sex roles; that is to say, with an inquiry as to whether sex roles have an ontological status and therefore take on the supertemporal qualities of archetypes. Or, the alternative possibility, that they are primarily culture-specific to the milieu in which they appear, will be considered.

It is in reaction to such questions that much of the contemporary debates about sex roles have appeared. Margaret Mead, for example, after an anthropological field study in New Guinea in the 1930s, became convinced that "natural sex temperament" was a fiction, and that prevailing sex and temperament traits appropriate to males and females were determined by the social conditions of particular cultures. The cultural values and the social structures with reference to the family organization—the modes of child-rearing—filtered out some characteristics and reinforced others. She concluded that "many, if not all, of the personality traits which we have called masculine or feminine are as lightly linked to sex as are the clothing, the manners, and the form of hair dress that a society at a given period assigns to either sex."[1] To cite another example, feminists who wish to promote equality between the sexes have argued that stereotypical sex roles are culture specific and therefore lack any logical justification. They insist that therefore there is no inherent reason why the changes which they advocate cannot be effected and enforced by law. Consequently, it becomes all the more urgent for scholars who possess an understanding of the evolution of sex roles to deal with this issue in an informed manner.

Sexual archetypes are not merely categories of human experience indicative of the psychological structuring of the human mind. They should be understood more on the model of Platonic ideas; not in the sense that they exist in some transcendent sphere, but in the sense that they are rooted in the objective order of reality. This view appears in classical traditions and in modern developments of thought in the East as well as in the West. The male/female polarization in life and experience is understood as reflecting the polarity in the sexual archetypes themselves. I am not simply abstracting the sexual archetypes from the experience of the interaction between the male and the female with its tension and complementariness; however, sexual archetypes for us are exemplified in such a relationship.

Perhaps under the influence of the model of the physical sciences, some of the early seminal figures who worked with these problems, such as Freud and Jung, tended to treat sex roles as having a status that went beyond the simple psychological understanding of the issue under consideration. Although it is Jung who gave currency to the word "archetype," Freud himself clearly believed that such a configuration as the Oedipal complex and such depth-psychological structures as the *ego* and the *id* were universal.

However, in this book it is necessary to clarify in which precise sense we are using the word, modifying the Jungian conceptualization of the category. Jung understood the structure of the human psyche in more than the empirical, psychological sense of the term, as something verifiable in terms of experience. Jung's theory of archetypes proposes to universalize certain culture-specific patterns which he found in his own culture.

Other interpretations of these patterns are possible, however. We know that a number of Jung's archetypes, such as that of the "quest," for example, are not present in widely diverse cultures. To cite another example, he discusses the Trinity as an archetype, though it is a concept formed within a specific patriarchal culture. It may be said that cultures and cultural patterns arise in response to their own socio-historical context. All human activity takes its distinct shape within a cultural setting, and it tends to bear the mark of that culture.

In this volume, the term "archetype" is used in a rather loose sense. If we may permit ourselves a generalization, the term may be described as having reference to the ontological nature of things: it is more reflective of the way things are, and as pertaining to the objective order of reality. The male-female aspect nevertheless is termed archetypal in that the psyche or the unconscious perceives the order of reality.

Like Platonic ideas in which reality participates, archetypes also refer to something supra-temporal, eternal, or perennial. That is, if we find discernible structures in the male-female interaction, we treat them rather as instantiations of a more primal relation. The reality provides the grounds for such an instantiation. Instantiation means that the biological, cultural, and psychological dimensions of the male/female polarization are equally to be viewed as dimensions of a more primordial reality.

The essays in this book analyze a generally neglected aspect of sex roles, namely, their religious origins and ritualistic significance. Without such treatment, we would be dealing with a purely sociological controversy. While sex and religion may seem opposed—since sex is physical and temporal, so to speak, and religion is spiritual and eternal—in reality, their interaction has provided the internal dynamics for many societies.

From the very beginning, patterns of interaction between the sexes have provided religion with its chief imagery and this in turn has had a profound effect on the way physical men and women have been able to view their respective existences. For example, although three great monotheistic religions of the world—Christianity, Judaism, and Islam—have no sexual duality in their conceptions of the deity, they nevertheless endow sex roles with divine authority. If we are ever to transcend intellectual parochialism, we must understand that in most societies throughout history sex roles have taken on a religiously defined meaning. Thus, religious equivalents for concepts which have recently become fashionable, such as androgyny, equality of the sexes, and so on, may be found at various times in human history. No one can question that in this age, when sexual roles are being redefined, both men and women can benefit from investigation of the spiritual dimension of this debate.

I

In the history of Christianity, women, like men, have had spiritual significance—but with certain reservations applied. It is true that in the Middle Ages woman was acknowledged as the inspiration as well as guide on the path to spiritual progress, as personified in Dante's Beatrice, for example. The gnostic sects conceived that the third person of the Trinity—the Holy Spirit—was feminine in gender, and therefore, the Trinity for them included a father, a son, and a mother (a counterpart, as it were, of the Hindu depiction in art and literature of divinity as the Holy Family consisting of Śiva together with his spouse Parvati and Skanda their son). Although such concepts do not have any place in the official theology of the Greek Orthodox Christian Church, such concepts have found covert expression in art and literature, again, as in Dante's *Divine Comedy.*

There was a trend toward quaternity in Christian thought, as for example, in the elevation of the Holy Virgin to the position in which she roughly came close to the status of divinity, almost a *persona* within the divine life, a sort of co-savior with the Christ. In any event, for the devotional perspective of many Roman Catholics, her significance surpassed the Holy Spirit and occasionally approached indeed the other *personae* of the Trinity. However, Protestantism, in its struggle against all human mediators between God and man, removed this symbolic meaning of the Holy Virgin. The female element in the symbolic expression of the divine came to be eliminated.

Against this background, Professor Cousins in his paper "Male-Female Aspects of the Trinity in Christian Mysticism," attempts to redress the balance and to recover the deeper spiritual significance of God for Christianity. His paper explores male-female aspects of the divinity as a basis for human relations through a study of the Christian mystical texts of Bonaventure. The analysis turns on the distinction between "mystical" and "theological" understanding of the Trinity and what lies beyond it. The images of Father and Son, the Trinitarian archetype, are patriarchal in character, since they are rooted in the ancient Hebrew culture, and reflect the exclusively male symbolism of Judaism. But beyond these lies the "abyss" of

Godhead, the *Wüste* of the Godhead (reminding one of the Hindu Brahman and Buddhist *śūnyatā*), which Professor Cousins interprets as the female aspect of the Trinity. Extending the principle of consubstantiality of the Trinity to the female "abyss" of the divinity, Professor Cousins contemplates the relation between the male and the female in the archetype as one of coincidence of opposites, of mutually affirming complementarity, which provides a divine grounding for the relation of male and female in terms, not of subordination, but of mutuality.

Taking Karl Jaspers' theory of the Axial Period between 800 and 200 B.C. as a point of departure, Professor Cousins believes that at present we are passing through a Second Axial Period in which the female archetype is emerging as the characteristic aspect of the new consciousness. In this integral and multi-dimensional consciousness the human community is rediscovering on a global level the female characteristics of the Pre-Axial Period without sacrificing the distinctive male values of Axial consciousness. Such a consciousness will integrate the two archetypes according to the principle of coincidence of opposites of mutually affirming complementarity.

Professor Barnhouse makes the same point in her paper "A Christian Speculation on the Divine Intention for the Man-Woman Relationship," when she states that we are in the process of evolving toward a new form which will be characterized by mutuality. She examines scripture and tradition to show the implications of the notion that the God of the Judaic-Christian tradition is androgynous and, further, that in order to create us in God's image it was necessary to create *both* man and woman. The relation between men and women is only one aspect of the relation between the masculine and feminine principles in the world. The proper relation is one of harmony and balance, which in turn depends on full equality between the two, and a theology of sex in which sex is regarded as a symbol of wholeness, reconciliation and at-one-ment. Western patriarchal culture, which has governed the world for at least some 3,000 years, makes it difficult to understand and implement such an ideal.

The patriarchal society itself is cause for the question, "Eve, where are you?" raised by Ms. Pascaline Coff. From time immemorial masculine qualities have been developed to the exclusion of the feminine. In men and women alike religions primarily have contributed to this imbalance. She exhorts Christians, especially monastics within the church, to reflect deeply on the place of the feminine in Christianity. Her paper therefore examines the divine intention for male-female relationships, the polarity that permeates not only creation but also the Godhead. The investigation proceeds by examining the concepts of *yin/yang, anima/animus* and androgyne. *Yin/yang* are viewed as the "gates of change," *anima/animus* as "gateways" to the self in the movement toward "wedding within," and androgyne is seen as the symbol of supreme identity in religious systems. She maintains that unless the fullness of receptivity, the feminine quality, is discovered in every human being so that receptivity to the spirit can be realized, the entire realm of the mystical will lie dormant and integration of human personality will not be achieved.

Thus, it is of paramount importance for a Christian to explore the female aspect of the Trinity at the present time. Ms. Newman investigates the divine intention for humanity as manifested in male-female relationships. Each human being has the potential for divinization, i.e., the process of becoming fully human. However, very few of us know how to claim this experience. The process of becoming fully human is a process of transformation into Christ, the recovery of the image of God within one's soul. This can be achieved through spiritual discipline, the systematic guidance of the soul in such a manner as to remove all obstacles in the achievement of this awareness of God.

Whereas Newman emphasizes the role of male-female imagery in creating psychological wholeness, Thompson studies the role of male-female in creating social harmony which will benefit society as a whole. He maintains that the divine intention for female-male relationships is one of mutuality. Woman and man are equal before God. Therefore, they should cooperate in serving the community. In spiritual matters there is no male or female. In reality, according to Jesus, there probably are no sex roles. Historically, however, men have dominated women and have enjoyed putting them in their "place." This subjugation can perhaps be attributed to man's fallen nature, because the biblical tradition has been interpreted to dignify the male and degrade the female. But a closer examination reveals that tradition, experience, and reason call both men and women to mutuality and cooperation.

The question asked by the essays in this volume on the relationship between women and religion in the Judaic-Christian tradition is one of the single most important issues that can be raised in our time. As is obvious from the summaries given above, and though presented in many different forms, all the essays have one basic question in mind. In simple terms, the authors ask, how can we reform religious thought so that both men and women can enjoy dignity and equality? Correlatively, the question applies to individual and cultural values, styles of life, ethics—in short, every facet of life as it is lived and perceived. These are not disparate questions, but various aspects of one central question that is and must be asked.

Judaism and Christianity are not different from other religions insofar as sexual imagery is concerned. However, they are distinguished from most religions in their elevation of an exclusively male, patriarchal God, without a female consort, as the sole master and the ruler. Correspondingly, there is a repression of feminine imagery of the divine and feminine roles in rite, rituals, and worship.

Until this century it was generally assumed that the gender of deity was masculine in the Judaic-Christian tradition. However, contemporary theologians and Christian feminists have argued that a closer examination of the texts reveals that there is a wealth of feminine as well as masculine imagery pertaining to God in the biblical writings. As one scholar observes:

> All the evils which have resulted from dignifying one sex and degrading the other may be traced to this central error: a belief in a trinity of masculine God in One, from which the feminine element is wholly eliminated. And yet in the scriptural account of the simultaneous creation of man and woman, the text plainly recognizes the feminine as well as the masculine element in Godhead, and declares the equality of the sexes in goodness, wisdom, and power.[2]

But, the fact still remains that in the history of Christianity such imagery has been eclipsed by the dominant masculine image of God. In Hinduism, on the other hand, feminine imagery is more explicit, more central, and more consistently expressed (as we shall see shortly).

Many theologians and social analysts argue that religion concerns the very foundation of human life. It provides "a set of symbolic forms and acts that relate man to the ultimate conditions of his existence."[3] As Clifford Geertz observes:

> A religion is a system of symbols which acts to establish powerful, pervasive and long-lasting moods and motivation in men by formulating conceptions of a general order of existence and clothing these conceptions

with such an aura of factuality that the modes and motivations seem uniquely realistic.[4]

Thus, they believe that sexual imagery is central to religion, and this in turn has had a profound effect on the way in which man and woman have lived and perceived their respective lives and existences.

This raises a very interesting question about the relationship of religion to feminine imagery as well as to the actual, social and self-images of women. Erikson[5] believes that there is a strong correlation between male sexuality and our cultural beliefs and behavior. Exclusive masculinization of patriarchal society has been dangerous for mankind. Cultivation of the feminine component in religious symbolization is badly needed if humankind is to be saved from a potential catastrophe and become whole.

II

Polarity symbolism on the other hand, is very ancient in the Hindu tradition. The earliest expression of it is found in the *Ṛg Veda* where it is stated:

From him Virāj[6] was born, and from Virāj came the Man. When he was born, he ranged beyond the earth behind and before.[7]

Who really knows? Who will *here* proclaim it? Whence was it produced? Whence is this creation? The gods came afterwards, with the creation of this universe. Who then knows whence it has arisen?[8]

The earth was born from her who crouched with legs spread, and from the earth the quarters of the sky were born. From Aditi, Dakṣa was born, and from Dakṣa Aditi was born.[9]

Thus, the polarity symbolism, at least, goes as far back as the *Ṛg Veda.* There are scholars who believe that it may even be older than the Indian tradition itself. There is some indirect evidence of the significance of male-female symbolism in the Indus Valley civilization. Professor Carmody maintains:

Since the Harrapans left no literature, our knowledge of their religion is inferred from figurines, seals, and the like, which archaeologists have excavated. They suggest a central interest in fertility—in the worship of a Proto-Shiva (a three-faced God, in yogic posture, with *penis erectus,* surrounded by animals) and a Mother Goddess. The ascetic concentration on Shiva as the divinity of life-force and the veneration of feminine power that characterizes later India, are probably both latent in Hindu Harrapan ancestry.[10]

The most systematic and developed expression of polarity symbolism is, however, found in the Sāṁkhya school of Indian philosophy. Sāṁkhya is the oldest systematized school in India. There is some indication that this school might have flourished in the eighth century B.C. (if Kapila is regarded as an historical person). The most important codification of Sāṁkhya doctrines is ascribed to Īśvarakṛṣṇa, who lived in the second century A.D. Sāṁkhya is a radically dualistic philosophy and central to its philosophy are *prakṛti* (a material principle) and *puruṣa* (a conscious principle). Whatever happens in the universe, happens in and through *prakṛti;* because *puruṣa* does not act, it is pure witness. But *prakṛti*—active, repository of all actions—could not act, if *puruṣa* was not there. Although the two are opposed to each other, it is only by their cooperation that the evolution of the world takes place. How the two interact is a postulate of intuition and cannot be explained by reasoning.

This male-female polarity symbolism, however, found its most pronounced expression in the tantric tradition. In general, tantrism has been associated with a particular system of practice and thought which employs the symbolism of opposition and seeks through various means to overcome this opposition. Both Hindu and Buddhist tantrisms conceive of a non-dual noumenon,[11] that can be expressed only in terms of a diametrical polarity because of their belief that the noumenon is ineffable, inexpressible, i.e., it is entirely transcendent. The paradigm chosen to illustrate this polarity is man and woman, or rather man and woman in their cosmic aspects, god and goddess. To put it differently, the creative function of the supreme is polarized into the static and dynamic aspects.

Hindu tantrism assigned the static aspect to the male principle *(śiva),* and the dynamic aspect to the female principle *(śakti).* Central to this system is the concept of *śakti:* the female as the projected "force" or "energy" of the male. Male and female, God and Goddess, are the polar manifestations of a single transcendent principle: though in appearance two, they are in essence one. It is only when *śiva* is united with *śakti,* that he is able to exert his powers as lord; without *śakti,* he is not able to move. *Śiva* in its transcendent aspect is *sava,* "dead" as it were.

Professor Gupta's paper explores male-female polarity symbolism in a particular tantric school, viz., Kāshmir Śaivism; and its influence on a contemporary Hindi classic, *Kāmāyanī.* The paper is divided into two parts: Part I explains the philosophies of Kāshmir Śaivism, highlighting the significance of the symbolism in this school; and Part II illustrates how the male-female symbolism is expressed through the structure of the entire classic under consideration.

Ultimate reality, in Kāshmir Śaivism, is ineffable and beyond any descriptions. It is transcendent as well as immanent. As transcendent, it is *śiva;* and as immanent, it is described as *śakti.* The manifestation of the universe is effected through the *śakti* of *śiva* which is not different from it. *Śiva* and *śakti* are two different aspects of the same ultimate reality. Because of the limitation of the language, we are forced to use expressions which imply that they are different. In reality, however, both are one and the same. *Mokṣa* signifies not only freedom from duality, but also one's identity with the ultimate reality. In this state there is no emergence or absorption of the universe: it is a state of perfect harmony between being and becoming.

Kāmāyanī also illustrates that man and woman, *śiva* and *śakti,* are not two different powers but rather two aspects of one undifferentiated reality. Everything in the universe is organically related. The 'without' appears as without only because it is 'within.' The conflict between the two cannot be resolved by suppressing one or by giving one up in favor of the other. Only when both elements coexist together on the same level can peace and harmony be attained. The inseparability of the two is a symbol of true personhood. It is only when both elements are aligned that a long-lasting relationship can be realized.

Professor Srinivasan, in his paper "Polar Principles in Yoga and Tantra" introduces the concepts of cosmology and psychobiology of yoga and tantra with reference to the polar principles of female-male duality within ultimate reality. The female is the active principle initially dormant. However, with the emergence of consciousness, its arousal is experienced as *kuṇḍalinī* force which merges with the passive male principle. Thus, it is not the externalized woman-man whose physical union is sought; it is rather the symbiosis and the synthesis of the female-male in each individual. Yoga recommends specific transactional and transcendental methods for achieving this unification. The mind-body continuum of individuals undergoing yogic practices can be measured in a laboratory, and the progress of the practitioner observed, during this convergence of the polar principles.

Srinivasan maintains that present interest in the hemispherical specialization of the brain suggests that the concept of bi-polar principle can serve as a useful working model. The left brain is analytical and transactional while the right brain is holistic and transcendental. A psychosomatic balance in an individual is achieved through an integrated functioning of the two halves of the brain. Thus, it may be said that the polar principle is not mere speculation, but that, rather, it has a physiological basis. The reintegration of these into one whole is required for experiencing ultimate reality. The symbolic language of most religious utterances and mystical experiences can be interpreted in terms of the polarity model and the unity in all approaches thereby understood.

Professor Sivaraman's paper draws upon the richness of the Indian philosophical and religious tradition, to address the question: "Is there a Divine Intention for Male-Female Relationships?" While affirming the transcendence of God, the Hindu tradition gives eloquent expression to the male/female aspects of the divinity. The Hindu approach cannot be expressed except in terms of paradoxes, the central one being the coincidence of 'enjoyment' and 'renunciation'. The heart and center of Hindu religious experience is identity or immediacy which makes religion interchangeable with mysticism. This allows for a reconciliation of the motifs of asceticism with love as exemplified in male-female reaction. Bi-sexual polarity in the deity itself serves as the ontological basis for the use of sexual symbolism and purports to show the continuity between the Upaniṣadic language and imagery with the later Hindu development of tantra. The theological, mythological, and soteriological implications of the Hindu concept of androgyne *(ardhanāri)* are elaborated from certain religious texts.

A separate section explains the layout and the esoterics of a fifth century Tamil lyrical text which highlights the theme of the paper, viz., the romantic coincidence of idealized human love and divine love. The author states:

> The close embrace in love of the male and female is the most perfect representation in the world of nature *(saṁsāra)* of the divine transcendence of all opposites, and paradoxically it also points to the absence of an ontological distinction between creativity and liberation. It is the Hindu version of the identiy of *'saṁsāra'* and *'nirvāna'*.

Professor Payne's major concern centers around the problem of the spirituality of masculine and feminine relationships. He seeks an answer to the question, "Can we rediscover the divine laws that operate to make human love a sacrament, an instrument of grace for our sanctification?" (p. 51) While such a problem stated in such a way seems innocuous, it becomes evident that it is a Pandora's Box of complexity and perplexity.

The author maintains that in the Judaic-Christian tradition, sexual activities are commonly regarded in the light of their possible harmful effects. A theology of sex must be written that encompasses not only male and female sexuality but also marriage and passion in sexual relationships. He attempts to articulate such a spirituality of sexuality by drawing upon his own religious experience, Christian mystical tradition, Jungian archetypes, and tantric *maṇḍalas.*

Thus, Western society has a lot to learn from the Eastern meditative traditions. The author states (pp. 69–70):

> The church, the new creation within creation, and within the church the sacrament of marriage, is the basic *maṇḍala* for a Christian tantra. Through this *maṇḍala,* internalized in disciplined sexuality, the great archetype of the original man, wholly united to the divine, can be personally reintegrated in the deep psycho-physical being of men and women. We might learn from ancient Eastern meditation traditions in order to fully realize the potentialities in our sacrament of marriage. For a Christian tantra may be one way to paradise regained.

Payne's project has much relevance for our troubled times and one may readily distinguish in it two different aspects, the personal and the institutional:

1) *Personal:* One can readily imagine that family therapists would find Payne's suggestions applicable to their own work.

2) *Institutional:* Whatever else Christianity may be, it is an institution embedded in Western society as philosophers since Kierkegaard have observed. The problem still remains: how to confront the very substantial inertia of societal attitudes about sex which are held by people who call themselves Christians. Mere theology, and theology alone, cannot bring about the changes in attitudes. We need to think of the way which will give impetus to the changes in sex roles which are already occurring—often with the open opposition of theologians.

When we view the issue of the relationship of feminine imagery to religion in the Indian framework, we get interesting results. In

Hinduism, we find the use of feminine imagery in an obvious way. However, that has not immediately led to a higher status of women in India. Thus, there does not seem to be a direct correlation between feminine imagery and the higher status of women. The question then may be asked: if there is no direct correlation, what kind of correlation does, in fact, exist? How do the images of God affect the self-images of men and women? The images of God grow up within a certain historical and cultural context and eventually become established. What happens when the context changes? Are the traditional symbols any longer effective? Should anything of the tradition be retained or should there be an entirely different religious language to meet the needs of the new situation? To what extent is it worthwhile trying to hang on to the traditional images? Is tradition itself something that has the ability to change? These are some of the related questions which a person interested in the problem of women *via-à-vis* religion might wish to explore.

III

It has become a clichè or a truism among social analysts and critics to observe that we live in a transitional era. The range, the scope, the scale and complexity of the social changes that we all experience are probably without historical precedent. We live in an era in which change occurs faster than ever before—in terms of life-styles, values, functions of institutions, politics, and so on. We feel most acutely the sense of an interregnum, a space between what has been and what shall be. The future is always problematic, but there is more uncertainty attending the future now than perhaps ever before because science and technology have unleashed dynamics whose consequences we cannot foresee, nor can we, in some cases, truly anticipate these with any confidence of accuracy.

If ours is an era in which the symbols, structures, and agencies of the past no longer seem adequate for dealing with the present, then it is natural for us to sense disequilibrium, a loss of stability, and therefore, to look for anchors, sources of stability, of continuity. This forces a reexamination of traditional images and symbols—the acceptability, the viability of traditional images and symbols—which, after all, originated and were inspired by very different cultural situations than our own. Consequently, our reappraisal of the adequacy of old images and symbols is both necessary and inevitable. We are forced to confront anew our past and ask: What is viable in it? What is new in it? What still speaks to us at a level that is meaningful to us? Are old forms intelligible in any negotiable sense any longer?

Traditional images of divinity, for example, seem to be modeled often on acceptance of authority, hierarchy, obedience, devotion, conformity, and compliance. They have centered around the idea of stability, security, and the prevalence of order. But contemporary culture calls for symbols and images of a quite different kind. We need today a symbolization of divinity that reflects modern humanity's reluctance to accept authority and conformity in some unquestioning fashion. This is especially manifest with regard to the images of man and woman. What kind of an image of divinity can be abstracted from traditional cultures and enlisted to cope with the demands of equality and today's affirmation of individual freedom in a changing society? Instead of appealing to traditional gender-linked stereotypes, what we need today is due recognition of the need for changed or revised interpretations of old images, consistent with the growing demands of the times.

More importantly, we need to recover the often obscure sense of the equiprimordiality of the sexes, as when the religions talk about the masculine/feminine component in the divine. In the Western tradition there is a very special need to rediscover the significance of the importance of the role of the feminine in the image of God. In Eastern religions, too, the overworked image of the feminine as mother goddess and as a power inherent in God *(śakti)* needs to be reinterpreted to underscore the equal and not the secondary role that women play in individual and corporate life. How is this principle of the equality of the sexes acknowledged in the Hindu religious tradition with its polarity of *śiva* and *śakti*? How is this principle to be translated into practice to cope with real life situations? This is a dilemma that the East must face.

The problem that religious traditions confront today is the paradox of a belief in the equality of the sexes and the prevalence of a divine image which has contributed to the oppression of women and an entrenchment of patriarchy. Does this mean that the traditional images of man and woman can no longer give an adequate expression to contemporary values as they effect gender and gender-linked roles within modern society? Can these symbols be legitimately reinterpreted to meet the present needs? Or, should we employ new symbols? Can such new symbols be created, as it were, *de novo?*

One method of exploring these questions involves a reexamination of the nature of tradition itself. Is tradition something frozen in time or is it something that has the ability to change? Is tradition diametrically opposed to modernity? Is it an "either-or" choice? So far as the images of men and women are concerned, it seems that there is an over-reliance upon this dichotomy between tradition and modernity. However, in real life situations, what women in contemporary culture around the world face is not so much a choice between traditions and modernity, as it is a question of creative tension and the selection for preservation of those elements out of the traditional past that deserve to be perpetuated, and to be embraced in a self-conscious and deliberate way in the light of modern needs.

Thus, the basic issue in the recovery of tradition, whether one is talking about the East or the West, is one of reinterpretation and reorientation of traditional images, bringing out their creative potential for answering the consistent and recurring problems of time and history. But there is another equally important aspect of the recovery of tradition, which is to see what light traditional images can shed upon the limits and inadequacies of that which besets the present itself. Instead of becoming overly preoccupied with the requirements of today, we must be in a position to contemplate these issues in the light of the more enduring aspects of the symbols and images of tradition.

NOTES

1. Margaret Mead, *Sex and Temperament in Three Different Primitive Societies* (New York: Mentor Books, 1950), p. 280.
2. Matilda Gage, *History of Woman Suffrage* (New York: Fowler and Wells, 1981), Vol. I, p. 796.
3. Robert N. Bellah, *Beyond Belief: Essays on Religion in a Post Traditional World* (New York: Harper and Row, 1970), p. 21.
4. Clifford Geertz, "Religion as a Cultural System," in Michael Banton's (ed.), *Anthropological Approaches to the Study of Religion,* A.S.A. Monographs, III (London: Tavistock Press, 1966), p. 4.
5. Erik Erikson, *Identity: Youth and Crisis* (New York: Norton, 1963), p. 261.
6. Virāj is the active female creative principle that was later replaced by *prakṛti* or material nature.

7. Wendy O'Flaherty (tr.), *The Rig Veda: An Anthology* (New York: Penguin Books, 1981), p. 30.
8. O'Flaherty, p. 25.
9. *Ibid.,* pp. 38–39.
10. It seems more appropriate to use 'noumenon' rather than 'divine', which will not be appropriate for Buddhism, or 'absolute', which appears to be too scholastic. The 'noumenon' being the opposite of 'phenomenon' seems to be the correct choice.
11. Denise L. Carmody, *Women and World Religions* (Nashville: Abingdon Press, 1979), p. 40.

2

Eve, Where Are You?

PASCALINE COFF, O.S.B.

I

In the beginning of creation when God made heaven and earth, the earth was without form and void, with darkness over the face of the abyss, and a mighty wind that swept over the surface of the waters. God said, "Let there be light," and there was light; and God saw that the light was good (Genesis 1:1–4).

Similarly, by his creative word God said:

"Let us make man in our image and likeness" . . . so God created man in his own image; in the image of God he created him; male and female he created them . . . so it was; and God saw all that he had made, and it was very good (Genesis 1:26–27, 31).

The whole of creation has been interwoven with this complementarity of feminine and masculine elements to maintain the cosmic harmony. This sexual polarity not only exists on psychological levels, but the human duality expresses an antithesis at the very heart of things, an antithesis "unceasingly striving for synthesis, eternally in an act of anticipation and restitution of unity."[1]

Cosmic Level

In ancient Chinese thought (4th Century B.C.) all things were classified as partaking of the *yin* (female principle), or the *yang* (masculine principle), two archetypal poles that set the limits for the cycle of change, underlying the rhythm of the entire universe. The *yin,* the female principle, is symbolized by the earth, the moon and water, while the *yang,* on the other hand, is symbolized by the sun and fire. However, both are eventually seen as transformed into each other, e.g., winter *(yin)* into summer *(yang),* unceasingly striving for synthesis. Confucius said: "*Ch'ien (yang)* and *k'un (yin)* are indeed the gate of change."[2]

Fritjof Capra, a renowned physicist of our day, describes these poles as *yang* (expansive, demanding, aggressive, competitive, rational, and analytical) and *yin* (contractive, conservative, responsive, cooperative, intuitive and synthetic).[3]

Nothing is only *yin* or only *yang,* but rather, everything is continuously oscillating between the two poles. The natural order is one of dynamic balance wherein all forces are harmonized.

Human Level

Being the warp and the woof of the whole of creation, these feminine and masculine qualities are obviously also two sides of human nature, two sides of the human brain. For each of us is androgynous, both female and male, and both elements, in harmonious balance, are essential. Berdyaev, the Russian philsopher, speaks of our being not only sexual but bisexual beings, combining the feminine and masculine principles in ourselves in different proportions and often in fierce conflict:

> A man in whom the feminine principle was completely absent would be an abstract being, completely severed from the cosmic element. A woman in whom the masculine principle was completely absent would not be a personality. . . . It is only the union of these two principles that constitutes a complete human being.[4]

The balance of feminine and masculine elements and the understanding of them is central to the wholeness of the human person, both individually and collectively. For without understanding one of these elements, "we cannot have a true sense of the other, let alone mature into a whole . . . person," claims Ann Ulanov in her study of the feminine.[5] This sexual polarity of feminine and masculine is not only experienced by us as we relate to our outer world, i.e., parents, friends or spouse, but is vital to our own inner experience, our integration and true religious experience. It is, in fact, the primary mode of achieving harmony and wholeness, individuation and, therefore, holiness.

Psychological Level

C. G. Jung coined the terms *anima, animus* for the two archetypal figures in the individual consciousness which are rooted in the collective unconscious and, therefore, form a bridge between the personal and impersonal in each of us. These psychic realities are function complexes behaving in ways that compensate for the outer personality, as if they were inner personalities, and exhibit characteristics lacking in the observable conscious personality. Normally both are present in each individual, but these are conditioned in their character by the past experience each individual has had with persons of the opposite sex and by the collective image of the opposite sex carried in each one's own psyche. Jung's wife describes the end product of this threefold meeting as forming a quantity behaving as if it were a "law unto itself," "interfering in the life of the individual as if it were an alien element; sometimes helpful, sometimes disturbing, if not actually destructive."[6]

Therefore, to achieve quality behavior, integration and wholeness, we must understand the influence of the *anima* and *animus,* and through whatever praxis, *sadhana, tapas,* or asceticism that is necessary, allow the inner spirit to be transformed, allow the "marriage within" to happen. In religious terms, this is called redemption.

As the *yin* and the *yang* are the gates of change, so the *anima* and the *animus* are considered to be "gateways" to the self, and only through the fullest relationship and expression of the feminine and masculine polarity can this "inner wedding" take place: "These archetypal aspects of the psyche . . . can never be known directly in themselves but only as we encounter them in images, patterns of behavior and emotional response."[7]

The marriage "without," i.e., the sacrament of mutual self-gifting, is one of the greatest opportunities for encountering, understanding and converting one's opposite quality, through wholesomeness of the oppositeness in one's partner in deep selfless relational love. For the Christian, especially for those called to celibate love, whether female or male, this is indeed to "put on the mind (heart) of Christ." In the incarnation we have been gifted with the perfect wholesome other in history and mystery which not only supplies the oppositeness for both sexes but, through total self-giving in paschal love, leads each of us into the depths of inner communion with ourselves and the divine and with every other. This is the very meaning and fruit of eucharist.

Spiritual Level

That the original human being was believed to be androgynous is found in many ancient traditions, such as the Persian, Greek, and

Talmudic myths. In India the androgen is usually conceived as Śiva and his consort, Parvati, fused into one being. As a matter of fact, the androgen is the symbol of supreme identity in most religious systems. In his work, subtitled "Reconciliation of Male and Female," Elemire Zolla says: "The model of a well-tempered androgyny hovers above either sex as the new criterion for both as incarnation of the cosmic man."[8]

Yahweh, the God of Israel and therefore of Jew, Christian and Muslim, is believed to be an androgynous being: "Let us make man in our image and likeness. . . . He made him in the likeness of God, male and female he created them. He blessed them and gave them the name man" (Genesis 5:1–2). God's image is to be found, therefore, in this polarity of female and male; the very relationship of woman and man is the primary concretization of the covenant God made with Noah and, therefore, with all people, with each person. This interpretation highlights the importance and essentiality of the feminine:

> If the feminine is neglected, in its contrasexual form within the masculine, or is misunderstood as a second-best category of human sexuality, then not only is the fullness of the human being damaged, but the relation of the human and the divine is damaged as well.[9]

II

In view of the extreme importance of the feminine for the wholeness and holiness of both female and male and of the whole human race, we will look for a moment at what is most characteristic of the feminine, realizing that what is good for Eve is good for Adam—each being utterly both.

Receptivity—The Feminine Quality Par Excellence

Receptivity is an unarmored stance of one's heart toward the other, the truly other. It is a profound attitude of openness, sensitivity to the other, involving the ability to let go, to be fully present, to adapt, to laugh, to cry, to clown, to play, to lay down one's life. It is essential for physical, psychological, and spiritual growth. Receptivity is a process of hosting and being hosted by another. It could be called hospitality at its ultimate. For to be receptive is to be welcoming, not only to those we know but to the stranger, the other. And the most other is the divine. The feminine style of receptivity is the virtue of attention, wherein ultimately the other enters in and fills one's inner space.

In describing the heights of prayer, John of the Cross insists that the only business of the soul is "the reception of God." For the Christian called to constant prayer (Ephesians 6:18), this is to be a continuous stance or attitude. The ancient Eastern *ṛṣi* described this receiving of the divine through the medium of a profound dialogue wherein a wife begs her husband for spiritual knowledge. *Bṛhadāraṇyaka Upaniṣad* states:

> Verily, a husband is not dear, that you may love the husband; but that you may love the Self, therefore a husband is dear.
>
> Verily, a wife is not dear, that you may love the wife; but that you may love the Self, therefore a wife is dear. . . .
>
> Verily, everything is not dear that you may love everything; but that you may love the Self, therefore everything is dear.
>
> Verily, the Self is to be seen, to be heard, to be perceived, to be marked, O Maitreyî! When we see, hear, perceive, and know the Self, then all this is known.[10]

Thus, the receiving of the divine has been recognized in all relationships from time immemorial. Eve and Adam walked in the afternoon breeze with Yahweh, and this, in fact, is the inner journey described variously in the different religious traditions.

Beatrice Bruteau describes the inner life of the Christian trinity, father, son and holy spirit, as being an "irresistible impulse in each Person which mightily draws them One to Another—a 'reciprocal eruption.'"[11] In the spiritual journey, is not the integration of the feminine and masculine in communion with the self, the divine, a reciprocal eruption, in irresistible fashion, drawing the three into one? The Apostle Paul described it when he said, "I live now not I but Christ lives in me" (Galatians 2:20).

Another important facet of receptivity is the ability to meet and allow oneself to be met. This has much to do with the difference between focused consciousness (division) and diffusive awareness (unity) and the wholeness of nature—that attitude of acceptance and readiness for relationship which is deeply feminine.[12] Christ surely learned this art of reading between the lines, closing his ears to the irrelevant and focusing on the heart of the other: "I have no husband," the Samaritan woman said; "there is no other one to put me into the pool," the cripple complained. Jesus always trusted the heart of others beyond the words he heard from their lips.

Perfect receptivity, therefore, involves listening with understanding love, a love that gives complete attention and helps the other to be free and open; it requires a certain maturity and self-transcendence in order to listen discerningly to another, with patience and openness to possibilities and to change. We must have a real capacity to pierce the cloaking of the words spoken. Douglas Steere, the Quaker, suggests there is an invisible third party present in every speaker, a "spectator listener," within the one who speaks, who listens while one speaks so that "what is going on in the outward listener's conscious mind, as well as what is occurring in the outward listener's unconscious, is never fully veiled to the speaker's inward spectator listener."[13] And this inward listener in the other who is speaking is listening most of all for real feminine receptivity, even though unconsciously.

Receptivity is the gift of a genuine listening heart that not only cares but assists the climate of openness for self-disclosure. It is to listen to one in life as a mother does her infant, with limitless caring. We encounter this feminine quality of receptivity in God in the Old Testament story of David and Absalom (II Samuel 18:19) and in the New Testament stories of the prodigal father (Luke 15:11), the widow of Naim (Luke 7:11) and others. Jesus is constant receptivity bearing witness to other feminine qualities flowing from this mother virtue, such as vulnerability, compassion, gentleness, and the like.

If a listening heart is the flower of receptivity, dialogue is its fruit. Dialogue is communicating in depth with another in confidence, openness, humility, and honesty, seeking truth by trusting the other. A niagara of feminine qualities is involved. Authentic dialogue is a way to conversion and enlightenment, the lived reality of the "wedding within." Dialogue is an essential part of the religious act described first by Jesus in the Old Testament terms as loving God above all things and one's neighbor as oneself, and then, in his new commandment, as loving one another as he loves us. Prayer, which is itself dialogue with God, brings us to receptivity to the spirit, and this receptivity is the crown and queen of human stances—that aim of all prayer: resting in God. But dialogue at every level demands quality time, that deeply feminine dimension of time.

Passivity

While the soul in relational love toward the divine is passive, there is a great difference between mere inactivity and the passive activity involved therein. By *wu wei,* the Chinese word for non-action, Lao Tzu says, "everything can be done."[14] *Wu wei* is not passivity as such, but feminine activity. Lam Govinda, a Tibetan Buddhist, makes a helpful distinction toward this point; whereas female activity is by way of reproduction and transformation and is inwardly centered, male activity is by way of intensification or direction and is outwardly directed. Female passivity is a positive attitude, e.g., receptivity, latent creativeness, or potentiality (which does not exclude activity within the particular realm of female properties—attention, receptivity, relating), whereas male passivity is merely an absence or lesser degree of action. Passivity, therefore, as characteristic of the female attitude, is positive, whereas passivity, as characteristic of the male attitude, is negative.[15] This insight is vital to the real understanding of the female and male qualities in ourselves and others. We cannot stress sufficiently that everyone is fully female and male; activity and receptivity belong to both women and men "not as feminine and masculine poles of their being, but as full possibilities as precisely as feminine and precisely as masculine."[16] However, Helen Luke warns us well that we are predominantly either female or male, and we forget this at our peril. We will never arrive at equality of value until we have learned to discriminate and accept the difference. For the biological difference between the two is never a "nothing but." "It is a fundamental difference of psychic nature."[17]

Unless the fullness of the feminine quality is discovered and developed in every woman and man so that receptivity to the spirit can be realized, the whole realm of the mystical will lie dormant, together with wholesome human integration and, needless to say, the whole cosmic harmony.

III

Patriarchal Society: Eve, Where Are You?

In our Western culture, Christianity and monasticism included, we have developed the *yang* qualities—the masculine, rational, scientific—to the absolute limit and to the exclusion of the feminine quality. The Chinese say the pendulum swings back every 500 years. Some say as many as 5,000 years are involved in the present patriarcate.[18] Fritjof Capra speaks of the slow and reluctant but inevitable decline of patriarchy, claiming the time associated with this era is closer to 3,000 years. The power of it is extremely difficult to understand because it is "all-pervasive." Today, the disintegration of patriarchy is in sight, being the one system never before openly challenged.[19] The feminist Rosemary Ruether agrees that women must recognize that "they represent the oldest and ultimate ideology of patriarchal culture, who serve to maintain its patterns of male domination and world exploitation."[20]

Capra, too, insists that our present profound cultural imbalance, which lies at the root of the current crisis, stems from the strikingly consistent preference for *yang* values, attitudes and behavior patterns: "The turning point we are about to reach marks, among other things, a reversal in the fluctuation of the *yin* and *yang*."[21] Even as God called out in Eden, "Adam, where are you?" so does God's cry come forth from "the very stones" in this our day: "Eve, where are you?" In the beginning Adam hid himself from God, but far worse, he has hidden Eve for centuries behind his analytical, rational, competitive, aggressive, expansive, demanding and conditional attitudes and behavior, his constructs and systems. God intended the sexual polarity to climax in the "marriage within"—in ultimate wholeness in our communion with the divine. Yet "our very language betrays us" in the totality of its patriarchal frame of reference with its "man," "his," and "he" exclusiveness even in our world scriptures. God, who is beyond all our divisions and categories, is both female and male and yet neither female nor male. However, in patriarchy we honor only his "maleness."

The dangerous and brazen exploitation of nature in our own times has gone hand in hand with that of women, for down through the ages there has been a natural kinship between feminism and ecology. Life itself has become unhealthy as a result of the excessive technological growth. We lack sincere receptivity to any other but self: domination, achievement, wealth and aggrandizement, to say nothing of the heavy climate of crime and war everywhere.

Religion

No realm of life remains unscathed in this regard. While most of the world religions have all been deeply colored by our long-standing patriarchal culture, Hinduism incorporates somewhat of a balance.

a) Buddhism. Buddhist research finds that the early tradition often had intrinsic problems with women practicing the spiritual path since, for monks, women are potential objects of lust. Therefore, they were considered threatening to men's meditative discipline. Also, the feminine emotionality innate in women made them unlikely and unsuitable candidates for enlightenment. At its most extreme, this view led to the conclusion that it would be best for pious women to spend their time praying that they might be reborn as men, in order that enlightenment might be possible for them. In fact, some 500 years after Buddha's *parinirvāṇa* (death), certain minor Mahayana texts directly stated that women had to become men before they could be enlightened. But an earlier, more subtle understanding of sex identification in some of the most revered Buddhist texts in the world, shows how fixation on sex identification can become a serious obstacle in practice. Moreover, "opinions about the relative merits of being a man or woman indicate a pernicious form of ego-clinging, making spiritual progress impossible."[22] The early Buddhist sūtras teach, through the medium of a wise woman or goddess in dialogue with a Buddhist monk Sariputra, that "womanness" cannot be grasped or apprehended at its core. In fact, *śūnyatā,* in the Buddhist tradition, is egolessness, neither womanness nor manness. Enlightenment cannot be attained by virtue of a female or male body. To prove this, the wise woman changes herself into a man and then back again. There is no achieving perfect enlightenment in any way.[23] In characteristic koan paradox form, the Buddha has said: "In all things there is neither male nor female."

b) Hinduism. Hinduism has much to offer to our dilemma in regard to the feminine. God as mother is one of the deepest intuitions of the Indian soul. Among the great world religions, Hinduism has remained closer to the notion of the androgynous ultimate than others, with her wisdom regarding the supreme self, the ground of human being and consciousness, the supreme person to be worshipped and adored, the one without a second, yet the subject of human love and unity. In the *Ṛg Veda,* probably the oldest book in the world, God is addressed as "my mother, my father."

Another symbol of the Godhead which comes to us from the Vedas is that of the mother goddess, the feminine aspect of God in each of his manifestations. The feminine power in creation is highly regarded, so much so that the feast of mother nature, feminine power, is the most universal of all feasts in India. There was a strong masculine tradition in earlier Hinduism, but with tantra the feminine power came into its own with its worship of the great mother, i.e., energy in nature, in the body and even in feelings. Contemporary Hinduism has a healthy blend of the feminine and masculine.[24]

c) Christianity. This calls Christians to reflect deeply on the place of the feminine in our own religion where the father, son and holy spirit are all masculine words and concepts. We need to recover this feminine image of God, remembering that God is both and yet neither. There is a strong leaning today toward seeing the holy spirit as feminine.[25]

The concept of wisdom *(hokhma)* in the Old Testament is feminine. That wisdom that "plays before God" (Proverbs 1:22) and that "issues from the mouth of the most high" (Siroch 24:3) is truly a feminine aspect of God. Feminine qualities are notable in the masculine God of the Old Testament: "A mother may forget her child, yet I will never forget you" (Isaiah 49:15). But there is a difference between a father and a father's love: the mother stands for unconditional love and the father stands for conditional love. Yahweh's love is usually described as conditional as a result of our patriarchal language: if you obey my commandments I will be God to you. The father has to challenge the child to move out from the mother and face the world. But the mother's love is unconditional. We desperately need to recover the concept of God's unconditional love in the full reality of the God who is love. Our language suffers not only from its masculinity but from its anthropomorphic descriptions of God as "angry" and "punishing," whereas, when we refuse God's love, we bring "punishment" on ourselves. Punishment is not from God. Recall the good shepherd, the woman caught in adultery, the Judas story, Mary Magdalene, and others.

Jesus, like Buddha, made no mention of changing from male to female, rather, he insists we change and become as "a little child" in order to enter the kingdom (Luke 18:3) with the powerless qualities of receptivity, trust, sensitivity, unarmored love—pure presence. While the church, Christ's bride, in her systems and institutions, is dominated by patriarchal values of our day, Jesus was and is the perfect androgen, never allowing laws, customs, time or the lack of it, to be cause for acting or being out of character and full truth, or to deny the other this same fullness of being. Jesus, rather, invited the other to wholeness and holiness, to receive the divine by virtue of his presence to them, for this was his very mission. St. Paul, echoing Jesus, insisted "there is neither male nor female, for you are all one" (Galatians 3:29).

Mary, Mother of Jesus and the Church

Until recently, the place in Christianity where the feminine had been strongest had been in devotion to Mary. Her place and role on all three levels—physical, psychological and spiritual—had been given by God to us as vital to our wholeness. Her place in the mystery of the incarnation, the birth, life, death and resurrection of Jesus, her place and role as our spiritual mother down through the ages, had been salvific for all concerned. In Mary there was the perfect balance of feminine and masculine: "Be it done to me"; "Do whatever he tells you!"; "Son, they have no wine."

Unfortunately, this devotion to Mary has declined in our age, and declined for reasons closely linked with the present disorientation of women by their loss of identity, individually and in the collective unconscious. In addition, devotion to Mary, while itself in great need of our new and true perception, is not enough. It is not sufficient that we see the feminine in a holy person, no matter how beautiful and perfect. The feminine is in God and we must discover that aspect.[26]

It would be unthinkable for a Christian considering femaleness and maleness in the history of religions not to surface the unique breakthrough of Julian of Norwich, Mechtild of Magdeburg, and saints Bernard of Clairvaux and John of the Cross in their descriptions of the soul as feminine in relational love with God. In apocryphal language, all God's people are seen as feminine, coming to the new earth as bride, a symbol of the soul with God (Revelation 21:2).

An overwhelming cry for a new attitude today rises from every corner of our earth. The feminine must be recovered on every level by each of us soon.

IV

Possibilities and Responsibilities for Integration, Transformation and Wholeness

The *yin* is moving in and we are already moving into the more feminine age, the age of spirituality. Counter-culture movements have been astir all through the 1960s and 1970s so that feminine awareness, which stresses the human, holistic and spiritual, is challenging and profoundly changing the old value system: small is beautiful, voluntary simplicity is in demand with a return to the earth in the vital effort at growth and development. Justice is again being seen as "God's fidelity to his promises" as there rises an ever greater sensitivity in relating with the other, the foreign other, the truly other. Nineteen seventy-five saw the international year of woman. But the perpetual pendulum is not the answer. We do not want to move back to what was without spiraling to a higher level of consciousness and growth. Calling this age "neo-feminism," Dr. Beatrice Bruteau describes its characteristics as holistic, with a fundamental and ultimate sense of the specialness, the unique preciousness of each particular individual. She sees participatory consciousness as essential to the "revolution," a participation introduced by Jesus at the Last Supper where he demolished forever the domination and submission structures through total receptivity to the spirit in himself and in his apostles and, therefore, in all of us.[27] But a new consciousness is only a beginning, because the transformation of a consciousness is the "servant of a struggle to transform this entire social system in its human and ecological relationships."[28]

Role of the Church and Monasticism

The church and monastics within the church have an enormous responsibility for the evolutionary leap with which humanity is presently involved toward wholeness and holiness—toward the recovery of the feminine. Surely the church cannot do everything, but her primary task of leading worship and coping with crisis transitions in human life is vital. Liturgy and spiritual direction, then, are her two most important tasks in her mission on earth as she enables life on every level to come to its fullness. As people of the word, the members of the church receive the gift of the word through proclamation and celebration, through catechesis and guidance, wherein Christian conscience is formed, discernment of spirits is learned, self-knowledge is gleaned, defenses are dropped, virtues are formed, and transformation to wholeness and holiness can happen. The word is sharper than any two-edged sword (Hebrews 4:12). Liturgy is the primary school for Christian prayer and spirituality, enabling Christians to live justly, peacefully and charitably in the world.[29]

Whether through the communal channel of good liturgy or privately directed, one to one, spiritual guidance is an effort to enable another to live in the eternal rhythm of life ever more integrally. And accountability for this weighs heavily upon the church, Christ's bride, for she is the only "institution" in the society that could understand it fully and implement it through adequate leadership. If she fails, it has been said by behavioral scientists, the whole society suffers greater division, sickness and injustice.[30] Is it not, then, the awesome overall task of the church and monastics within the church to provide and implement such leadership toward wholeness through spiritual awareness, and also her task to be in the forefront of the integration of the feminine quality in society as a whole and individually, while helping restore the sacredness of our earth by intuitive ingenuity with her own best foot forward?

Spiritual Direction

Spiritual guidance or direction involves enablement, assisting another in coming to total receptivity to the spirit. It is like trying to make rise from another's chaos all that is divine, human and capable of entering the harmony of the kingdom.[31]

A good spiritual guide must be endowed with all the feminine qualities we have considered above: receiving and hosting the divine, the ability to meet and allow oneself to be met with diffusive awareness of unity and the wholeness of nature, the "reading between the lines," listening beyond the words, having an understanding heart, being a channel of participative rather than domineering or servile love, assisting the climate for self-disclosure in the dialogue of in-depth communication which allows for conversion and ultimately contemplative communion and enlightenment.

The eternal rhythm in life is itself grace permeating the spiritual atmosphere even more than the air we breathe. While grace cannot be produced or demanded because of its very nature as gift given, we can prepare to be fertile ground for the gift. This is one of the tasks of spiritual direction. Preparation for grace entails looking beyond the appearances to the reality in each thing, in each event. This is the difference between meaning and meaninglessness. In our very scientific age we are liable to become discouraged because scientific information has replaced our human myths, for the most part, and myths are vital for meaning in life. But this same science permits us to perceive the reality of grace itself, and, once perceived, our understanding of ourselves as meaningless and insignificant dissipates. This is the purpose of spiritual exercises—to allow the inner spirit to bring us to this breakthrough.[32]

In the spiritual journey, there is a phenomenon referred to as positive regression (extradependence) which is a movement toward some trust source outside one's ego. It is a step beyond intradependence which is focused and analytical, seeking to master or adapt to one's own environment. Extradependence is an unfocused, symbolic consciousness and is marked by an adult search for someone or something to depend on. This is a period of disengagement. Thomas Merton referred to this in one of the final articles of his life when he studied the existential moratorium that takes place in final integration.[33] At this time, ordinarily, spiritual guidance is vital. However, good liturgy, as we know, is itself a mode of extradependence, "when fully and undefensively experienced, with a transforming sense of transcendent trustworthiness," which enables people to shift to intradependence with greater capacity for risk-taking and for exploration of the unknown.[34] This inner process—"path" or "way"—is recognized in most traditions, yet each path is uniquely personal. For the Christian, Christ is both the way and the inner guide on the way.

Spiritual guides are few and far between. The church has an enormous task ahead of her to provide for the training and availability of such guides. A director is not a re-creation. Good programs can be developed, but good directors are God's gift. It is an awesome responsibility to provide for this immediate need. Humanity, in its unbalanced polarity, and the earth, in its ecological nightmare, are "groaning" to be brought to integration and restoration. This is the paschal mystery—that redemption is already given to us by Christ yet not yet received individually.

Liturgy

The church's task is equally weighty to provide good liturgy and good leadership in liturgy. Liturgy is communal worship. The liturgy of the hours, the liturgy of time, is sacramental prayer, in which the church, i.e., the members of Christ's body, in union with their head, Christ, are engaged in the manifestation *par excellence* of the church at prayer, Christ at prayer, always making intercession for his people, everywhere in the world.

The world and its history are the terrible and sublime liturgy, breathing of death and sacrifice, which God celebrates and causes to be celebrated in and through human history in its freedom. This liturgy of the world is as it were veiled to the darkened eyes and the dulled heart of those who fail to understand their own true nature. This liturgy, therefore, must, if the individual is really to share in the celebration of it in all freedom, as self-commitment even to death, be interpreted, "reflected upon" in its ultimate depth in the celebration of that which we are accustomed to call liturgy in the more usual sense.[35]

Liturgy obviously partakes of the fullness of that eternal rhythm of life that is the ebb and tide of everything, welling up unexpectedly everywhere. There is a gift called serendipity that enables us to discover unlooked-for treasures in the very ordinariness of our lives. This gift is for everyone willing to receive it. Grace permeates the universe. We only need to be disposed. Liturgy is one of the channels that not only makes us aware of the presence of grace but actually disposes us to receive it.

Liturgy is time made holy, sanctifying the whole year by months and days, feasts and fasts. This broad understanding of the liturgy of the world, the sacredness of all time, is therefore our bridge between the sacred and the secular, between worship and work.

A contemporary anthropologist offers an insightful distinction involving the female/male polarity, dynamically at work in every group, including the community at worship: *communitas* vs. "the social structure." *Communitas* is marked by spontaneity, immediacy, quality, lack of status, comradeship, active passivity and sacredness. *Communitas* comes about as a result of "I-thou" relationships. When *communitas* needs are repressed, people can go mad, whereas obsession for excessive structure can be a defense mechanism to hide the urgent need for *communitas.* The social structure, on the other hand, is marked by roles, status, and differences of all kinds, necessary for a society's functioning, or which may have accumulated over the years. Rooted in the past, the social structure extends into the future through language, law and custom. Little wonder there is deep concern for updating old laws and customs, with efforts presently under way to revise sexist language in the liturgy.

The ideal is to acknowledge the marriage of *communitas* and social structure as they make up the one same stream of life, within us and without us, acting with *communitas* values while playing structural roles. United States bishops are being called upon to do this even now.[36]

Liturgy at its best involves the relationship of *communitas,* that trusting exchange and atmosphere of participative love. The formative power of the liturgy can never be exaggerated. It is the dynamic channel for a new consciousness of world peace and justice and international harmony. It is, as we have seen, the place where personal transformation can happen. Therefore, it was right that liturgical reform precede many other concerns in the process of the church's renewal through the Second Vatican Council and subsequent years. The responsibility for forming good leaders in both liturgy and spiritual guidance weighs heavy upon the church. Both the structure and content of worship must be such that people are guided through the process of personal breakthrough to wholeness, a process which includes: owning responsibility for one's life; forgiveness; experiencing dependent, trustworthy relatedness as the other; a sense of worshipping with others and on behalf of others; an awareness of symbols that point to mystery beyond themselves with values transcending the unmodified culture; crossing over the threshold of feelings of separateness from power, goodness and wholeness, to union with these and, ultimately, to transformation which brings intradependence.[37]

Hindrances which impede this process must be studied in an effort to avoid them. Leaders of worship themselves must be aware that the quality of this time of the sacred liturgy must be different from ordinary work time, even in view of the "liturgy of the world." For during this special time, deep positive regression and its power to transform need to have space and grace to happen. Leaders may refuse to allow people to let them be the "sacred authorities" they need them to be. Worship leaders may hinder the process of personal awakening by carelessness with the structure and content of the liturgy itself.

Symbols

Within the process of that personal breakthrough, the place of symbols in our day needs serious attention. For the recovery of symbolism as an experience of life is one of the greatest needs of our age. Since the symbol is the power which unites opposites, it is vital to new consciousness, to feminine consciousness. "Symbols are bridges between body and soul, mind and matter, feeling and intellect, knowledge and life. The symbol reunites meaning and event, understanding and life."[38] Symbols and the awareness of them allow us to move through them to the mystery beyond. Without symbolism, which puts things back together, the mind loses its contact with life. Helen Luke says the safeguard for the individual woman in our patriarchal society today lies in "her ability to connect the theories expounded and the emotions aroused in her with her symbolic life; for only when the connection is made do the changes in her actual life become real."[39] In order to help put things back together today, women must look for a myth, not only for themselves but for men as well, to nourish the inner imagery as new personalities struggle for birth. From our own unconscious our numinous meaning must break through in order to come to "a new synthesis in both woman and man."[40]

The scriptures of all the world religions are written in symbolic language. They need quality time to burst open in the depths of our hearts. The Christian scriptures are loaded with symbols and imagery which we already carry within. It is here that we must begin to discover the feminine still unknown in our day. While the spirit is not confined to time and place, good liturgy, sacred reading and meditation are the most ordinary channels for this breakthrough to new consciousness, to ever greater individuation and wholeness, to new meaning and new life. But there can be no transforming effect even though there may be some understanding of meaning, without the feminine mode of perception in the reception of these religious symbols in our midst.

The implications for monastics are staggering in regard to all that has been considered. The challenge for monastic women is especially overwhelming. How fitting that St. Benedict, "father of Western monasticism," should have had a twin sister!

Conclusion

Adam will again walk humbly with God in the "cool of the evening" when Eve returns to his side, both within and without. Eve is beginning to surface everywhere, yet by her very nature she is elusive and unassuming. Only in the struggle to achieve total integration of the human personality in all its dimensions will a vital effort toward perfect contemplation be attained. Receptivity to the spirit within and without is crucial to our physical, psychological and spiritual growth as individuals and as a people. Only when Christians allow themselves to become the very justice of God, no longer perceived as an "eye for an eye" but as a sacrament of fidelity to God's promises with limitless love, will humanity begin to recognize and seek the "new Adam" who is Christ, our way. The church has an awesome responsibility and primary task to bring all to this receptivity through forming good leaders of liturgy, which sacralizes time and individuals, and by providing fruitful spiritual direction which invites transformation into wholeness and holiness within the gift of time, the church, i.e., as perfect androgen.

NOTES

1. Karl Stern, *The Flight from Woman* (New York: The Noonday Press, 1966), p. 10.
2. Wing-Tsit Chan, *A Source Book in Chinese Philosophy* (New Jersey: Princeton University Press, 1973), p. 249.
3. Fritjof Capra, *The Turning Point* (New York: Simon and Schuster, 1982), p. 38.
4. Nicholas Berdyaev, *The Destiny of Man* (New York: Harper Torchbooks, 1960), pp. 61–62.
5. Ann Ulanov, *The Feminine in Jungian Psychology and in Christian Theology* (Evanston: Northwestern University Press, 1971), preface x.
6. Emma Jung, *Anima, Animus* (Switzerland: Spring Publications, 1972), p. 2.
7. Ulanov, p. 157. Also Kenneth Woodward, *et al.*, "Vows of Defiance," *Newsweek* (March 19, 1984), pp. 97–100.

8. Elemire Zolla, *The Androgyne: Reconciliation of Male and Female* (New York: Crossroads, 1981), p. 6; also John Sanford, *The Invisible Partners* (New York: Paulist Press, 1980), p. 4.
9. Ulanov, p. 292.
10. F. Max Müller, *The Upanishads* (Delhi: Motilal Banarsidass, 1982), pp. 109–10.
11. Beatrice Bruteau, "In the Cave of the Heart: Silence and Realization," from a conference recorded in Kansas City, KS, at East-West Monastic Seminar, "Formation and Transformation from an Eastern Perspective" (August, 1983).
12. Iréne de Castellejo, *Knowing Woman* (New York: Harper Colaphon Books, 1973), pp. 11, 20.
13. Douglas Steere, *On Listening to Another* (New York: Harper and Bros., 1955), pp. 4, 7.
14. Lao Tzu, as quoted in Fritjof Capra, p. 37.
15. Lama Anagarika Govinda, *Creative Meditation and Multi-Dimensional Consciousness* (Wheaton: Quest, 1976), p. 164.
16. Walter Burghardt, S.J., *Woman, New Dimensions* (New York: Paulist Press, 1977), p. 63.
17. Helen Luke, *The Way of Women, Ancient and Modern* (Three Rivers: Applegate Farms), p. 11.
18. Beatrice Bruteau, "Neo-Feminism and the Next Revolution in Consciousness," *Cross Currents* (Summer, 1977), p. 172.
19. Capra, p. 29.
20. Rosemary Radford Ruether, *New Woman, New Earth: Sexist Ideologies and Human Liberation* (New York: Seabury Press, 1975), p. 204.
21. Capra, p. 45.
22. Judith Simmer Brown, "Women and Enlightenment," *The Naropa Bulletin,* 1983, p. 18; also of Diana Y. Paul, "Buddhist Attitudes Towards Women's Bodies," *Buddhist-Christian Studies,* Honolulu, Vol. 1 (1981), p. 65.
23. Nancy Shuster, as quoted in Judith S. Brown, p. 19.
24. Bede Griffiths, "Riches from the East" (Kansas City: NCR Cassettes, 1984), tape 34.
25. Cf. Joan Schaupp, *Image of the Holy Spirit* (Denville: Dimension Books, 1975); also Yves Conger, "The Spirit of God's Femininity," *Theology Digest,* Vol. 30, No. 2 (Summer, 1982), p. 129.
26. Griffiths, tape 4.
27. Bruteau, *Cross Currents,* pp. 173–74.
28. Ruether, p. xiv (preface).
29. "The Church at Prayer: A Holy Temple of the Lord," pastoral letter, November, 1983, *Origins,* Vol. 13, No. 25 (December 1, 1983), #2 and #48.
30. Tilden Edwards, *Spiritual Friend: Reclaiming the Gift of Spiritual Direction* (New York: Paulist Press, 1980), p. 71.

31. Anthony Bloom, as quoted in Tilden Edwards, pp. 2, 256.
32. See St. Ignatius of Loyola, *Spiritual Exercises* (Chicago: Loyola University Press, 1951).
33. Thomas Merton, "Final Integration: Toward a Monastic Therapy," *Cistercian Studies* (December, 1968), p. 96.
34. Bruce Reed, as quoted in Tilden Edwards, p. 77. A full reading of this whole section will be rewarding (pp. 77–82).
35. Karl Rahner, "The Person in the Sacramental Event," *Theological Investigations* (New York: Seabury Press, 1976), Vol. XIV, p. 169.
36. Cf. Archbishop Quinn's "Dialogue and the Bishop's Pastoral Service to Religions," Report to U.S. Bishops, November 15, 1983, *Origins,* Vol. 13, No. 25 (December 1, 1983), p. 427, insisting on "quality time" for dialogue with local religions.
37. Cf. Archbishop Quinn, p. 79.
38. Bede Griffiths, O.S.B., Forward to Jyoti Sahi, *The Child and the Serpent* (London: Routledge & Kegan Paul, 1980), p. xii.
39. Luke, p. 1.
40. Luke, p. 1.

3

Male-Female Aspects of the Trinity in Christian Mysticism

EWERT H. COUSINS

In exploring the divine intention for male-female relations, we can follow several avenues of investigation. One of the most fruitful approaches is to examine male-female aspects of the divinity. For, according to the metaphysics of exemplarism, God has imprinted his image on human beings in his very act of creation. Therefore, by contemplating male-female aspects of God, human beings can discern a divine model for their male-female relations. Yet Christians immediately encounter a problem—glaringly manifested in the fact that I used the form "his" in speaking of God. I was constrained to do so by a linguistic convention rooted in over three millennia of patriarchy. Derived from its patriarchal Jewish heritage, the Christian image of God is masculine. This masculine conception is intensified by the archetypal images associated with the Hebrew God: king, warrior, lawgiver, priest. Unlike members of archaic tribes or present-day Hindus, Christians cannot draw from a rich tradition of goddesses and divine consorts. The mother goddess of the Mediterranean world was suppressed by the masculine sky god of ancient Israel. For Christians, the maleness of the Jewish God was intensified by the fact that they believed his unique incarnation occurred in the male Jesus of Nazareth, who called God his father. This male image of God reached a peak in the doctrine of the Trinity. It is here that patriarchy triumphed. Although the doctrine of the Trinity introduced differentiations within the divinity instead of opening up the male-female aspect of God, it was formulated exclusively in the patriarchal terms of Father and Son.

In the course of Christian history a number of attempts have broken through this exclusively masculine image of God. For example, both the divine Wisdom and the Holy Spirit have been described as feminine. Because of their care and concern, God and even Christ have been called mother. The most powerful feminine image in Christianity has been Mary, the "mother of God." Although this has offered some compensation for the dominant male image, it has always been done on patriarchal terms, since Mary, as a creature, is never subsumed into the divine level. At the present time, when consciousness of the feminine is emerging in many quarters in culture, it is important for Christians to explore female aspects of the divinity and to see these in relation to the masculine.

In this paper, I propose to examine male-female aspects of the divinity that stand behind the patriarchal image of the Trinity. To do this, I will first draw upon the classical mystical writings of Bonaventure and Eckhart. Second, I will analyze these in the light of the principle of the coincidence of opposites, which operates through mutually affirming complementarity. Third, I will situate this form of mystical consciousness and the principle of the coincidence of opposites within the extensive transformation of consciousness which is occurring throughout the world on the eve of the twenty-first century—a decisive era in history which I will describe as a Second Axial Period.

Patriarchy and the Trinity

In his essay entitled, "A Psychological Approach to the Trinity," C. G. Jung presents the Trinity as a primordial archetype, which in Pythagoras and Plato had a mathematical formulation involving the numbers one and three. In the Christian tradition it took on a concrete form through the patriarchal names Father and Son, and by the exclusion of the feminine. According to Jung, the form is concrete "in that the archetype is represented by the relationship 'Father' and 'Son.' Were it nothing but that, it would only be a dyad. The third element, however, the connecting link between 'Father' and 'Son,' is spirit and not a human figure." Jung draws out the implications of this for the exclusion of the feminine:

> The masculine father-son relationship is thus lifted out of the natural order (which includes mothers and daughters) and translated to a sphere from which the feminine element is excluded. In ancient Egypt as in Christianity, the Theotokos [the mother of God] stands outside the Trinity.[1]

After treating the male figures of father and son and the figure of spirit as life, Jung identifies this formulation of the archetype as distinctively patriarchal:

Father-son-life (or procreative power), together with rigorous exclusion of the Theotokos, constitute the patriarchal formula that was "in the air" long before the advent of Christianity.[2]

It would be interesting to speculate on what concrete formulation the Trinitarian archetype would have acquired in a matriarchal culture: for example, mother-daughter-life. It is possible also to penetrate patriarchy and matriarchy, to perceive in the Trinitarian archetype an inner dynamic which is imaged in the love between man and woman and in their procreation of offspring. I personally do not believe that there is only one manifestation or concretization of the Trinitarian archetype. I might note here that I am using the term "archetype," not in an exclusively psychological sense, but to mean an objective structure of reality which can be perceived by the psyche, especially the unconscious. If we are dealing with God as Trinity, then the divine reality—the divine Trinitarian archetype—in all its richness would provide the ground for many concretizations. In a correlative fashion, the mystery of the masculine and feminine is so rich that it can be realized in many modes, not only in the biological male and female.

With this as a preamble, I would like to focus on the central point of this investigation. I will not attempt to recast the patriarchal Trinitarian formula in matriarchal or male-female terms. Rather, I will accept the patriarchal formula as expressing the male aspect of the divinity; but through the writings of Christian mysticism I will go beyond this male element to a primordial female ground of the Trinity. My position is that, in spite of its patriarchal dogmatic formulation, the Christian experience of God, in its deepest mystical states, is of a feminine ground of the divinity. It is of crucial importance for Christians to recover this feminine ground of the divinity because of the demands of our time in the dialogue of world religions and in recovering our rootedness in the earth. It is equally crucial that we not only recover this feminine ground but that we discover it as creatively related to the masculine aspect of the divinity.

The Trinity in Christian Mysticism

In exploring this primordial male-female aspect of the Trinity, I will draw from two medieval theologians and spiritual writers: Bonaventure, the Franciscan interpreter of Francis of Assisi, and Meister Eckhart, the controversial Dominican preacher in the

Rhineland. From Bonaventure I will derive the male aspect of Trinitarian mysticism and from Eckhart, the primordial female ground.

In his treatise *The Soul's Journey into God,* Bonaventure opens with a prayer which reflects the patriarchal Trinity: "In the beginning I call upon the First Beginning, from whom all illuminations descend as from the *Father of Lights,* from whom *comes every good and perfect gift*" (James 1:17). He continues with the formula: "I call upon the Eternal Father through his Son, our Lord Jesus Christ. . . ."[3] It is not surprising that Bonaventure should begin his treatise with an invocation to the Trinity, since he is one of the most explicitly Trinitarian theologians in Christian history. Throughout his writing he spells out his Trinitarian theology in great detail, not only in the inner divine life, but in its vestiges imprinted on creation. In Franciscan fashion he contemplates the reflection of the Trinity throughout the material universe.

For Bonaventure, however, the Trinity is not primarily concretized in the patriarchal names of Father and Son, nor in the mathematical pattern of three and one. For him, as for the mainstream Christian mystical tradition, the Trinity is primarily the archetype of divine emanation, expressed in the mystical symbol of the fountain. Bonaventure perceives the Father as an eternally flowing fountain of creative energy, generating the Son and resulting in the spiration of the Holy Spirit. He describes the Father as *fontalis plenitudo* (fountain-fulness).[4] The divinity possesses the fulness of all perfections but is not envious, holding its perfections back in a miserly fashion. Rather, it shares these perfections; it is a fountain flowing out of its own fulness, bringing creatures into being to share its perfections. But this flowing out of the divine fountain-fulness is by no means completely actualized in the creation of the world. Rather, it is grounded on another fountain-fulness which is in the inner life of God: namely, in the Trinitarian processions. From all eternity the fulness of the divinity wells up in the person of the Father and expresses itself in his Son, who is the Image and Word of the Father. According to Western theology, the Father and the Son as one principle breathe forth the Holy Spirit. The Trinitarian processions, then, are actualization of the fountain-fulness of the Father. Bonaventure expresses this through the principle of the fecundity of primacy:

. . . but the more primary a thing is, the more it is fecund and the principle of others. Therefore just as the divine essence, because it is first, is the principle of other essences, so the person of the Father, since he is the first, because from no one, is the principle and has fecundity in regard to persons.[5]

There is reason to perceive this emanation archetype as a male aspect of the divinity. It consists of power which flows out, expressing itself in intelligence or *Logos,* which is also the divine Word, as the Son is designated. It is imaged as well in the mystical symbol of light, shining out from its source, penetrating and illumining darkness. Although a number of these archetypal qualities can be associated with the feminine, I am focusing here upon their distinctive masculine aspect. From this point of view, then, the patriarchal Trinity would coincide with the emanation archetype.

But the emanation archetype does not exhaust the divinity. There is also the divine silence out of which the word is uttered, the divine darkness out of which the light shines, the abyss out of which the fountain flows. It is this silent, dark abyss of the divinity that I would associate with the primordial feminine as the ultimate ground of the divinity. Although there are hints of this dimension in Bonaventure, the major articulator of it in the Christian West is Meister Eckhart.

It is important to note that Eckhart did not ignore the patriarchal Trinity nor the emanation archetype of fountain-fulness. However, his more characteristic approach is to go beyond the Trinity to the desert of the Godhead. This desert is the abyss out of which the fountain-fulness flows, the silence out of which speech is uttered, the darkness out of which light shines. Eckhart states:

. . . it is stripped of matter that the soul attains to God. It is only thus that it succeeds in uniting itself to the Blessed Trinity. But its happiness can become even greater yet if the soul search out the naked Godhead, for the Trinity is only the manifestation of the Godhead. In the pure Godhead there is absolutely no activity. The soul attains to perfect beatitude only in throwing itself into the desert of the Godhead there where there are neither operations nor forms, to bury itself there and lose itself there in that wilderness where its ego is annihilated and where it has no more care than it had in the days before it existed.[6]

Eckhart evokes the mystical experience of the divine desert in the following statement:

> I speak in all truth, truth that is eternal and enduring, that this same light [the spark of the soul] is not content with the simple divine essence in its repose, as it neither gives nor receives; but it wants to know the source of this essence, it wants to go into the simple ground, into the quiet desert, into which distinction never gazed, not the Father, nor the son, nor the Holy Spirit.[7]

In another passage, Eckhart evokes the same experience:

> But if all images are detached from the soul, and it contemplates only the Simple One, then the soul's naked being finds the naked, formless being of the divine unity, which is there a being above being, accepting and reposing in itself. Ah, marvel of marvels, how noble is that acceptance, when the soul's being can accept nothing else than the naked unity of God![8]

I believe that Eckhart has penetrated the other side of the Trinitarian archetype. If we accept Jung's principle of polarity, we can say that this is the dark side, not in a destructive or evil sense, but in a positive sense. If the emanation archetype, as presented by Bonaventure, is that of light, then Eckhart's presentation is of darkness; if Bonaventure's is of fulness, then Eckhart's is of emptiness; if Bonaventure's is of speech, then Eckhart's is of silence; if Bonaventure's is of the patriarchal male Trinity, then Eckhart's is of the matriarchal female ground of the Trinity. I believe that we can associate the feminine with the abyss of the divinity, since it reflects the mysterious ground, the cave or abyss of the divinity, the undifferentiated mysterious hidden depths of the divine reality.

Implications of the Divine Feminine

What are the implications of the feminine ground of the divinity? According to the principle that everything on the level of the divinity shares consubstantially in the divine nature, this feminine ground is fully divine. In fact, it has a certain primacy of order over the male Trinity, since it is the abyss out of which the Trinitarian processions flow. It is important to note that this ground is not a "fourth person" of the Trinity in a technical sense, for such has been excluded by the theological tradition, and rightly so, since it would merely subsume and transform the female element into the male Trinity. Rather, it stands as the presupposition and ground of the Trinity: the complementary other side of the Trinitarian archetype. It means that the male Trinitarian archetype alone is not the ultimate structure of reality and hence cannot subordinate the female to itself.

Where the Trinitarian archetype in its male form dominates, the female is identified with matter, which is relegated to the lowest level of the hierarchy of being. In the history of Christianity, the female principle has been imaged in the person of Mary the mother of God, through whom matter is given a new status. Jung has pointed out how Mary has been lifted up to produce a quaternity, which is the figure of completion. For Jung the Trinitarian three is incomplete without a fourth: "Medieval iconology, embroidering on the old speculations about the Theotokos, evolved a quaternity symbol in its representations of the coronation of the Virgin and surreptitiously put it in place of the Trinity." Jung saw the doctrine of the bodily assumption of Mary into heaven as the completion of the Christian quaternity:

> The *Assumptio Mariae* paves the way not only for the divinity of the Theotokos (i.e., her ultimate recognition as a goddess), but also for the quaternity. At the same time, matter is included in the metaphysical realm, together with the corrupting principle of the cosmos, evil.[9]

I agree with Jung that the quaternity manifests the ultimate completion of reality, but I do not believe that it can be achieved by assuming Mary and hence matter into heaven, because for Christians there always remains the infinite gulf between creature and creator. Therefore, to resolve the problem of the female aspect of the divinity through Mary is doomed to failure, for it subsumes the issue into the patriarchal hierarchy of being. While maintaining their patriarchal Trinitarian principles, Christians cannot admit into full consubstantiality with the divinity Mary, who is a creature, and matter, which is the lowest of creatures. On the other hand, if we locate the female aspect in the abyss of the divinity, we establish a quaternity in Jung's sense by situating the female at the very ground of the divinity.

Discovery of the female ground of the divinity challenges us to reexamine our understanding of matter. If viewed from the perspective of the patriarchal Trinity, matter stands at the lowest rung of being—below divinity and spirit. From the Greek philosophers, Christianity had assimilated the hierarchical structure of being. For example, Plato and Plotinus chartered a spiritual path from matter to spirit to the divine. For Aristotle, matter was pure potentiality, open to a variety of specifications through form whereby it acquired intelligibility. Although matter is relegated to the lowest position in the patriarchal universe, it bears remarkable similarities to the female abyss of the divinity. Eckhart saw that in this abyss all differentiations fade and all hierarchies collapse. On the human level we see a reflection of this in the unconditional and undifferentiated quality of a mother's love. It may well be that there is a divine dimension of matter that lies undetected under the patriarchal archetype. If so, this would open to the theologian a female dimension in the Christian mysteries of creation, incarnation, redemption. A sign of the spiritual power of matter, hidden in the female abyss of the divinity, may be discerned in the paradoxical fact that the mystical symbols which reflect the loftiest level of the divinity are drawn from matter: water, light, darkness, abyss, ground.

This leads us to the question of the relation between the male and the female in the Trinitarian archetype. I believe that they should be seen according to the coincidence of opposites of mutually affirming complementarity.[10] By this I mean that they are on an equal level, according to the Trinitarian principle of consubstantiality. By viewing the Trinitarian archetype as I presented it—with its male and female aspects—we avoid the problem of subordination, to which Jung has called attention in his treatment of Mary. The relation is complementary, not merely in a static way, but in a dynamic mutual affirmation of each other. The more female one pole is, the more it affirms its complementary male pole. In the history of Christian theology, the persons of the Trinity have been viewed as being constituted by their mutual relation. The foundation of this was laid by Augustine, was explored from the standpoint of human interpersonal relations by Richard of St. Victor, and brought to a climax by Thomas Aquinas' treatment of the divine persons as subsistent relations.[11] This rich theology of mutual relationship could be transposed to the female-male aspects of the Trinitarian archetype.

This paper has focused on the divine archetype. How the divinity is or should be exemplified in human beings is a complicated issue. I do not believe that we can look at the divine reality and find there a photo-like model of relations between men and women; rather we can discover ultimate principles of and a divine grounding for such relations. I believe with Jung that these archetypes filter through the unconscious and cannot be analyzed in minute detail by the conscious mind. However, when the archetype is awakened from the unconscious—as I believe is happening at the present time in the case of the female side of the divine archetype—it works its way into consciousness and into social structures and personal lives. However, there is one point that should be made here. As Jung has abundantly illustrated, the male-female polarity is found within each psyche and is not relegated exclusively to the interrelation of the biological male and the female. This means that Christians have the task of differentiating and assimilating in a new way the female divine archetype as this is imaged in their individual psyches.

The Axial Period

There are many signs that the female archetype is emerging at the present time: for example, in the widespread movement to achieve equal rights for women in economic, social, and political spheres. I would like to situate this emergence of the feminine within a large historical and geographical context, seeing it in relation to the history of consciousness as this has been studied by Karl Jaspers in his book, *The Origin and Goal of History.*[12]

Observing the phenomena of the first millennium B.C., Jaspers notes that a striking transformation of consciousness occurred in three geographical regions: China, India and Persia, and the Eastern Mediterranean, including Israel and Greece. This transformation took place apparently without significant influence of one area upon the other. Jaspers calls this era the Axial Period because it "gave birth to everything which, since then, man has been able to be." He continues:

> It would seem that this axis of history is to be found in the period around 500 B.C., in the spiritual process that occurred between 800 and 200 B.C. It is there that we meet with the most deep-cut dividing line in history. Man, as we know him today, came into being. For short, we may style this the "Axial Period."[13]

In the Axial Period the transformation of consciousness was mediated by great spiritual teachers who emerged in the three pivotal regions. Confucius and Lao-Tzu appeared in China; the Upanishadic sages, Mahāvira, and the Buddha in India; Zoroaster in Persia; the prophets Elijah, Isaiah and Jeremiah in Israel; and the philosophers Socrates, Plato, and Aristotle in Greece. These teachers mediated a transformation from the mythic, cosmic, ritualistic, collective consciousness of primitive peoples to the rational, analytic, critical, individualistic consciousness that has characterized the mainstream of human history since the Axial Period. Or, we can characterize this shift in terms of female and male archetypes, claiming that the feminine, organic, holistic, nature-centered consciousness was supplanted by a masculine, differentiating, individual, patriarchal form of consciousness.

We can grasp the significance of this transformation by comparing the qualities of Axial consciousness with those of primitive consciousness. The nature of primitive consciousness can be examined through archeological research, through a study of the surviving forms of primitive culture—for example, the American Indians—and through the residue of this form of consciousness within the consciousness of the Axial Period. First, it is important to note that the transformation was not abrupt but was prepared for by an intermediate period of the great empires of Egypt, Assyria, Persia, and China. Granted this intermediate period, the radical nature of the transformation can best be seen by contrasting Axial consciousness with its primitive antecedents.

The most distinctive quality of primitive consciousness is a lack of the foundational element of Axial consciousness: distinct individual identity which allows one to separate oneself from the tribe and the cosmos. Primitive peoples experienced themselves as part of the totality. They felt that they were linked in an organic fashion to the cosmos and the cosmic cycles, whether they were food-gatherers, hunters, herders, or farmers. They grounded their religious life in the change of the seasons and the fertility cycles; they were sensitive to nature symbolism in a much deeper way than the Axial peoples, often naming themselves from animals or objects in nature. They related to life through myth and ritual, drawing from nature powerful symbols which gave expression to their deepest spiritual longings. A similar sense of fusion existed also with the tribe. They experienced corporate, not individual, identity, for their psychic and spiritual energy flowed through the collectivity of the tribe. Ostracism from the tribe was the worst of fates, for it cut them off from their vital roots, leaving them to psychological and even physical death.

The Axial Period altered this structure of consciousness, producing a more masculine form with a new type of relatedness to the world and the community. In the Axial Period there emerged a sense of independent individual identity. No longer was the human person fused with the cosmos and the tribe; rather, he could separate himself from the cycles of the seasons and the fertility of nature and embark on his own individual spiritual journey. No longer was he embedded in the matrix of the tribe; rather, he could radically criticize the structure of society, as did Socrates and the Hebrew prophets. No longer was he related to the universe and events through myth and ritual; rather, he would use his newly acquired analytic reason to determine the scientific structure of the natural world and record the events of history. With his capacity for abstract reasoning, he created philosophy, analyzing the very structures of being. In fact, he could turn his analytic, reflective consciousness on himself, arriving at a new awareness of himself, his capacities, and his place in nature and history.

It was during this period that the world religions as we know them came into existence. Although they have roots in the Pre-Axial Period, their present form embodies the distinctive consciousness of the Axial Period. In fact, their message can be seen as a charting of the spiritual path within the horizon of Axial consciousness. This is true of the religions that crystallized in this period: Hinduism, Buddhism, Jainism, Zoroastrianism, Taoism, Confucianism, and Judaism. It is true also of the religions that appeared later but with roots in this period: Christianity, Islam, and Sikhism. In the great religions of the Axial Period, the individual spiritual path became a possibility. Because of the emergence of individual identity, the person could now come to a self-reflexive grasp of his psyche in relation to the "good," according to the Greeks, or of his *ātman* in relation to Brahman, according to the Indians. He could then pursue his journey toward his goal through the inner way, disengaged from cosmic rhythms and rituals, and from the collectivity of the tribe.

Monasticism as a way of life came into being in the Axial Period. Equipped with the new individual identity, one could take the stance of a marginal person in society, become a beggar, free oneself from the tasks of the tribe and from the cycle of sexual reproduction. Having made a radical break from nature and the community, he could pursue his spiritual path as a hermit or a member of a community of monks with a similar structure of consciousness. Although mythic, ritualistic, cosmic, and collective forms of consciousness survived in the Axial religions, they were subordinated to the new Axial consciousness, often remaining subliminal or unconscious.

It is safe to say with Jaspers that "in this age were born the fundamental categories within which we still think today, and the beginnings of the world religions, by which human beings still live, were created."[14] Or, in terms of this paper, it was in the Axial Period that the male archetype emerged into full ascendency in the form that has perdured until the present. It is true that there has been in world religions a difference of degrees in the dominance of the male and suppression of the female, with Western religions registering high on the scale. Yet Axial consciousness, with its male modes of thought and its patriarchal priorities, has determined the pervasive awareness in world religions.

Although the Axial Period opened many spiritual possibilities, it produced negative effects. In differentiating a masculine form of consciousness, it suppressed the feminine. At the same time that it generated individual consciousness, it alienated the person from nature and the community. In opening up to the individual spiritual journey, it produced an other-worldly attitude, directing attention away from matter and the rootedness of the human community in the earth. If we look at the maps of the spiritual journey charted in the Axial Period, we will find that they are directed to the individual and present a path which proceeds in an ascent from matter to spirit to the divine. There is, of course, a spectrum of attitudes, with Taoism at one end upholding an organic relation of the human with nature. Nevertheless, the approach of the great religions has assimilated Axial consciousness, with its patriarchal modes of thought.

Second Axial Period

I believe that we are passing through a Second Axial Period.[15] For centuries, forces have been building up which are now reaching a climax. I call this the Second Axial Period because I believe that it is producing a transformation of consciousness as significant as that of the First Axial Period and that this transformation is affecting the great religions of the world in a profound fashion. According to Teilhard de Chardin, the forces of history are moving toward "planetization": an organic global consciousness brought about by the spherical shape of the earth, the development of science, technology and communication, and the increase of population. According to Teilhard, the forces of divergence, which for millennia have caused the human community to separate, have shifted to those of convergence. Like the meridians on a globe that separate at the equator and converge at the pole, the human community, after its long history of divergence, is moving toward convergence in global consciousness.[16]

What are the characteristics of the consciousness of the Second Axial Period? It is global in two senses: (1) in a horizontal sense, it is global in being comprehensive, encompassing the entire world and the human community as a whole; (2) in a vertical sense, the Second Axial Period is pressuring the human community to extend its consciousness back into the earth, into matter and the biological substratum that supports life on our planet. The pollution of the environment, the exhaustion of natural resources, the threat of nuclear holocaust are forcing the human community to reexamine its roots in the earth, to relate itself harmoniously to its ecological base, if life is to survive at all on our planet. To state it briefly, in the Second Axial Period the human community is rediscovering on a global level the female characteristics of the consciousness of the Pre-Axial Period without losing the distinctive male values of Axial consciousness. We must rediscover the cosmic and collective consciousness of primitive peoples—but integrated into the individual consciousness, with its analytic, critical modes of self-reflection. Thus the consciousness of the Second Axial Period would be more integral and multidimensional than the consciousness of either the Pre-Axial or the Axial Periods, for it would integrate the male and female archetypes according to the coincidence of opposites of mutually affirming complementarity.

The impact on religion of Second Axial consciousness will be enormous, comparable in its own way to the transformation of consciousness in the Axial Period that produced the world religions as we know them. Already this influence is being manifested in the major religious phenomenon of our time: the meeting of world religions in an atmosphere of dialogue and solidarity. Such a meeting as this conference gives concrete evidence of the emergence of global consciousness, bringing together people from the various religions to discuss their ultimate beliefs about God and to address contemporary problems in this Second Axial Period. In keeping with the dynamics of the Second Axial Period, we should explore the male-female archetypes in the world's religions. As suggested in this paper, Christians can explore the female dimension of the Trinitarian archetype, bringing this to light through dialogue with other religions in which the feminine has been more prominent than in the West. Together, members of the various religions can share their wisdom creatively to explore the religious, social, and personal implications of the emergence of the feminine archetype in the Second Axial Period.

NOTES

1. C. G. Jung, "A Psychological Approach to the Trinity," in *Psychology and Religion East and West:* Vol. 11 of *The Collected Works of C. G. Jung,* 2nd ed., trans. R. F. C. Hull (Princeton: Princeton University Press, 1969), p. 132.
2. *Ibid.,* p. 133.
3. Bonaventure, *The Soul's Journey into God,* Prologue, 1; the English translation is my own, from *Bonaventure: The Soul's Journey into God, The Tree of Life, The Life of St. Francis* (New York: Paulist Press, 1978), p. 53.
4. Cf. Bonaventure, *I Sent.,* d. 27, p. 1, a. un., q. 2 and 3.
5. *Ibid.,* d. 2, a. un., q. 2; the English translation is my own.
6. This quotation is from the sermon *Expedit vobis,* which is printed as #76 in *Meister Eckhart,* ed. Franz Pfeiffer (Göttingen: Vandenhoeck and Ruprecht, 1924). Although previous editors considered this sermon to be Eckhart's, it was not listed by Joseph Quint among Eckhart's authentic works in his critical edition (cf. note 7, below); yet it is from the Eckhart school and represents in a concise fashion the essence of his position.
7. Eckhart, *German Works: Sermon 48;* translation from *Meister Eckhart: The Essential Sermons, Commentaries, Treatises, and Defense,* trans. and ed., Edmund Colledge and Bernard McGinn (New York: Paulist Press, 1981), p. 198. This translation has been made from the critical text: *Meister Eckhart: Die deutschen and lateinischen Werke,* herausgegeben im Aufträge der Deutschen Forschungsgemeinschaft (Stuttgart and Berlin: W. Kohlhammer, 1936–).
8. *Ibid., Sermon 83;* trans., p. 206.
9. Jung, "A Psychological Approach to the Trinity," pp. 170–171.
10. For a study of this form of the coincidence of opposites, cf. my book, *Bonaventure and the Coincidence of Opposites* (Chicago: Franciscan Herald Press, 1978).
11. Cf. Augustine, *De Trinitate,* V; Richard of St. Victor, *De Trinitate,* III; Thomas Aquinas, *Summa Theologiae,* I, q. 29, a. 4. corp.
12. Karl Jaspers, *Vom Ursprung und der Geschichte* (Zürich: Artemis, 1949); English translation by Michael Bullock, *The Origin and Goal of History* (New Haven: Yale University Press, 1953).
13. Jaspers, *The Origin and Goal of History,* p. 1.
14. *Ibid.,* p. 2.
15. For a further exposition of my theory of the Second Axial Period, cf. "Teilhard and Global Spirituality," *Anima,* 8 (1981), pp. 26–30.
16. Pierre Teilhard de Chardin, *Le Phenomene humain* (Paris: Editions du Seuil, 1955), pp. 268–269.

4

Circles of Love: In Search of a Spirituality of Sexuality and Marriage

RICHARD PAYNE

We live today in a desacralized world; the physiological acts, such as sexual union, which can be rightly used as a sacrament, have been deprived of spiritual significance and therefore of their truly human significance. If we could understand sexual union fully, in all of its infinite possibilities—psychopathological, drive for power, biological urge, sensual, sacred, and sacramental—we would be liberated from the demonizing influences of Freud, Darwin, and our profaning rational mind. Sexual union reached exceptional prestige in Asian tantrism,[1] where it strikingly demonstrates how it can be transformed into a religious ritual, or a mystical technique. As a tantric text expresses it: "The true sexual union is the union of the supreme *Shakti* (nature, ed.) with the spirit; other unions represent only carnal relations with women" (*Kulārṇava Tantra V,* 111–112). There is no longer any question of a physiological act—there is a mystical rite, and a transfiguration of the carnal has taken place. Can we rediscover the divine laws that operate to make human sexual love a sacrament, an instrument of grace for our sanctification? Carl Jung's rediscovery of symbolic thinking, archetypal events, and *maṇḍala* structures are invaluable aids to lead us from darkness into light, and I shall use insights of his in this essay.

Jung needs no introduction. What does need to be clarified about the man and his work is that his understanding of Western (European) life came largely from his patients, while his understanding of Eastern (Asiatic) life came primarily, if not exclusively, from the lives of Eastern saints and from their scriptures. To the best of my knowledge, he never interviewed a Jewish or Christian saint, nor did he ever treat any wide number of psychological disorders of Asiatics. If we are to compare the consciousness of East and West, we should compare the ideal, the holy of the East with the holy of the West. If we are to compare the ideal of East and West, this should be done with "the normals" of each culture, and the same for psychopathology within each culture. Furthermore, the studies should be interdisciplinary; that is, the psychologist, the anthropologist, the theologian, the sociologist, the statistician, the historian, and even the mathematicians, physical scientists and economists, as well as poets and artists, should pool their findings into a holistic picture of consciousness and culture. Bearing in mind the experiential limitations of Carl Jung, we can proceed to a study of a small part of his very significant contribution to our understanding of ourselves and our spiritual nature and needs. With proper caution, he can be our guide into the psychology of personal and collective unconscious.

Intellect, detached from the soul, is death, according to Jung.[2] Intellect, self-confident and isolated in arrogant complacency, does not ennoble us. It humiliates us, deprives us of our personality and freedom; it kills the loving participations in the life of things and creatures of which the soul with its emotions and intuitions is capable. It enslaves us to the mechanical creations of our own finite mind. Intellect by itself becomes the principle of disintegration. Only the soul, with its special capacity for receiving and manifesting eternal truths, can save us from a nihilistic, meaningless existence. These special capacities of the soul, which transmit divine knowledge to the mind, function through symbols, archetypes, and *maṇḍalas.*

A symbol always stands for something more than its obvious and immediate meaning; a sign is always less than the concept it represents. A symbol implies something hidden, vague, unknown: for example, the lamb represents Christ; the apocalyptic lion, eagle, ox and man represent Mark, John, Luke and Matthew, the Evangelists. A sign denotes the objects to which it is attached and acquires recognizable meaning through common usage or deliberate intent: USA or UNESCO.

According to Jung, there are two main classifications of symbols: individual or private symbols that belong only to the user, and collective symbols which are chiefly religious. It is these collective symbols that form a "forgotten language" and are used by the mind to explore ideas that lie beyond the grasp of reason. Because there are innumerable things beyond the range of human understanding, we constantly use symbolic terms to represent concepts that we cannot define or fully comprehend. This is one reason why all religions employ symbolic language or images.

But this conscious use of symbols is only one aspect of a psychological fact of great importance. We produce symbols unconsciously and spontaneously, in the forms of dreams (sleeping and waking) and visions. They also occur in any intermediary state when the conscious mind gives way to the unconscious and releases subliminal content. Such states can occur after discursive prayer, while gazing upon sacred pictures, and almost always when one has mastered the basics of contentless meditation as practiced in Zen and elementary *rāja-yoga.* The Buddhists discard the world of this unconscious language as useless illusions, e.g., *makyo* (Zen). Many Christians put the church and St. John of the Cross between themselves and their unconscious. We are so entangled and captivated by our rational consciousness that we have forgotten the age-old fact that God speaks chiefly through dreams and visions. In spite of the fact that the Catholic church admits the occurrence of *"somnia a Deo missa"* (dreams sent by God), most of its thinkers make no serious attempt to understand dreams or to stimulate "symbol states" of consciousness where the same symbolic thinking can take place in the waking state. Basing their opinions upon a few lines from a sixteenth-century Spanish mystic, St. John of the Cross, who had no knowledge of twentieth-century empirical psychology, they turn away from experience of the subliminal unconscious as a temptation or even invitation to the sin of pride, with such conviction that many Catholic contemplatives succeed in repressing such material until it emerges in neurotic behavior.

I agree with Jung in recognizing no difference in principle between organic and psychic growth. As a plant produces its flowers, so the psyche creates and releases its symbols. And whether or not the new plant will live long enough to bear fruit depends entirely upon whether it is encouraged or actively discouraged. It is folly to dismiss these symbol states because in rational terms they seem to be absurd or irrelevant, or to be terrified that remembering them will lead us away from truth and into an abyss of pride and inflation. They are important constituents of our psycho-spiritual make-up and vital forces in the bridge-building between the temporal and the eternal, and they cannot be eradicated without serious loss. Where they are repressed or neglected, their specific energy disappears into the unconscious with unaccountable consequences. Even tendencies that might be able to exert beneficial effects can be transformed into demons when repressed.

We do not understand how much our "rationalism" has destroyed our capacity to respond to numinous symbols and ideas, and has thus put us at the mercy of the psychic underworld. We have freed ourselves of superstition, or so we believe, and in the process have lost our spiritual awareness to a positively dangerous degree. The plenitude of being has been replaced by a plenitude of books about the plenitude of being.

In the last seventy-five years since the development of modern thought, experience has been to feel oneself meaningfully linked up with the whole of being. An unknown, powerful fascination radiates from the situation, which explains the extraordinary lucidity of the experience, its very strong after-effects, and its intensity. The genesis of this experience cannot be solely from within the individual. Something from outside oneself stimulates the flow of psychic energy in the form of symbols, just as the pleasure of smelling a flower is stimulated by the perfume in the flower.

Jung preferred not to deal with this initial cause, and therefore made many enemies, but his specialty was the psychological, not the metaphysical, process. What makes an experience of "feeling meaningfully linked up with the whole of being" meaningful? The whole experience of being linked up becomes a symbol. There lies its real sense. The reality of the symbol is proved by its fascinating power, by the impossibility of bringing the experience down to a logical formula without robbing it of its essential parts, and by the transforming effects it has upon the life of the experiencer. Thus contemplation of a natural landscape, very often the first and strongest incitement to this religious experience, may suddenly lead to this feeling of linked-upness with the whole of being, and thus become symbolic.

It is not given to everyone to think in symbolic structures, just as not everyone can hear the range of sounds and tones that Bach did. So it seems that among several conditions needed to make this primary religious experience possible, there is also the power to see symbolically. To those who do not understand symbolism, the experience will be denied.

What power is this? Perhaps something resembling what Husserl calls *Wesensschauu,* viz., the power of feeling one's inner self germinate the seed of that on which one has been concentrating purely and earnestly. Then the symbol arises, followed by the moment of interpretation. When the inner and outer worlds unite in a new way, with symbolic vision we experience something of a reality which we do not yet, nor ever shall, know in our rational thoughts. It follows that we meet such symbolic visions only at the borders of our knowledge, and it seems certain that symbol-blindness and subsequent rational-intellectual thinking always go together.

Archetypes

There are archetypes, archetypal events, and archetypal treatment of symbols. For instance, a god-man is an archetype known throughout the whole world since time immemorial. Examples of archetypal events are the stories about the meaning of life and death, and the dramas of the creation of the world. The archetypal treatment of symbols is the function of the psyche in its natural attempt to reconcile and reunite opposites, and thus direct itself to wholeness.

The forgotten language of primordial images or archetypes varies to some degree individually and culturally, but Jung demonstrated how their universality and their persistent basic patterns show that they are unlearned. Archetypal symbolizing is an instinctive trend in the human psyche, as marked as the impulse of birds to build nests or ants to form organized colonies. This implies that collective thought patterns function in more or less the same way in all of us. They appear in dreams, visions, thoughts, whenever the archetypal mind has been freed from the tyranny of the rational discursive mind. The subject matter, always of a philosophical or religious nature, is intuitively grasped by the unconscious, submitted to archetypal treatment, and translated into action in daily life. The archetypes have their own initiative and specific energy, enabling them to produce meaningful interpretations, and to redirect conscious thought and behavior. They create myths, religions, philosophies that characterize whole nations and epochs of history.

The universal hero myth, for instance, always refers to a powerful god-man who vanquishes evil in the form of dragons or demons, and liberates his people from destruction and death. Sacred texts and ritual describe this event, and the worship of such a figure by hymns, prayers and sacrifice exalt the individual to an identification with the hero and an attempt to imitate him. This does not mean that a god-man did not exist in history or is "only a myth." It means that just as all men know to walk on their two feet, so all men have known instinctively that a god-man is required to produce certain events.

To be properly called archetypes, images must have a powerful emotional charge and through their numinosity or psychic energy, become so dynamic that some positive consequence must flow from them. Archetypes "come alive" only when they give meaning to the life of the individual to whom they are relating, when the whole being is suffused with their numinosity and a link is made between the creator and the creature: when purpose and meaning are given to both life and death.

Maṇḍalas

Jung's research clarifies the "centering" process in the human psyche seeking "wholeness," and the function of the *maṇḍala.* A *maṇḍala* can be a picture or drawing of a psychogram or a cosmogram. It can be a place to enter, as a temple. Or, it can be verbal, such as a Catholic mass. It can be a ritualized, formalized human body, a microcosm of the whole cosmos of creation.

The function of a *maṇḍala* is to bring persons to beatitude, to unite them with God, with the one, the all, to transcend the human condition, and to recover the divine condition—as a Christian or other Semite would say, the condition before the fall of the original man.

The basic components of a *maṇḍala* are the representations of the individual, of God, of time—past, present, and future—and the forces of good and evil. It is a symbol map of the whole universe in its essential plan, and the process of intersection between earth, heaven, and hell. Pictorial *maṇḍalas* have been drawn by North American Indians in sand, by contemporary Americans on canvas, but most powerfully and intricately developed by Tibetans of the Vajrayāṇa system in the tantric school. The word *maṇḍala* in Sanskrit means "circle" or "that which surrounds," and is in fact a series of circles inscribed within a square, drawn on consecrated ground by means of colored threads or colored rice powder, with the various divinities of the tantric pantheon arranged in order. The *maṇḍala* thus represents an *imago mundi* and at the same time a symbolic pantheon. Minute care is taken in every step so that the consecrator will provide the psychological condition needed for the process of redemption.

Basically the Tibetan *maṇḍala*[3] contains an outer enclosure and one or more concentric circles, which in their turn enclose the figure of a square cut in transversal lines. These start from the center and reach to the four corners so that the surface is divided into four triangles. In the center and the middle of each triangle, five circles contain emblems or figures of divinities. The circumscribing circle represents the mountain of fire which must burn out the ignorance and error that prevents us from the light we are seeking. Immediately after this circle is one of diamond symbolizing illumination, cosmic consciousness, which is outside time and space but is every place and every instant when it is realized. Next comes a circle in which eight graveyards are represented, which are symbols of the five senses, the intellective consciousness, the thinking faculty of the individual, and the store-consciousness, which produces *saṁsāra,* the rounds of births and deaths. A girdle of lotus leaves follows the graveyards, signifying spiritual rebirth. In the center is seated the god at the journey's end on a lotus bud symbolizing original synthesis. In the middle of this first circle is the "palace," flanked by seven walls in different colors, constituting the walls of the sacred city, and appropriate arches, vases, a tree of paradise, an eight-spoked wheel and various other symbols. The basic pattern of the *maṇḍala* corresponds to the ground plan of a royal city.

The pattern of divine cycles which form the *maṇḍala* are not the result of arbitrary construction, but the reflection of personal intuitions on the eternal contrast between the essential luminosity of man's consciousnsess and the forces which obscure it. By combining this introspection with cosmological concepts, rules were defined and classifications were established in patterns. The interior impulse which is translated into a *maṇḍala* becomes a support for meditation, an external instrument to produce the images and visions that help rediscover the way to reach secret reality. Through the symbols the neophyte can give form to the infinite possibilities in his subconscious, to primordial impulses, to disintegration and reintegration, and finally to that liberating experience which has been described as entering the kingdom of heaven.

The initiation of the neophyte begins by the entering into the different levels of the *maṇḍala* in a ritual manner. These first stages have the twofold effect of initiating the practitioner into a space where we can concentrate and find our own center. They also have a psychological and magical sense of protecting one from harmful influences and forces from outside. Above all, the ceremony performed within the *maṇḍala* is a royal "coronation" with baptism by water and a baptism of the tiara, because the neophyte, when his head is crowned, must become a king, raised above all the play of cosmic and psychic forces and reintegrated with the origin of all things, returned to primordial unity in primeval unity.

Some tantric schools reject the external *maṇḍala* and have recourse to interiorized *maṇḍalas.* These can be of two kinds: first, a purely mental construction, which acts as a support for meditation, or alternatively, an identification of the *maṇḍala* in one's own body. The discovery of the *maṇḍala* in one's own body indicates a desire to identify this "mystical body" as a microcosm of the universe. In this system of mystical physiology the reactivation of the *cakras,* those wheels or circles which are regarded as so many points of intersection of the cosmic life and the mental life, is homologous with the initiatory penetration into the *maṇḍala.* The "awakening" of the basic life energy, *kuṇḍalinī,*[4] is equivalent to breaking through to the ontological plane—that is, to the plenary realization of the symbolism of the "center." Every human tends, even unconsciously, towards this center, towards his own center where he can find integral reality—a sacredness, a place of communication with "heaven." The dynamic forces of the universe are not different from those of the human soul, and to recognize and transform those forces in one's own mind, not only for one's own good but for that of all living creatures, is the aim of Buddhist tantras, or psycho-physical-spiritual disciplines.

The Buddhist of the Mahāyāna school does not believe in an independent or separately existing eternal world, to whose dynamic forces one is a stranger. The external world and the inner world are only two sides of the same coin, in which the thread of all forces and all events, of all forms of consciousness and of their objects, are woven into an inseparable net of endless, mutually conditioned relations. The Buddhist tantras are of a mystic nature trying to establish the *inner* relationship of things: the parallelism of microcosm and macrocosm, mind and universe, ritual and reality, the world of matter and the world of spirit.

In tantric symbolism, the Buddha becomes one with knowledge *(prajnā)* and compassion *(karuṇā),* just as man and wife become one in the embrace of love, and this becoming is the highest, indescribable happiness. The embodiment of the active urge of enlightenment finds expression in the all-encompassing love and compassion, and is represented in the Buddha's sexual embrace of a female deity, the embodiment of highest knowledge. Though the polarity of male and female principles is recognized in the tantras of the Majrayāṇa, and is an important feature of its symbolism, it is raised upon a plane which is far away from the sphere of mere sexuality. It is the *union* of the male and female principles which must take place. After this, sexual polarity becomes a mere incident of universal polarity.

Sexual Symbolism in the Internal Maṇḍala

Although the "awakening" of the *kuṇḍalinī* or basic life energy is equivalent to breaking through the *cakras* or centers of the body to union with the first source of creation, tantric scriptures are full of warnings to the uninitiated. If not properly controlled, and without many years of spiritual training as a prerequisite, the aroused *kuṇḍalinī* may rush downward, bringing union with a lower order of creation. The carnal appetites are then vastly intensified: worldly ambitions are stimulated, together with the will to satisfy them at any cost. Lust, anger, grief, violence, hate, destruction, and the whole catalogue of evil passions take control. Rasputin is an example of this, and in recent times Charles Manson is another.

For these reasons, tantric texts and practices have been kept secret, and only a small select number are permitted to enter into the highest practices and initiations. A Tibetan Abbot of the Kagyupa sect recently told me that only four Tibetans living today have gone beyond multiplicity by these sexual practices. Further, it seems that the high degree of spiritual advancement required before such practices can be safely engaged in reduces the candidates to those who have actually achieved transcendence, or are so close to the border that it is imminent.

However dangerous this tantric use of sex and sexual imagery is for the Tibetan Buddhist, or his Hindu brother, or the American in our contemporary bedroom playground, we should examine it more closely, as it may throw much light upon our Christian Catholic sacrament of marriage, a sacrament which is not complete or valid without sexual intercourse.

As I have said before, the purpose of the *maṇḍala* is to bring the practitioner to the beatitude of the infinite and the eternal. On the exterior *maṇḍala* is projected the drama of cosmic integration and disintegration, which also takes place in the individual psychic life.

So the external *maṇḍala* is transferred to the internal *maṇḍala,* namely the human body, in which the same symbols as those of the former are placed in similar arrangements: a series of wheels, or *cakras,* rising from the base of the spine to the top of the head. In cosmic correspondence, the spine is the central mountain of the universe, and the wheels leading to it are various celestial planes. The body demands to be looked after, to be satisfied, to be favored in its desires, but at the same time without this body we could not enjoy the beauty of things, not catch that first glimmer of divine omnipotence which is displayed in the magnificence of nature. If it is tamed by a suitable discipline, the psycho-physical complex will be directed towards the divine. The practitioner knows that the principle of salvation is within him.

Thus, the two worlds, the physical and the spiritual, though opposed, acting through the medium of the psyche, cooperate in redemption, in the living unity of the individual. The procedure in using the human *maṇḍala* is to take the *citta,* i.e., the psyche's volitive, effective, and intellective activity, to the highest *cakra,* situated on the summit of the head, the *sahasrāra,* the lotus of the thousand petals, or in tantra, the archetypal original human, the androgynous man-woman. It is towards this reconstitution of this primordial man-woman that many years of laborious effort are directed, and its realization is beatitude *(ānanda).* Thus, unity is illumination, which unites itself indissolubly in itself. At this point the universal process is transferred into the microcosm, and more specific sexual symbolism is introduced into the system. The male seed and the female ovum are reintegrated in the primordial unity. In some tantric schools this conjunction takes place in reality or allegorically between the initiate and a woman, and here arise diverse practices, abuses, distortions, and rank superstitions. But such is the fate of all human institutions, and the corruption of the sacred ideal in sexual union has suffered the same fate in the West.

The idea of original unity and of its successive disintegration from which arises the desire to regain the initial paradise represents the spiritual basis of religions East and West. We need only note here the familiar Old Testament account of Adam and Eve in Eden. In a similar way, the Hindus recount that Prajāpati at the beginning of creation felt alarmed at his own solitude:

He did not feel joy, because no one when he is alone feels joy. And he was desirous of another. So he became the same size as are husband and wife in the moment of mutual embrace. So he divided into two and thus husband and wife were produced. However, this was only part of himself, like a pea divided into two. The void was, in a way, filled by woman. He approached her. Thus were men born.[5]

It was these intuitions and yearnings towards essential unity that inspired the tantric sexual practices. The tantricist's final goal is to unite the two contrary principles, male with female, wisdom with compassion. We can note in passing Jung's insights into the function of the *anima,* the feminine aspect of the psychological makeup of the male, and the *animus,* the masculine aspect of the female, in personal individuation.

In a man, the *anima* manifests itself in archetypes such as the harlot, the witch, the martyr, the sister, the peasant, the gypsy, the beloved, the saint, the goddess or a spiritual guide. Mythologically it is represented in stories having to do wtih the eternal feminine in all its forms, such as mother earth, love, and wisdom.

For a woman, the archetype of the *animus* is represented by such male images as the laborer, the judge, the teacher, the monk, a Prince Charming, prophet, magician or rapist. Mythologically it is represented in tales about the conquering hero, the great king, the wise man, Zeus, Apollo, the devil, and so on.

The function of the *anima* and *animus* is to mediate the contents of the objective psyche to the conscious ego.

Individuation is the reconciling of all opposites or polarities, within and without the person, into an integrated "whole." The sense of new being and wholeness that is felt when the tension of opposites is resolved is of greatest significance for the religious life. It is often felt as "following God's will," and is the basis of the numinous experience which is antecedent to creeds and religions. The individuated or whole person is, then, for Jung, the contrasexual person in whom the male and female polarities circulate and complement each other rather than fight and extinguish each other.

Creation as we encounter it now in our lives represents the state after an explosion of the primal unity and the separation of the two contrary principles, creating duality, suffering or, in our Christian mythic terms, "exile from paradise." "Paradise regained" would be the result of union of opposites, wherein the experience of duality is abolished and the phenomenal world is transcended, and a state of bliss *(nirvāṇa)* is achieved. Certain tantric schools teach that this state is achieved principally by ritual union of the sexes *(maithuna).*

Others teach that this same union of the opposites can be achieved within the body of one individual through meditation and other religious practices, as every individual retains within him both the male and female principles. In Hindu tantra, *śakti,* the female principle or nature, dwells at the base of the body and is moved by spiritual physical disciplines upward to the skull where *śiva,* the male principle or the divine source of nature, dwells and there unites with him. The union of the divine pair within his own body transforms the practitioner into a kind of "androgyne" and a state of cosmic bliss is experienced together with the other qualities of transcendence. In our Western Christian tradition we might see this as the Rhineland mystic Suso's coincidence of opposites *(coincidentia oppositorum)* realized within his own body and spirit.

It must be stated quite clearly that this return to a man-woman state, characteristic of primordial man, is not to be confused with satanic hermaphroditism as in the case of Aleister Crowley or some current movements which encourage decadent sexual practices for their own sake. These deviations are concerned not with the wholeness of man, resulting from the fusion of the sexes, but with carnal erotic diversions. The androgyne is not heterosexual, homosexual or bisexual. He is an *arsenothelya,* "male-female," and has become transsexual in the etymological sense of the word, not in its current usage of sex-change operations. Jung's term "contrasexual" is descriptive of a state prior to androgyna and must be considered in the content of his entire thesis. Clearly our vocabulary is not adequate to describe states that are beyond the usual and approaching the transcendent. When Ramakrishna was practicing the *madhura bhāva,* identifying himself with Rādha in her devotion to Krishnā, he wore women's clothes, imitated women's behavior and lived with women as a woman.

> If the devotee can make himself seriously believe for a while that he belongs to the opposite sex, he will be well on his way to overcoming the illusion of sex-distinction altogether; for he will then know that the distinction is not absolute, as he had supposed. . . . All of the devotional attitudes I have described above are *sādhanas* of the Vaishnava sect.[6]

Similar techniques are practiced, for the same androgynous ends, by Moslem *sufis* but with a great deal more secrecy.

It should also be noted that the preparations required of the tantrist to reach this undivided state, whether there is transcendent sexual unity within one's own body or unity achieved with another person, are extremely stringent and require much heroic discipline and ascetic preparation, compassion, and "*karmic* predisposition." Projected into a liturgy, purified by asceticism and prayer, exalted and transfigured by religious ideals, the tantric practices intended to repeat the drama of the universe. When the original man-woman has been reconstituted and maintained in a state of unity, and accompanied by a sublimation of personal satisfaction, an ecstasy of complete spiritual fusion exists. Tantra does not deny the senses, but uses them transformed towards a more noble path.

Sex as Sacred in the Judeo-Christian Tradition

Every soul and every spirit coming into this world is composed of a male and a female united in one being. Descending to earth, these two halves separate and go off to animate different bodies. At the time of marriage, the Holy One, blessed be He, Who knows all souls and spirits, unites them as before, and they become again a single body and a single soul. . . . But this union is consistent with the actions of man and the ways he has traveled. If he is pure and behaves piously, he will enjoy a union exactly like the one that preceded his birth (The Zohar).

The theme of mystical marriage in a religious ritual appears in the practices of the Jewish Kabbalists whose Torah scholars used to perform marital intercourse precisely on Friday night when the Sabbath began; the exile of the *Shekhinah,* or, in other words, the separation of the masculine and feminine principles in God, is usually imputed to the destructive action and magical influence of human sin. Adam's sin is perpetually repeated in every other sin. Instead of penetrating and contemplating the whole of the Godhead, Adam, when faced with a choice, took the easier way of contemplating only a part.

Instead of preserving the unity of God's action in all the worlds, which were still pervaded and governed by the secret life of the Godhead, instead of consolidating this unity by his own action, he shattered it. Since then there has been, somewhere deep within, a cleavage between the upper and lower, the masculine and feminine. . . . The reunion of God and his *Shekhinah* constitutes the meaning of redemption. In this state, again seen in purely mythical terms, the masculine and feminine are carried back to their original unity, and in this uninterrupted union of the two, the powers of generation will once again flow unimpeded through all the worlds. The Kabbalists held that every religious act should be accompanied by the formula: "This is done for the sake of the reunion of God and his *Shekhinah.*"[7]

This divine myth became a model for human union—the cosmic structure of the conjugal ritual transforms his conjugal union into a sacred act. A portion of a hymn used for the Friday evening meal runs:

> "Her husband embraces her
> In her foundation,
> Gives her fulfillment,
> Squeezes out his strength."

(The "foundation" is correlated with the male and female sex organs.)

These intuitions of sexual intercourse as a sacrament to help men and women find the supreme divine principle have not been absent in Christianity. The concept of divine love flowing through sexual union into the heart and souls of humans has been clearly defined by many Christian theologians, in spite of anti-sex religious trends. So convinced were they that married love is the work of grace that they concluded it was indissoluble except by death. Some theologians in the Eastern Orthodox church went further in their high esteem of marriage, which they believe cannot be dissolved, even by death. And it is worth noting here that while the Asian tantric schools have limited their secret practices to a select elite of male initiates in monasteries, with female partners clearly inferior, in the West sexual love as a sacrament is available to all baptized Christians, in *equal* measure to both partners. Until very recently in Asian societies, marriage for lay people was always arranged by the respective families. In Tibet, marriage was such a sad and traumatic affair that it was traditional for the bride's parents to send a *pakgyoma* (young woman appointed for the purpose) to stay with the bride for one month to console her when she encountered difficulties in her new life.

For the earliest Christians, the clergy did not intervene in marriage, because it was God who gave permission for them to marry, and the angels were witnesses to the union and protected its continued existence. Augustine called marriage between baptized Christians a sacrament and a continuation of the other sacraments; he saw it as a sacred symbol of Christ's marriage to his church. Ivo of Chartres maintained that according to Genesis, sexual intercourse constituted marriage, which was indissoluble on this basis. Astenasus defined the essence of marriage as sexual intercourse. With time and the expansion of Christianity, the definition of marriage widened to include interpersonal relationships, and a social framework for the rearing of families. It became necessary to prohibit child marriages by placing an age limit, and to prevent marriages arranged for financial and political reasons. For these reasons and other abusive practices a nuptial liturgy was developed, and the sacramental nature of marriage was defined. The discovery of marriage as a sacrament was made in the light of "virginity for the sake of the kingdom of God." Marriage and virginity were seen as complementary spiritual states of life within the church and each supporting the other, the nuptial liturgy and the liturgy of the dedication of virgins being strikingly similar. It is an incontestable fact that whenever virginity and celibacy have been denied the right to exist within the church, the sacramental nature of marriage has also not been recognized. This concept of both the celibate and noncelibate states as being equally effective in bringing the individual to salvation is found with remarkable similarity in both tantra and Christianity. Thus, although the Catholic church officially defined sex as a sacramental dimension of marriage, in practice they extinguished the concept before it ever took root.

The clergy has been more concerned with the failure of marriage than with exalting its sanctifying powers. The sacrament of matrimony has long been said to excuse concupiscence in that weaker part of humanity which did not have the courage to practice perfect chastity. Novices are still led to believe that the highest mansions in heaven are reserved exclusively for the professed religious, and that their greatest merit is that they have escaped the dangers of sex.

Of the seven sacraments, the most frequently used by the largest section of the population is the sacrament of sex, yet a theology of sex remains to be written: nowhere in existence in our day is there an exhaustive delineation of the male-female relationship on the spiritual, psychological, and physical levels insofar as this relationship is willed by God and leads to him. Current textbooks on the subject used in seminaries are written by clerics, for clerics, in defense of clerical chastity, with the intention of proving that it is the absolutely superior way of life. Sexual activities are considered, not in their potential perfection, but mostly in regard to their possible harmful effects. As a result of the prejudices of Gothic chastity, all sexual activity became tainted, and all virginity became holy. Woman was either temptress or virgin. The theory of the absolute perfection of virginity, enthroned as a dogma, was not supported by evidence, human or divine, and so frequently repeated condemnation of sex was used to protect this position. This prevented any reasonable investigation of the facts and actually led to misogyny, with sex viewed as something derived from the devil. The sacrament of sex was handed over to the secular world as a tool for advertising goods and making coarse jokes.

Biographies of saints who were once married invariably include the length of their widowhood, which purified them, or a statement that they had renounced sex during most of their marriage. The church fought the two sources of these negative views on sex, gnostic and Manichean dualism, for centuries, but only on the doctrinal level. On the level of human life it reduced the sacrament to a state lesser than natural love: to one of duty for the purpose of procreation. Even animals are not condemned by nature to such a mechanistic state, except perhaps domestic cattle in places where artificial insemination is practiced.

But we should not be harsh with those celibates who have been responsible for this. They have no deeper understanding of the celibate way than they do of the married way. Nowhere in seminaries or monasteries have I heard of any intelligent instruction available on sublimation of sexual energies. Jung called this process "canalization of the libido," with symbols being used to effect the transformation, a process which was known three thousand years ago in India in Patañjali's time as *pratyāhāra.*

The theology of sex must be rebuilt, both for the celibate and for the married. The tantrists who have used sex for transcendence have their own saints, scriptures, liturgies, teachers, art, and a long history of accomplishments. The Western Catholics have the sacrament of marriage which is like a diamond lost in a dungheap, surrounded by an immense wall of ignorance, fear, falsifications and silence.

The problem of opening ourselves up to the sacrament of sexual union is exactly the same as opening ourselves up to the imperishable power of grace conferred by Christ in any of the other six sacraments in the church. The psychological and spiritual ladder of ascent to this condition is precisely the same for baptized Christians as it is for the tantrist, and we could employ many Eastern forms of *maṇḍalas* in a Christian tantra. However, the baptized Christian clearly has more immediate help from the active presence and participation of Christ. This search for the noumenon is a difficult path for both Buddhist and Christian, but precisely because it is so different, we need any help that we can obtain. The baptized Christian has the advantage of the great mysteries, the sacraments of the mothering church, who has so much of the responsibility for her children's ascent to truth. It is not necessary for baptized Christians to repudiate their own values; rather, they should use all of their own spiritual resources and heritage but pay due respect to how divine laws operate within other spiritual traditions.

One of the divine laws that operate for Christians is the interaction and integration of the various sacraments. The divine law that operates universally is that of the living force of love taking possession of one's inward essence, rescuing one from the self-assertion that is the parent of hate and division. Love, by abrogating egoism, is the salvation of all. Egoism, not only separating one from God, also separates one from half of humanity, as it causes one to assert the two mutually exclusive ideas: either *I am a man* or *I am a woman.* Most spiritual traditions are concerned with transcending the ego, but it seems to be that using sex for this purpose is found in those traditions that have as their *final* goal love and compassion for all humanity. Not in vain is it that the sexual relation is not merely termed love but by general acknowledgement represents love *par excellence,* exhibiting the type and ideal of all other kinds of love. How can we synthesize our own lives with the new-old vision of divine love made flesh, through the flesh, in the spirit and throughout eternity? How can we understand ourselves going into God and God coming into us through sacramental sexual union?

Realizing Sex as a Sacrament

Let us examine more closely how Christ loved us, which might suggest a Christian tantric way to reach divine love: "I give you a new commandment: love one another; just as I have loved you, you must also love one another" (John 13:34–35).

The living ideal of the divine love, antecedent to our love, contains in itself the secret of the idealization of our love and the map of how to reach the summit of love. There is the simple carnal, physiological union in animal nature; there is the legal union in a social-moral order; and there is the union through God which leads to immortality by partaking of the divine principle and forming a link with the source of all life and creation. The third kind of love, which is the first in the true order with the claims inherent in it, is wholly natural to us in our entirety as being with souls and created in the image of God, forming a link between God and the world. In the province of one's sex it is not only disordered love, the deficiency of the highest spiritual consecration, and the satisfaction of emotional needs after the fashion of lower animals that are contrary to nature. Equally contrary are the two lower elements, the animal nature and the law of society (likewise natural in their proper place), when they are kept apart from what is higher and relied upon in place of it. But such things are especially contrary to nature from the point of view of the human being in its entirety, since this displacement of all true relations gains the upper hand in existence and is acknowledged as "normal." This is the most common perversion of life today.

The following is an excerpt from the Old Testament book of Tobit. Tobias married Sarah, whose previous husbands had all died because they married for the wrong motives. Even though their marriage was arranged by God, Tobias "fell so deeply in love with her that he could no longer call his heart his own." Tobias and his bride pray together before they lie down on their bridal night:

> It was you who created Adam.
> You created Eve to be his wife
> to be his help and support;
> and from these two the human race was born.
> It was you who said,
> "It is not good that man should be alone;
> let us make him a helpmate like himself."
> And so I do not take my beloved
> for any lustful motive;
> I do it in singleness of heart.
> Be kind enough to have pity on her and on me
> and bring us to old age together (Tobit 8:6–7).

The principal requirement for the third kind of love, which alone brings in the wish to participate in the divine order, requires the model of Christ's love for us. He died for love of us. He transmuted the temporal into the eternal by renouncing inferior ties bound up in ego, self-will and self-love. It was not his denial of the flesh but his denial of self-love which made him victor over the exile we experience. Not without reason, the Orthodox church in her marriage ceremony makes mention of the holy martyrs and compares the bridal wreath to their crowns. A Christian tantra would require a special *ascesis,* as well as the sacraments, as its foundation.

It must be understood that in order to have a relationship with the beloved which transcends into the sphere of the divine, one must have laid the foundations for this within oneself. Only by affirming God in the beloved, God in oneself, and God himself as the center and root of all existence can one find a triune faith that is the prerequisite to the true union of man and woman, and a union that has a sacramental quality. It is not enough to have this sense of God's presence as a concept or an abstract idea. It is a fundamental law of being that God must be experienced in a general way in order to be experienced in a particular way. It is not possible to isolate oneself and one's spouse in a separate spiritual existence. God must be recognized in every facet of life and love, so that the boundaries of a personal love include all that is encountered. With constant attention to God and to the spouse as an incarnation, or intermediary, of the divine power and love which activates and permeates the entire universe, the life of the married couple becomes as prayerful as that of the most pious monk and their sexuality essential to their mystical unity with God.

Eastern Orthodox Christian theology, comparatively unaffected by the heretical Manichean doctrines, influential in Western Christianity, which bitterly denounced sex and the body as evil, recognizes that sexuality was sanctified to become part of the exchange of love in Christ's eschatological kingdom, which marriage signifies and makes present. As Christ loved the church, his bride,

> In the same way men are also bound to love their wives as they love their own bodies. In loving his wife a man loves himself. For no one ever hated his own body; on the contrary, he provides and cares for it; and that is how Christ treats the church, because it is his body, of which we are the living parts . . . it applies also individually; each of you must love his wife as his very self; and the woman must see to it that she pays her husband all respect (Ephesians 5:28–33, *The New English Bible,* Oxford).

As God is in relation to his creation, as Christ is in his relation to his church, so man ought to be in relation to woman.

> Therefore shall a man leave his father and his mother, and shall cleave unto his wife; and they shall be one flesh. And they were both naked, the man and his wife, and were not ashamed (Genesis 2:24–25).

The church, the new creation within creation, and within the church the sacrament of marriage, is the basic *maṇḍala* for a Christian tantra. Through this *maṇḍala,* internalized in disciplined sexuality, the great archetype of the original man, wholly united to the divine, can be personally reintegrated in the deep psycho-physical being of men and women. We might learn from ancient Eastern meditation traditions in order to fully realize the potentialities in our sacrament of marriage. For a Christian tantra may be one way to paradise regained.

NOTES

1. For a general discussion, see Agehananda Bharati, *The Tantric Tradition* (London: Rider, 1969).
2. C. G. Jung, *Modern Man in Search of a Soul* (New York: Harcourt, Brace and World, 1933).
3. For a detailed discussion, see Herbert Guenther, *Treasure on the Tibetan Middle Way* (Berkeley: Shambhala, 1976).
4. Gopi Krishna, *Secrets of Kuṇḍalinī in Panchastavi* (New Delhi: Kundalini Research Publication Trust, 1978).
5. *Bṛhad-āraṇyaka Upaniṣad,* I.4.3.
6. Christopher Isherwood, *Ramakrishna and His Disciples* (New York: Simon and Schuster, 1965), p. 112.
7. Gershom Scholem, *On the Kabbalah and Its Symbolism* (New York: Schocken Books, 1965), p. 108.

5

The Masculine-Feminine Symbolism in Kāshmir Śaivism and Its Influence on a Contemporary Hindu Classic, *Kāmāyanī*

BINA GUPTA

The notion of two interacting, opposing, yet complementary metaphysical principles, one feminine, the other masculine, is very ancient in human thought. Inspired perhaps by the obvious biological duality of the species, the ontological description of femininity and masculinity appears quite early in the religious and philosophical assumptions of many disparate cultures: Father Heaven and Mother Earth among the North American Indians, *Śiva* and *Śakti* in tantrism, Zeus and Demeter in Homeric Greece, Izanagi and Izanami in Japan, Thunder-lightning and Mother Earth in Hittite Turkey.

Whenever and wherever a philosophic dualism is enshrined, whether among the native American Indians, in classical Chou-dynasty China, among the aborigines of Australia, or throughout the magico-religious traditions of Southeast Asia, the association of two competing but reciprocal powers with masculine and feminine traits is as commonplace as it is perhaps inevitable. Thus, for example, in the *Tao Te Ching, yang* is characterized as the life-breath of heaven, while *yin,* its polar opposite, is the vital energy or "life-breath" of the earth. The former metaphorically is strong and associated with light; the latter is weak and dark. *Yang* is the masculine perceiver, *yin* is the female principle, passive receiver of the masculine *yang.*

In the religio-philosophic tradition of India, male-female polarity symbolism has played a very important role. The presumption of two opposing but complementary principles has pre-Buddhist philosophical roots tracing back to the Sāṁkhya system, one of the oldest Indian metaphysical schools.[1] Although the historical antecedents of the school can be dated back to the Upaniṣads, the main codification of the school occurred in the 2nd Century A.D. Sāṁkhya is a dualistic philosophy expressed in terms of two fundamental and opposing principles, of *prakṛti* and *puruṣa: Prakṛti* as active but not conscious, *puruṣa* as conscious but inactive. Activity is inherent in *prakṛti,* it is continually changing, and is one substance. *Puruṣa* does not change but there are many *puruṣas.* Thus, whatever happens, occurs in and through *prakṛti,* since *puruṣa* does not act. However, *prakṛti* could not act if *puruṣa* was not there. Although the two are opposed to each other, it is only by their cooperation that evolution takes place. How the two interact is a postulate of intuition and cannot be explained by reason.

There is no doubt that the pre-Aryan religion of India was characterized by mother worship, and the female deity was ranked supreme. However, the Vedic doctrine and the Aryan invaders, because of their own religion and belief in the male supremacy, assigned goddesses a somewhat inferior position. In time, the idea of the power of the female in worship and ritual regained the importance which we find in tantric schools.

> We do not know how and when popular imagery and speculative proclivity blended into the trantric pattern, but one fact emerges with clarity: *Prakṛti,* the active *natura naturans,* and the goddess of pre-Aryan India were merged into the religious style which we encounter forthwith, as were the inactive conscious, witnessing *puruṣa* and the (Vedic?) male deity. The indigenous element having reasserted itself, it found its most refined diction in the words of the tantric scholar and the poet, based on what by this time had become fundamental doctrine: *If Śiva is united with Śakti, he is able to exert his powers as Lord; if not, the God is not able to stir.*[2] [Emphasis supplied]

Both Hindu and Buddhist tantrisms employ the fictive device to refer to what is otherwise conceived of as an absolutely ineffable and inexpressible noumenal realm. The tantrics attempt to convey this noumenal polarity by having recourse to male-female symbolism, that is to say, static and dynamic expressions of otherwise undifferentiated unity. The purpose of this paper is to explore the use of this polarity symbolism in a particular tantric school, viz., Kāshmir Śaivism, with particular reference to its formal congruence with, and undoubted influence on, a contemporary Hindi classic, *Kāmāyanī.*

For the sake of clarity, I have divided the paper in two parts: Part

I of the exposition treats the male-female opposition in Kāshmir Śaivism by analyzing their respective expressions of ultimate reality, their manifestations of the world process, and related themes of bondage and liberation; Part II explains the theme of *Kāmāyanī* and how the masculine-feminine duality is expressed through the structure of the exposition of the work as a whole.

The Śaiva system, in general, is known as Śiva-*Śāsana* or *Śaivāgama.* The non-dualistic Kāshmir Śaivism is known as Trika-*Śāstra,* or Trika-*Śāsana,* or simply, Trika. The term 'Trika' implies its acceptance of a trinity or triad, whether it be Śiva, Śakti, and Nara (bounded soul); or *para* (the highest), *parāpara* (identity in difference), and *apara* (difference).

Although the Trika school of Śaivism seems to have made its first appearance in Kāshmir in the beginning of the 9th Century A.D., Śaivism as such can be traced back to an earlier period. However, it is difficult to state with exact certainty how and when Kāshmir Śaivism first appeared, although its beginnings can be traced back to the Vedic period. The scriptures of this school, regarded as authoritative, are called the tantras. The leading exponents of this school are Vasugupta, Somānanda, Abhinavagupta, Kṣemarāja, and these were also the reputed names in the tantric tradition. The literature of Kāshmir Śaivism has been classified under three headings, viz., (1) the *Āgama Śāstra,* (2) the *Spanda Śāstra,* and (3) the *Pratyabhijñā Śāstra.* In this paper, we will be mainly concerned with the *Pratyabhijñā Śāstra* for two reasons: (a) this *Śāstra* expounds the philosophy proper of the school under consideration with arguments and discussion, and (b) this *Śāstra* seems to have influenced the Hindi classic *Kāmāyanī,* the focus of the second part of my paper.

1. Ultimate Reality as Unitary and Bi-Polar

Monistic thought which underlies Hindu theism affirms the One as also the transcendent *(atītam, turiyam, cathurtham).* Its transcendence may be described in the language employed to represent the Semitic god, viz., 'as the wholly other,' provided it is not overlooked that the term carries its own nuances of meaning so typical of Hindu religious experience. The One which alone truly merits the dignity of 'being' *(ekam sat)* in one sense is so 'other,' so transcendent, that it outreaches the sweep of mind and speech. Even the highest categories of thought fail to represent it, and speech even of the most extravagant kind, simply fails to refer or denote it. This, however, is only one side of the coin. The other side is how the One despite its severe otherness stands in a positive relation to the many. The One is also the creative source and consummation of everything. All oppositions and diversities, marking the sphere of the many, subsist in the One emanating from it and resolving into it. Likewise, while it (the One) is not itself speakable, all speaking is grounded in it. It is the creative logos. It is because of it speech 'speaks.'

The Trika system is a model of monistic thinking refined and defined to make the monism, in one sense, more rigorous and, at the same time, more integral *(pūrṇa)*. The refinements that it introduces into the general pattern of monism outlined above are, in effect, aimed at demonstrating that God's or Godhead's unity *(Īśvarādvayam)* is not, and indeed, cannot be, opposed to multiplicity. Godhead, to be God, can simply have no opposite by which it can conceivably be conditioned and limited. It is 'wholly other' and is also at once supremely the 'non-other.' Its unity has to be understood in a manner compatible with its being the 'I,' the pure or transcendent 'I' *(pūrṇo 'ham, śuddho 'ham)*, which cannot (1) assert itself as a subject or agent *(kartṛ)* over against 'object' (as the transcendent subject overreaches the epistemological divide of the subject and the object), and also (2) cannot assert itself *against* you and me (as the true 'you' and 'I' are on the side of the subject and never also object or objectifiable).

When it was said that the One could not thus be opposed to the many, what was described was the structural characteristics of the One which precludes, by virtue of its omnipervasiveness or ubiquity, admission of an 'other' to it. It does not imply any limitation on the part of the One. While there could not thus be an 'other' to it, in the very nature of the case, its unity, nevertheless, admits of an internal distinction of aspects in its essence, roughly that of will and being. This is the bi-polarity of the One imaged as the male and female and phenomenologically identifiable in terms of consciousness, as 'I' and 'this': The former refers to the purely luminous or shining aspect *(prakāśa)* of awareness and the latter, to the self-objectifying pole of consciousness, or as the tradition would conceputalize, consciousness being conscious *(vimarśa)*. *Vimarśa* is the heart of the luminous essence combining in a germinal form the entire universe, the moving and the non-moving.

2. Śakti and Śiva: The Archetype of Male-Female

The innermost nature of the supreme Lord who is imaged as the male, representing the unrestricted freedom of his reflexive (reflective) consciousness of perfect 'I-ness' is *śakti,* the primal feminine. It is interesting to note that the *śakti*-idea implies a kind of separate existence as a category without at the same time entailing an ontological dualism. The relation is essential identity with distinction of function, technically termed *'samavāya'* (*Mālinī-Vijaya,* 3.5), *tād-ātmya* (*Bodhapañcaśika,* 1.2), all of which affirm the inherent unifying character. It is not a case of two disparate things being in a state of indissoluble connection *(a-yuta siddha),* but more, as Kumārila would say, as referring to the essential nature of the way things are *(svarūpa).* The relation between *śaktimān-śiva* (male) and *śakti* (female) is that of perfect non-distinction ('in flesh one'). If he is the supreme lord *(parmeśvara),* she is the supreme lordly nature *(paramaiśvarya).* She is the manifestation of the highly wonderful *śakti* holding within her the mass of phenomenal existences. These are endlessly wrought by *māyā śakti,* invested so to speak, by intentionality, the rising of the tendency of the reflection of objectivity. (What is intrinsic to the conceptualization of the feminine is indicated by the phrase *'aunmukhya,'* which means the "intentional existence" of the many.)

Kallata, the author of the *Vṛtti* on the *Spanda Kārikā* (18) brings out the essence of the feminine as precisely what is distinguishable from the male and yet what does not fall outside the self of the male *(sva-avyatirekiṇī).* This may seem on a superficial reading to imply that *śakti's* operation is (reduced to one) of perfect harmony with *śiva's* illumination of consciousness and that the role assigned to the 'archetypal' feminine is only 'reflexive.' This, however, is not the case. As Ramakaṇṭha, the later commentator of *Spanda Kārikā* indicates, the inseparable internal relation of *śakti* is the very condition of the possibility of *śiva. Śiva* comes to recognize his lordship *(aiśvarya)* only when he knows *śakti* as his and not standing outside of him. Consciousness of the 'I' in its fullness *(pūrnahamvimarśa)* in which consists the *śiva*-hood of *śiva,* is possible if and only if *śiva* is also *ipso facto* holding the entire phenomenal world within himself in his aspect as the feminine. Just as when one desires something, the object or 'accusative' of desire, not yet actualized, still exists or rather 'inexists' intentionally undifferentiated from the volition of the psyche of the desirer, *śakti* remains inseparably united with *śiva* as the creative impulse within him (Ramakanṭha's *vivṛti, Spanda Kārikā* 1.1). As *Vijñānabhairava Tantra* (18) states, *śakti* is nothing but the 'own form' *(svarūpa)* of *śiva* in the aspect of the one who fashions, sustains, and withdraws the world.

The scorching power of fire cannot be told apart from fire, i.e., cannot be perceived to exist separately, however meticulously one may make the distinction in conceptual terms. In such experiences as 'this fire,' what is immediately experienced, when phenomenologically analyzed, is at once the scorching power and its source, viz., fire. *Śakti* therefore is described as a category by itself *(padārthātma),* i.e., a datum and not simply an attribute having existence in abstraction. *Śakti* is *'dharminī'* (possessor of attribute) in her own right and the real character of her non-distinct relation to *śiva* must not be overlooked. *Śakti,* verily, has the attributes of *śaktimān* and therefore it is said that there is an essential identity between the two.

As to the question, why admit a duplication of principles instead of conceding that there is really one principle, the Kāshmir Śaiva writers give the following reply: The one principle, *śiva* itself, cannot be established unless it is also admitted that there is real dynamics in him, viz., *śakti (svarūpa pratipada anyathānupapatti).* The One will come to nothing without admission of consciousness *(samvittva)* and lordship *(maheśvarya),* and the generic name of these integral aspects is *śakti.*

3. Manifestation of Śakti

Śakti, from being a mere inner nature of perfect "I-ness" of *śiva,* slowly emerges in the course of the Śaiva thought into a full-bodied principle of autonomous existence capable of having things predicated of her. Śiva, the pure foil-like datum of all modes of consciousness, as it were, recedes into the background of "pure being," wholly transcendent to thought. *Śakti* reigns supreme as the sole principle of all becoming.

Before shining out in the different modes of her manifestation, *śakti,* as immersed in the being of *śiva,* is described by the general term *cit-śakti* (consciousness-power), *parā vāk* (the supreme logos), or *vimarśa śakti* (power of perfect I-ness). Abhinavagupta identifies this fundamental character of *śakti* with the power of 'self-determination' *(svātantrya śakti),* and as the basis of primal speech prior to all convention which comes to establish agreement between a particular word-symbol and a particular meaning. In the form of 'inner sound' *(sabdnam), śakti* encompasses within her the entire world of objects in its ideal form. While thus spanning the whole world of objects as the supreme word, she rests on her own self which is consciousness and in this sense is described as eternal *(nityā)*. The aggregate of objects in the 'pure experience' imaged as *śakti* in a continuous resplendent form as 'I am,' from which she throws out the aggregate of objects in gradual succession in diverse forms, giving rise to the distinctions of diverse cognizers *(pramātṛ bhedā)*. Unifying and separating every moment in various ways the cognizing subjects, *śakti* projects the world of names and forms by performing the cosmic functions of creation, etc. The independent play of *śakti,* the primal feminine, thus, may be seen to be what introduces diversity in unity and unity in diversity both in the external and in the internal world *(bhede abhedanam abhede bhedanam)*.

The idea of *śakti* is thus resolved into the factor of the power of determination of self by self into the two categories of subject-ness and object-ness (*ahamtā* and *idamtā*), or that of the perceiver and the perceived *(grāhya grāhaka)*. The *Mālinī Vijayottara Tantra* explains it thus:

> Here now she attains multiplicity, although she never ceases to be single. That by which a thing is known for certain to be 'this' and not otherwise, goes by the name of *jñāna-śakti.* When the idea emerges 'let this thing be thus,' the power making it so is called *kriyā-śakti.* Though *śakti* is thus of two forms, as determined by the limiting adjuncts of objects, she becomes of endless forms. Therein she attains motherhood, becomes divided two-fold and fifty-fold. She thus becomes Mālinī. Desire, knowledge, and actions are only 'points of views' or perspectives *(vyapadeśa)* from which *śakti* is looked at, owing to the play of *māyā-śakti* which brings objectivity into the uppermost level.[3]

The desire or will to affirm the object side of the universal experience is known as *sadāśiva,* while in the next state of *Īśvara* the object becomes a little more determinate, described as the blossoming of the universe. In the *sadvidyā* stage the 'I,' i.e., the subjective and the objective side of experience (namely 'this') are equally balanced. Thus what was in the beginning an 'I-experience' unfolds into 'I-this' experience and then into 'this-I,' and finally, an equipoised 'I and I' and 'this is this' experience. Thus far, in the manifestation of *śakti* the real nature of divine remains as yet unveiled.

From here on commences the order of manifestation through concealment, when *māyā-tattva* begins its play. *Māyā* is, literally, that which measures or limits experience, severing 'this' from 'I,' and 'I' from 'this,' and also severing one 'this' from another 'this.' *Māyā* throws, as it were, a veil on self, because of which there is a simultaneous 'self-forgetfulness' and a projection as a differentiated universe. There are five products: one reducing the omni-agency *(sarva kartṛtiva)* of *śakti* and thus effecting limited agency *(kalā tattva);* another reducing omniscience, bringing about limited knowership *(vidyā-tattva);* still another reducing the ever-fulfilled nature, and bringing about the desire for this or that *(rāga tattva);* still another reducing the eternity of the universal and bringing about limitation in respect of time *(kāla tattva);* and, finally, the one that reduces the freedom and pervasiveness of the universal and causes limitation with respect to cause. Thus, subjecting himself to *māyā* and wearing, as it were, the 'cloaks' *(kañcūka)* limiting his universal knowledge and power, *śiva* becomes the *puruṣa* (individuated subject/agent). *Puruṣa* is the subjective manifestation of 'I am this' experience of *sadvidyā,* while *prakṛti* (the next *tattva*) is the objective manifestation, existing in a state of equilibrium of *guṇas* as the pole of 'this' in such an experience.

Prakṛti thus undergoes further differentiation into the psychic apparatus, senses and matter or material elements. The details of the evolution of twenty-four *tattvas* are, with minor variations, concurrent with the account given in Sāṁkhya-Yoga. The significant difference in terms of our understanding of male-female archetype between the Śaiva and Sāṁkhya-Yoga accounts, however, is not to be forgotten. *Prakṛti,* for the latter tradition, typifies the female as existing by itself or rather herself through subserving the purposes of *puruṣa*—the exemplary male, who himself is devoid of sentiency or purpose of his own. The dynamic and the conscious are thus bifurcated though one, viz., the first is made to serve the purpose of the other. In the Śaiva thought, however, the two are fused inseparably, thus bringing out the essential identity of the two despite distinction of functions. The Sāṁkhya bifurcation of the two, in a sense, is preserved in Advaita Vedānta, except that it is transformed into a dualism of the negative and the positive, i.e., *māyā* and Brahman. Consequently, Brahman, the *cit*-principle, becomes pure knowledge or pure consciousness without the sense of I. *Māyā,* representing the sphere of 'I-this,' is equated with the illusory *(anirvacanīya).* It is only in the Śaiva account that a truer form of monism is claimed to be achieved in terms of a distinction that illumines, instead of distracting, the rigorous sense of the One, viz., the distinction and complementariness of the male and the female.

II

In his epic poem *Kāmāyanī,* Jayashankar Prasad conceives of an idealistic state of happiness attainable through a somewhat nonrational or suprarational faith. Humankind's salvation is the principal theme of *Kāmāyanī;* all characters and situations are instrumental to the elucidation of this principal theme.

Kāmāyanī etymologically means the daughter of *Kāma* (desire). In Indian thought, however, *kāma* is much more than simply 'libido.' It connotes 'libido' and the Eros of the Greek mythology. It is the basic urge to live, to protect, to expand, and to preserve. The daughter of *Kāma* is Shraddhā, which signifies faith as well as the determination to live with *satya* (truth) as the fundamental principle of life. It is the symbol of determination—determination to lead a conscientious and moral life. It denotes an unwavering faith in righteousness, in just and good human conduct.

The story of the epic poem has been taken from the Hindu myth of the Deluge. In Indian mythology, Deluge does not simply mean physical and universal inundation, but has deeper philosophical and metaphysical implications. It signifies the end of the urge to live—inertia, complete inaction. *Kāmāyanī* begins with this great Deluge, when Manu,[4] the protector of mankind and the sole survivor, finds himself on the peak of the Himalayan mountain. His idealism after the Deluge is soon fragmented as he faces the dreadful reality of the destruction of a civilization. At this point Shraddhā appears, gives him hope, and points the way to a life of action and fulfillment. Although Manu promptly falls in love with Shraddhā, his restless mind does not find satisfaction in her peaceful company. Instead, he deserts her, one day finding himself in the land of Idā, the Queen of the Sarswat kingdom. At her insistence, Manu rebuilds her kingdom, conferring upon it abundant material wealth and prosperity. This modern civilization based upon science and technology gives rise to competition and class struggle which in turn lead inevitably to stress, strain, discontent, and despair. Manu tries to possess Idā. His attempt to rape her prompts a mass revolution, forcing him to retreat. In the end, he is rescued by Shraddhā, who helps him to attain *mokṣa* (salvation).

The book is divided in fifteen cantos, each named after a character appearing in the Canto: *Chintā* (anxiety), *Āshā* (hope), *Shraddhā* (faith), *Kāma* (desire), *Vāsanā* (passion), *Lajjā* (Shyness), *Karma* (action), *Irshyā* (jealousy), *Idā* (intellect), *Swapana* (dream), *Sangarsha* (struggle), *Nirved* (renunciation), *Darshan* (vision), *Rahasya* (mysticism), and *Ānanda* (bliss). As the names of the cantos indicate, all the different characters of *Kāmāyanī* represent different states of the human mind. However, the three principal characters of *Kāmāyanī* are Manu, Shraddhā, and Idā. Manu is the mind; therefore, the different thoughts of Manu represent different conditions of the human mind. Shraddhā represents love, conscience, and faith. Idā epitomizes rationality and the scientific approach to reality.

From one perspective, *Kāmāyanī* deals with the history of mankind, the primal man—Manu and his consorts Shraddhā and Idā—and the propagation of the human species. From another perspective, it is an allegory in which a human being forsakes faith and reverence for logic and reason, so bringing about his own destruction in the end.

As discussed in Part I of this paper, Kāshmir Śaivism affirms the belief in two kinds of orders: *aśuddhādva* (impure order) and *śuddhādva* (pure order). In the impure order, an individual under the influence of *māyā* perpetuates distinction without resolving them. In the pure order, the real nature of the ultimate reality is not veiled and polarity between 'I' and 'This' is simply in the form of an idea only. The entire story of *Kāmāyanī* falls into these two orders. The first twelve cantos, from *'Chintā'* (reflection) to *'Nirved'* (renunciation) belong to the impure order, and the last three cantos from *'Darshana'* (vision) to *'Ānanda'* (bliss) belong to the pure order.

In the impure order, one is in the realm of *māyā* and the six *kañcūkas.* The chief function of *māyā* is to conceal, obscure, and thereby limit the experience respecting both the nature of what is experienced and the experiencer himself. At the outset of *Kāmāyanī,* we find Manu restless, alone, and feeling dejected. He fails to realize the truth and purpose of Shraddhā's dedication and gives himself over to lust, passion, and violence. He longs for enjoyment in the empirical world of names and forms. Desire breeds further desire. His behavior determined by desires consequently becomes morally polarized as good or bad leading to either enjoyment or suffering.

Manu, in the first twelve cantos, perpetually asserts his authority and supremacy over all living things—material as well as non-material. That is, he moves in the sphere of *karma.* He tries to possess Shraddhā, and she surrenders. However, the company of Shraddhā does not absorb him entirely. He deserts Shraddhā and meets Idā, who directs Manu's attention to worldly pleasures and prosperity. He perpetuates the sense of 'I' and 'mine,' with its built-in knowledge of reciprocal difference. His universe of discourse, as well as his universe of being, are now limited to the world of difference. He fails to comprehend all of this, only limited aspects of it, and regards himself as different from others. This is the predicament of every embodied soul which consequently is born and reborn in this world interminably, as it were, until it is freed from all desires. Those who attain *mokṣa,* free themselves from all desires and reach a state of bliss beyond the plurality of names and forms.

The last three cantos of *Kāmāyanī*—Vision, Mysticism, and Bliss—belong to the pure order where Shraddhā helps Manu attain the highest goal, namely, *mokṣa* (salvation). Shraddhā leads him to a place where one can find eternal peace. Manu gazes at the empty space and he has the vision of Lord Śiva—a vision of the delightful cosmic dance of Śiva.[5] He walks with Shraddhā, and on seeing three luminous colored dots—red, dark, and silvery—queries Shraddhā:

> What are these three spheres? asks Manu.
> Tell me, what are these explain, explain!
> To what universe have I traveled into
> Oh! Free me from this illusion, this chain.[6]

Shraddhā explains to him that these represent the three spheres of will, knowledge, and action. Each sphere is a universe in itself. The red one is the universe of desire. It is the kingdom of *māyā* and attracts souls. The dark-hued sphere is the sphere of action, a kingdom of conflict, turmoil, and frustration. And finally, the bright silvery one, the sphere of knowledge, is a world of indifference to pain and pleasure. These three spheres are divorced from each other, and unless the three meet in harmony, fulfillment of life is impossible to achieve. Soon the glow of Shraddhā's smile spreads into the three spheres, rendering them "one," dissolving their individual identities and transforming them into a happy harmony, casting thereby an augury of bliss:

> Dream and slumber and awakening vanished
> As wish and wisdom and action dissolved.

The heavenly music filled the earth and sky
And Manu in Shraddhā's spell was lost.[7]

They attain bliss, where there is no dichotomy, no division, only a single pure consciousness that pervades everything where:

Matter and spirit were in harmony
The form of beauty was exquisite
One consciousness was everywhere
Infinite Bliss, indivisible.[8]

Thus, at the close of the poem, the poet Prasad maintains that it is only with the help of faith that the three facts of life—desire, knowledge, and action—can be brought together in proper harmony. The idea of *"samrasatā"* (harmony) runs through the poem as a connecting link.

It should not be difficult to see the close similarity between the vision that the text of *Kāmāyanī* presents with that of Kāshmir Śaivism outlined earlier. *Parama śiva,* the ultimate reality, as stated earlier, has two aspects. The active aspect is called *śakti. Śiva* is the unchanging aspect, and *śakti,* its unchanging power, appearing and articulating as mind and matter. This is the ontological vision behind the Kāshmir Śaivite doctrine of ultimate reality with a duality of aspects which are brought into play through its trinity of power, *icchā* (desire), *jñaña* (knowledge), and *kriyā* (action). The phenomenal world where this trinity of power does not operate in unison is described as the impure order. In the pure order, one makes proper use of will, knowledge, and action and thus regains the integral perspective about the ultimate reality.

In the poem of *Kāmāyanī,* Prasad has also tried to show the complementary and yet conflicting principles operative as significant aspects of reality, and symbolizable as masculine and feminine. Reality is One, and it encompasses within itself all pairs of opposites. We find illustrations of this dual and complementary nature of reality in the case of human beings as they go through their daily lives. Internal and external worlds of human beings are often in conflict with each other: divine and demonic tendencies always in struggle. Man's unconscious mind pulls him in one direction and his conscious in the other. The inner conflict of Manu in *Kāmāyanī* is the symbol of the conflict of every individual.

Prasad maintains not only that masculine-feminine principles are equally significant parts of reality, but goes a step further in affirming that the two are complementary. The inseparability of the masculine and the feminine is a symbol for true personhood. It is only when both elements are aligned together, when both elements have attained the same level and are in a state of mutuality and interdependence, that a true relationship may be said to be recovered. In the words of a commentator:

Manu's transitory idealism after the deluge is soon fragmented as he faces the reality, of spiritual vacuity, of the need of Shraddha in his life. It is a series of sufferances that qualify him for an ideal seat. He is in this regard not the ideal but an idealistic real man of modern race. The weaknesses from which he suffers are not only characteristic of his but of modern man. His longing for possession of authority, for adventure, enterprise and the lust for sex are the human weaknesses in their misapplication. . . . It is in him that the readers most identify themselves.[9]

Kāmāyanī depicts the basic conflict of 'man'—his follies and faults, his shortcomings and limitedness, and the struggle in which he is involved and the lines along which such a conflict may be resolved.

Prasad also illustrates how man in his innate characteristic is potentially inactive, and requires a woman as the source of inspiration of all actions. In the first canto, Manu is desperate and desolate, he has lost the urge to live; it is Shraddhā who in the third canto, motivates and inspires Manu to a life of action. Shraddhā does not believe in inaction and false asceticism. Her message is the message of will to live—to transform the feeling of I-consciousness into that of world-consciousness. Therein lies the complete fulfillment of life, *ānanda* (bliss). From the very beginning, the idea of *mokṣa* (fulfillment) has been verbalized *vis-à-vis* the masculine-feminine symbolism; bliss consists in the harmonious union of the two opposites as well as their transcendence. To experience the opposition as union is to transcend the opposites. Towards the end of the poem, traversing the three spheres of desire, action, and knowledge, Shraddhā helps Manu to perceive the harmony of the macrocosm, reflecting the fact that enduring happiness is attainable in human life. Every other feeling of pleasure is transitory, as there is in it a residuum of unpleasant feeling which gives rise to a new series of activity.

Prasad also maintains that the intellect creates far too many complications and consequently makes the individual more miserable. Idā, in the poem, represents the rational and intellectual approach of the modern mind which is distanced and even divorced from the creative, compassionate aspects of the self. In the absence of faith, the intellect creates the sense of 'I' and 'you,' 'I' as standing over against 'you.' As this feeling of difference expands, it gives rise to conflict and estrangement. The way to obtain peace and happiness is to avoid the intellectual pursuit of happiness.

Faith represents the *sāttvika* (pure) tendency of mind. It makes one introverted, inspires one to self-examination. For this reason, it has been so much emphasized in the Vedic literature. However, in this regard, it must be stated that Prasad was at the same time also aware of the power of intellect (Idā) and its role in the onward process of creation. Toward the end, Shraddhā leaves her son Kumār in the care of Idā (intellect), because Kumār is compassion, faith, and Idā is sheer intellect. The harmony of the two is essential for the happiness of mankind. Manu gained knowledge in the company of Idā. However, in the long run it was faith that brought him *mokṣa.* Only faith can elevate the soul to the highest spiritual joy. Prasad says:

> Brain is the inspiration of reason
> Faith is the Queen of hearts
> Perfect Harmony of the two
> Is the immortal story of life.[10]

In general, Hinduism maintains that the world is an order or cosmos. It is not a chaos of things thrown together without any relation or rule. This world order is *dharma,* which sustains the universe. It is not a law imposed from outside, it is the very nature of things; that which constitutes them. As a follower of Kāshmir Śaivite philosophy, Prasad believed that *śiva-śakti,* man-woman, were two important constituents of the whole. A lasting harmonious relationship between the two cannot be established by suppressing one in favor of the other. Only when both elements co-exist together, and when both elements have attained the same level, can peace and happiness be realized. The interplay of the within and without makes *Kāmāyanī* a valuable contribution to the psychological and social aspects of human life.

Kāmāyanī, therefore, is an epic with a practical purpose and point of view combining human ethics and pathos in its poetic creativity. It couples individual with society, not merely with a contractual agreement but with a mutual organic gravitational pull. *Kāmāyanī* is not a pessimistic document of human failures. It does not agree to the philosophy of Schopenhauer or Nietzsche. It does not confirm the views of Darwin and Freud. In fact,

Prasad realized that the modern age with all these views, does not augur well for the future.[11]

Everything in this universe is organically related. Intrinsic and extrinsic factors, man and woman, *śiva* and *śakti* are not two powers but rather two aspects of One unitary reality. The 'without' appears as without only because it is 'within.' The conflict between the 'within' and the 'without' cannot be resolved by suppressing one, nor by giving one over to the other. Both must be taken into account.

This problem of the relationship between the male and the female is not an idle play of the rational mind; it affects our lives deeply. *Kāmāyanī* constructs an edifice enabling one to understand the true meaning and purpose of life and thus gain true self-knowledge.

It is refreshingly new and is traditionally and mythologically old. It is both the story of the 'first man' that is Manu and also of the modern man, who is equally symbolised and characteristically displayed in him. The enigma of Manu, his conflict and struggle, his lack of faith and determination, his pseudo-attachment and hedonistic interpretation and the way of life, psychological inhibitions, complexes and perversions are impressingly sane. Akin to modern man, he is psychologically abnormal, schizophrenic and nostalgic with a diseased auto-erotic base.[12]

Kāmāyanī points to a unique harmony of "masculinity-femininity," "reason-faith," "without-within," "intellect-emotion." It is only when both elements are equally represented that one can realize the essence of one's being, of which another name is *mokṣa* according to the tradition of Hinduism.

NOTES

1. Kapila may have lived in the eighth century B.C. and has been regarded as the founder of the Samkhya School. The systematization of this school is credited to Īśvarakṛṣṇa who lived in the second century A.D.
2. Agehananda Bharati, *The Tantric Tradition* (London: Rider and Company, 1969), p. 205.
3. *Mālinī Vijayottara Tantra,* III.5.9.
4. The scattered references to Manu are found in the Vedas, *Purāṇas,* and Epics.

The story of the Deluge is described in the *Śatapatha Brāhmaṇa,* the *Purāṇas,* and the *Mahābhārata.* Prasad accepts Manu as a historical figure and the 'first-born' of Indian history. Whether we accept Manu as a historical figure or not, in the Indian tradition it has always been assumed that the evolution of mankind continues through the active cooperation of Manu and Shraddhā—representing masculine and feminine principles.

5. Cosmic dance of Śiva is known as *Tāṇḍava* dance. Though it is dreadful, it is very auspicious and imparts bliss to the entire creation.
6. Jayashankar Prasad, *Kāmāyanī* (Allahabad: Bharati Bhandar, 1964–65), *Rahasya* Canto, concluding stanza, my translation.
7. Manohar Bandopadhyaya, *Kāmāyanī* (New Delhi: Ankur Publishing House, 1978), p. 16.
8. *Kāmāyanī, Ananda* Canto, concluding stanza, my translation.
9. Bandopadhyaya, p. 23.
10. Sushila Bharati (trans. and ed.), *Kāmāyanī* (Hyderabad: Milinda Prakasan, 1966), p. 167, my translation.
11. Jaikishandas Sadani (trans.), *Kāmāyanī* (Calcutta: Rupa and Co., 1975), p. v.
12. *Ibid.,* p. vi.

6

The Mysticism of Male-Female Relationships: Some Philosophical and Lyrical Motifs of Hinduism

KRISHNA SIVARAMAN

The myriads of the created It brought forth into being in Its (archetypal) likeness (*Taittirīya Āraṇyaka* 10, 12, 29).[1]

Thou art woman. Thou art man. Thou art the youth and the maiden too. Thou art the old tottering along with a staff. Being born Thou facest in every direction *(Svestāsvatara Upaniṣad* 4, 3).

The bi-unity of *śiva* and *śakti*[2] (which defines the essence of God) God hath let permeate the entire order of creation. The latter accordingly stands polarized as the male and the female, similar and yet dissimilar, characterized by characteristics unique (and yet complementing). From her, (side of God's bi-modality) indeed accrues the felicity that all this life is (as structured intra-sexually). Those not discerning it discern not also the (esoteric) nature of (the cultic symbolism of) the phallus-and-the-pedestal (*Śiva Ñāna Siddhi, Supakkam* 1, 69).

To one that is he as well as also a she, and assumed a corporeal form consisting of eight limbs (*viz.*, the physical elements) of earth, water, fire, air and ether, the sun and the moon (which measure out time and space) and the human soul (who is) the agent of (sacred rite like) sacrifice (as it were) to excoriate the good of immortal life for the benefit of those that spurned in recoil (the mixed good of) worldly life—To this dancing pair, the image-form is but single (androgyny). By use of what (gender-indicating pronoun) can I refer to it? One that is a he or one that is a she? But for a natural numeral term (luckily present in the vocabulary with a prefix-indicating singular number and a dual denoting suffix)[3] neutral in application as between the two (genders) how else indeed could I denote (Thee demonstratively)? (*Cidambara Seyyutkovai* 53)

I

In the religious setting of Hindu tradition with its characteristic nontheological tenor it is more appropriate to ponder the spiritual significance of sexual love, instead of exploring for an answer to the question of a 'divine intention for male-female relation.' Male-female relationship is itself an embodiment of what may be described mytho-poetically as 'divine intention.' Divinity and divine intention or will are strictly a symbolic and not a conceptual distinction for the generality of Hindu thinking,[4] even when it does not endorse the view of divinity as devoid of name, property, activity or relation to others. No religious tradition which contemplates God in personalistic terms views Him as a person among others whom we may come to know and add to the number of those we love. God's claim on us is incommensurable with the claim of persons who love us and whom we love.

The symbolism of intentionality that is employed to speak of divine nature draws from introspection of interior life. To the question 'who is this one whom we worship as the *ātman?*' (the 'theos' of Hindu tradition), the following answer is given by an Upaniṣad:

> That which is heart, this mind, that is consciousness,
> perception, discrimination, intelligence, wisdom,
> insight, steadfastness, thought, thoughtfulness,
> impulse, memory, conception, purpose or intention
> *(samkalpah),* life, desire, control, all these,
> indeed, are its names.[5]

This symbolism is rendered even more concrete in terms of yet another symbolism—this time deriving from a dimension of life at once more interior in the sense of 'non-objectifiable,' and at the same time more readily identifiable—that of love in sexual form between two distinguishable but inalienable aspects of deity. God is the eternal male and his power, the creative logos by which and through which all created order is as it is, is the eternal feminine. The 'happy interpenetration of the two'[6] accounts for the timeless procession of worlds and souls as the fruit of their union. Divinity of God thus both transcends sex—as the creative ground transcending the creation—and *is* sex, the union of the 'archetypal' male and female, 'ever chaste and yet ever productive,' a mystery, as the text continues, which even the sages, the very apotheosis of austerity,[7] cannot comprehend.

The view that all this sexual relation of the male and the female is a theophany does not, however, mean that *all* of the divine essence is thereby exemplified. That would be pantheism of the naturalistic kind in contrast to a 'religious' type which identifies divinity with the universal essence, the substance of everything rather than with everything. The latter type, it is needless to say, reflects the sense of any religiously significant equation of 'all' with God or God with all. To employ the symbolism of quantity as the Vedas do,[8] only a quarter of God's abundance suffices to fill up the worlds, however far-flung in space or however long they may endure. What remains exceeds the whole of that which suffices to fill up all that there is. The general view of Hindu religion, *vis-à-vis* the Upaniṣads, the fountainhead of Hindu philosophy, remains, in the words of R. C. Zaehner (whom one cannot accuse of being partial to the Hindu tradition on which he wrote extensively), that 'God is over all, through all and within all, as St. Paul puts it.'[9]

A more significant aspect of divinity of special relevance for discerning a possible theological meaning of male-female relationship is the understanding of God as supreme identity. The counterpart of biblical 'monotheism' on the Hindu side is the acnowledgement that God is identity, a 'connumerable' identity, and expressed in terms of negation, as 'without duality.' The descriptive discourse that matches the God-language of the West is also the name by which 'theological Hinduism' labels itself—*advaitam* (one without a second). What is conveyed by this nomenclature is that God is preeminently experienceable as 'immediacy,' the denial of every conceivable separation. The knower of Brahman, verily, *becomes* Brahman.[10] Immediacy is, literally, denial of what comes between. To the extent life in the world means becoming oblivious to its 'non-dual' dimension of depth, to that extent the world is the kind of intervening thing that immediacy denies. The way of life that is appropriate for being in such a world for one who yearns for a 'recovery of immediacy' can only be the way of the ascetic.

Ascetic spirituality need not mean monastic seclusion, abstaining *from* the world in a formally confessed manner. It surely involves abstention but as a positive function to be sought and won through life *in* the world. Monasticism itself is an institutionalization of the spirit of withdrawal at least from movement on the same plane. The starving anchorite with his extravagant austerities may not exactly typify this mood of abstention, but it should not be forgotten he is only a radical version of the householder who also, through a willing submission to a life of infinite obligations *(dharma),* strives for controlled disengagement from the world, which is reared and sustained by a sense of 'me' and 'mine.' The one which is beyond all dualities and opposition is not at the end of a straight line from the ways of a 'dualistic' world and is not reached as a simple extension of the merely pragmatic, mediated kind of knowledge.

One of the distinguishing descriptions of this 'one without a second' is pure bliss (even as it is pure awareness and pure being). *Anantam* (infinite), interpreted by Vedānta to mean bliss,[11] is really impartiteness or infinitude. "Where there is plenteousness there is happiness. There is no happiness in anything petty, only the plenteous is happiness. Infinitude alone thou shalt seek."[12] One of the clear implications of this mandate to seek the infinite is not to set final store on life in the world as it falls short of the ideal of infinitude. What is less than 'plenty' is coeval with unhappiness. The basic paradigm of Hindu spirituality, one may even generalize, is that bliss of fulfillment and renunciation are merely two sides of the same coin. 'Know that all this, whatever moves in this world, is enveloped by God. Therefore, find enjoyment by renunciation.'[13]

Infinitude is the 'plenteousness of all' and its experience implies abrogation of finitude or 'pettiness' *(alpatvam)* of every conceivable kind, whether it be in respect of space or time or even thing—or personhood. Bliss as experience of immediacy denies separation or distance and any interval of time. It denies the very basis of expressions like 'it is here and therefore *not* there' and 'it was then and *not* now.' The expressions 'at one' or 'within' *(antaram),* 'uninterrupted presence' *(anantaram),* express this sense of immediacy. Likewise divine nature experienced as impartite signifies 'overcoming' of finitude in respect of personhood. A is not B and I am not you. The expressions 'identity,' 'secondlessness' *(advitīyam)* bring out this sense of immediacy as one of recovering of a truer non-otherness of the 'other.' Experience of 'unlimitedness' is, then, to experience without the limitations that are imposed by the order of nature, *viz.,* of space, time, and thinghood, each of which is more insidious than the preceding. Spirit is non-dual experience.

However, union as between the sexes and mystical love in sexual form are also the commonplace of Hindu lyricism and art and even of later Hindu doctrine which thematize it as the natural and perhaps the highest manifestation of the ultimate reconciliation of all opposites in the One beyond all dualities. Sexual love scorned as the very stuff of the 'worldly' lure of which the ascetic should be most wary is also, paradoxically, celebrated as a sacramental reenactment of the truth of eternity and infinitude, the relation of sexual love, meaning precisely the abolishing, albeit temporarily, of the reciprocal distinctiveness of the sexual partners. Physical togetherness and interpenetration are symbolic expressions of love only because love is the regaining or recognition of non-duality. The two are of one flesh as a mode of recovery of their unity of spirit.

In human love sexual relation is the natural climax of the entire process of self-giving which is love. It is a sacrament. 'From Her accrues all this felicity,'[14] the seal, as it were, of divine consent set on a life of self-giving. Religious and literary traditions have not been slow to perceive the resemblance between the raptures of divine love and sexual union in which, as in ecstasy, the human ego melts away and one is taken outside oneself. In divine love, worship ripens into 'devotion' *(bhakti)* involving service, sacrifice, surrender and union. The soul abandons 'herself' entirely to the will of the divine lover who is conceived as the male, though (as it shall be shown in the sequel to this paper) a reversal of the symbolism also effectively brings out the sense of unity through union. In the Hindu view, sexual relation signifies a fuller identity than mere concern or sympathy or affection between two individuals facing each other. Coomaraswamy, in his memorable essay on *sahaja,* brings out the precise significance of erotic imagery for a mysticism which does not quite admit the existence of a God who is distinct from the self:

> . . . Each as individual has now no more significance for the other than the gates of heaven for one who stands within. It is like an algebraic equation where the equation is the only truth, and the terms may stand for anything. The least intrusion of the ego, however, involves a return to the illusion of duality.[15]

Whether contemplated in a forthrightly monistic way where mysticism is the process of the recovery of the infinite ambience on the part of the so-called finite, or theistically where the accent is on 'mystic union' between two in a 'non-dual' relationship, the experience of immediacy in the sense outlined above provides the only basis of faith for the generality of Hinduism. This is what makes it mystical through and through, marking it off from Judeo-Christian and Islamic traditions.

The Upaniṣadic ideal which conceptualizes such faith is describable as much in terms of a language of self-realization as that of 'union.' While it sets the stage for and bequeathes a common focus to Hindu religiosity, *viz.*, in espousing identity between Brahman and the individual self, it also discourses about identity from which relationship is *not* excluded. Realization of self *(anubhūti)* is also existentially stated true union *(sāyujya)*. The union is expressed in terms of sexual union in which the individual self, even when it sees itself as co-terminus with 'all,' may be said to copulate[16] with the One which 'abiding in all beings is other than all beings.'[17] The passage in the Upaniṣad which compares the bliss of *ātman*-intuition with the ecstasy of earthly lovers locked in self-forgetful embrace is an unambiguous anticipation of the later fusion of lyric and mystical experiences:

Just as a man closely embraced by his loving wife knows nothing without nothing within (or, more freely translated, naught of myself within or thyself without), so does this man *(puruṣah)*, closely embraced by the Self that is of the stuff of wisdom know nothing without, nothing within. This is his (true) form in which (all) his desires are fulfilled *(aptā-kāma)* in which self alone is his desire *(atmā-kāma)*, in which he has (indeed) no desire *(a-kāma)*, no sorrow.[18]

II

What serves as the ontological basis legitimizing the use of sexual symbolism in describing the religious goal of the vision of and participation in 'identity'—a goal which is avowed as transcending the pursuits of all legitimate goals of life—is the notion of bisexual polarity in the deity itself. The doctrine of a divine bi-unity in its theological articulations is surely a peculiarity of post-classical Hindu tantrism which celebrates the paradoxical interdependence of eroticism and asceticism. But the seeds of the doctrine are to be found in the Upaniṣads and in classical Hindu doctrines.

It is well known that in Sanskrit, grammatical gender is not always a sign of physical sex. An individual may be masculine from one point of view and feminine from another. Brahman is neuter grammatically but is indeed the principle of differentiation into the masculine and the feminine. One of the most evocative creation texts of the Upaniṣads begins[19] with '*ātman* alone in the aspect of a human male' *(puruṣa)*. This person 'in the beginning' was of such sort 'as are a man and a woman in close embrace' *(yathā strī-pumān-*

sau sampariṣvaktau). Desiring a second, 'he' caused the self to fall atwain *(ātmānam dvedhāpatayat)*. Thence came into being 'husband and wife' *(patiśca patnīca)*. He had intercourse with her, whence were engendered human beings. The first 'duality' having emerged—that of male and female—the universe in all its variety and multiplicity comes to be from the conjunction of the two (as may be seen, in the passages that follow, from the mention of a series of transformations of the original human pair into animal forms).

Scholars have compared this account to Plato's myth of the androgynous man (*Symposium,* 189c), but even more striking is the similarity it bears to the Genesis account:

And God said, let us make man in our own image, after our likeness . . . so God created man in his own image, in the image of God created he him; male and female, created he them.[20]

The likeness is exemplary. The 'image of God' is reflected in a creation 'male and female.' Adam (as Coomaraswamy rightly points out)[21] is in fact a 'Syzgy' until the deity brings forth the woman out of him, that he may not be alone. In the Hindu text the presence of the archetype of this polarity in God is rendered explicit by the description of it as bliss or plenteousness in essence, i.e., *in divinis.* In the order of existence (to which pertains the account of 'creation' of the world) the self in the shape of a human male *(puruṣavidhaḥ)* 'looking around saw nothing, nothing else than the self.' Then the text goes on to say that 'He was afraid,' and 'One who is alone is afraid.' But of what should he be afraid when 'there is nothing else than myself' *(yan mad anyan nāsti)*? 'It is from a second that fear arises.' The point is as the passage that follows runs: 'He verily had no delight.' 'He who is alone has no delight' *(ekākī na ramate)*. So he desired a second, when he became, as pointed out earlier, as large as 'a woman and a man in embrace.'[22]

Thus one may conclude that what came to be clearly enunciated and made the basis of a visual and ritual symbolism in the Hinduism of the classical period was also the Hindu ontological vision from its very inception in the Upaniṣads. God is an essence 'without duality,' apprehended as such ('How else is it intelligible save as the being of what is'),[23] but its essence subsists in two forms, being and becoming, as uncharacterized and characterized, ultimate and proximate, as *deitas* and deity, i.e, the absolute preceding creation and the God that creates and performs other functions. The tantra is a focus on the imaging of these two forms as the male and the female typifying two conjoint principles co-essential without signifying duality or division. Masculine gender and feminine gender logically distinguishable are yet 'one in Godhead' which is neither 'he' nor 'she' but 'it,' or alternately expressed, the essence whose 'nature' is inexpressible with clarity about gender identity save as 'He half of whom is woman' *(ardha-nāri)*.[24]

To render this important visualization as 'hermaphrodite,' one in whom both sexes are represented anatomically and physiologically, obscures the idea of 'wholeness and fusion of sexes' and the original 'oneness' imported by the symbolism. As Eliade would explain it, it rather represented an ideal condition which men endeavored to achieve spiritually by means of initiative rites, a 'ritual androgyne,' because it implied not an augmentation of anatomical organs but 'symbolically the union of the magico-religious powers belonging to both sexes.'[25] The ritual symbolism itself, one may say, partakes of an ontological insight into the identification of essence and nature *in divinis*. That is why the relation of marriage is a sacrament and rite.

The relevance of this insight into the original nature of 'what is' to the order of creation is the subject matter of *purāṇas* and hymnal writings inspired by *purāṇic* accounts. I give here below a summarized version of the account given at the beginning of a section of *Śiva Purāṇa:*

The Creator-God (Brahmā) originally was (created by Śiva) and bidden to create beings. The gods and beings were mentally created by him but they did not multiply. They were being created again and again . . . Then he pondered with his heart, lovingly and in devotion, Śiva united with his 'power' called Śiva and performed great penance. Ere long Śiva assuming the wish-yielding form of Īśāna (perfect consciousness) and in the form of half-male and half-female appeared and said 'may your desire for the increase of Creation be granted.' Thereupon He as it were detached Śiva from His 'body' to whom Brahmā the creator supplicated thus: O Śiva! O Mother! O beloved of Śiva! Give me the power to multiply the mobile and the immobile beings of the universe by giving me the power to create women. Hereafter I wish to make all my subjects flourish by making the creation originate from pairs. Thus, implored by the creator, the supreme goddess consented and bestowed that power upon the creator by creating *śakti* equal in lustre unto herself from the middle of her eyebrows. And further at the behest of Śiva and in compliance with the wish of Brahmā she became the daughter of Dakṣa the progenitor of the human race, himself the son of the Creator-God . . . Ever since then, women were created in the world and creation became copulatory.[26]

The implications of this mythic rendering of the coming to be of multiplicity from an original bisexual unity are obvious. The dynamism inherent in the masculine-feminine interaction, accounting alike for the procreative, enjoying dimension of physical life *(bhoga)* as well as for the redemptive, 'renunciant' dimension *(yoga)* in the service of the bliss of everlasting life, is born of the embrace of two within the one. The embrace also paradoxically combines within it the germ of opposition of a creative kind within the opposites. Translated in terms of psychic life, it is the creative tension between activity-passivity, procession-recession, motion-rest, illumination-vibrancy, independence-dependence, logic-intuition and so on. The archetypal generator of these divisions and tensions is that of male-female, a division which is a condition of the existence of composite things in the created order. The divisions are, however, coincident without opposition in the One who (or which) is no thing. 'Nature,' in the words of Thomas Aquinas, 'recedes from likeness to God, yet even insofar as it has being in this wise, it retains a certain likeness to the divine being.'[27]

The entire universe coheres through the conjunction and reconciliation of the opposites. The symbol of Śiva, the God-personification of the One who is no thing, is the phallus *(liṅgam)*, which unchanging in itself, never ceases to generate life. Sex is the bearer of the genetic molecules, which is the closest organic analogue to a deity's eternity. Phallus in union with the pedestal *(yonī)* is the natural symbol of supreme deity in the sense that it is the most pervasive aspect of the organic order. The natural being the highest, it is the emblem under which God himself, the worshipping devotee fancies, particularly delights to be worshipped. *Śiva-liṅgam,* the central presence of the Hindu temple (of the Śaiva kind) is the symbol of 'God above God' before whom even the gods bow down in worship.[28]

A thirteenth-century Śaiva text (from which was quoted the verse at the beginning of this article) beautifully gathers together the theological, mythical and soteriological aspects of the divine as exemplified by the mystery of male-female relationship. Describing how truly the divine remains the incomprehensible *(acintya)* despite the vogue of myths and metaphysical speculations, the text goes on to say how people fail to understand the mystery involved:

That the divine 'form' is inherently transcendent to the world people do not understand. That the world arises from His freely assumed personality-form, also, consequently they understand not. His 'presence' in the embodied self as well as the embodying world itself is inscrutable to their reason. He is like anyone in the world (though vastly big) they think—all these (of learned ignorance) are they who do not discern the mystery . . . His form 'in the beginning' being half of it woman is truly beyond their imagination . . . His primordial Form outstretching the comprehension of Creator-God himself and even of the God of providence (that protecteth) bespeaking of His nature as the unapproachable one knows not. The genesis of all from His 'personality' they cannot make sense of. By being (Himself) the 'enjoyer' *(bhogi),* He initiates and makes possible enjoyment of life in the world. By being Himself the withdrawing *yogi,* He helps show the way of yogic freedom. By being, as it were, the terrific, He, in his role as the judge, releases the human souls from being held in ransom by the effects of deeds done in the past by them. One self-identical being, He nevertheless assumes in freedom mutually discordant roles, whereby He stands transcendent to a world that is unfree, this is difficult to see . . . Such discordant personalities assumed against the exigencies of conferring 'enjoyment' and 'withdrawal from enjoyment' are all alike modal aspects of the function of bestowal of grace one cannot gauge (except in retrospect). . . (Such are some of the following roles and the 'events' illustrative of how the two—physical life and life everlasting alike *vis-à-vis* male-female love are rendered possible, and the rendering possible is itself grace benign—the feminine side of God's bi-modality).

The Beloved in a sport of euphoric play hid with her hands the eyes of her lover when, lo, the entire creation became enveloped in blinding darkness. Out of concern for the lot of creation, He opened the hidden eye in His brow, thus conferring shining light to a world which was devoid of illumination . . . When the Lord with the eye on the brow assumed the austere form of a *yogi,* creation (which includes gods) languished without sexual love, the God of love *(Kāma)* Himself rendered helpless. When the latter was sent to lure Him by a clever strategy of the 'god that protects' out of concern for the lot of creation pining away without love, He awoke from yogic absorption and burned the god of love to ashes by a stare, but uniting (in matrimony) with the Damsel begotten of the king of Himalayas conferred to beings supreme felicity . . .[29]

The close embrace in love of the male and the female is the most perfect representation of the world of nature *('saṁsāra')* of the divine transcendence of all opposites. Paradoxically it also points to the absence of an ontological distinction between creativity and liberation. It is the Hindu version of the identity of *'saṁsāra'* and *'nirvāṇa.'*

Love and marriage, one may say, may be 'sacramental' but still remain preeminently on the plane of being 'exclusivist.' It is a love of conscious preference. There is an egoism *a deux*. "Not for the sake of the husband the wife loves the husband but for the sake of the self. Not for the sake of the wife the husband loves the wife but for the sake of the self. . . ."[30] Does not married love become a wider and more entrenched selfishness in proportion to the completeness with which the partners have given themselves to one another? The danger of ego asserting its domination and spoiling the purity of the union is in a sense built into the very structure of the relation, which therefore makes it a challenge and an opportunity. The unity-in-duality is what love portends, which ideal will have to be won by surrender of the separate self-assertive will. Love as interchangeable with divine essence is not an extension of man-woman love taking the simple form of an expanding circle of ever-wider comprehensivenss. Love grows intensively and not extensively. This is the paradoxical union of asceticism and eroticism implicit in the conceptualization and imageries of the primary Hindu religious texts and made explicit in the later lyrical and philosophical reconstructions of it.

III

In this section (which may be treated as a lengthy postscript to the present article) an account will be given of the esoterics of sexual love as adumbrated through the medium of Tamil lyrical poetry which is part of the religious literature of classical Hinduism of the early Christian era.[31] Śaiva Siddhānta mystical tradition, which among other things, may be described in a pan-Hindu setting as a right-wing development of tantra, contemplates sexual love as the paradigmatic model for representing gnosis *(jñāna)* in its quintessential form by which one intuits the impartite *(a-kala)* essence of the *deitas (paramaśiva)*—the same as the Brahman of the Upaniṣads. The self-surrendering, self-regaining love between the lover and the beloved is the appropriate symbol of the true path *(sanmārga)* and of the love or devotion germane to such path as *descriptive* of its very life *(sādhya bhakti)*—not a mere prescription in the form of 'thou shalt love with all they heart,' etc. The mystic, unlike a non-mystic, knows what he means by the love of God when bidden to love God (as in the Upaniṣadic mandate 'thou shalt seek the infinite alone').[32] The beatitude of love—sexual love—is the exemplar of joy or happiness that is the very constitutive essence of Godhead.

All the different forms of sentiment or attitude through which religious consciousness expresses itself are typified in the models of 'suffering servant,' 'begotten son,' 'filial friend' and find their most comprehensive symbolism in the love of the paramour for the beloved which 'grows ever anew even as it is consummated.'[33] The mystic poet quoted in the preceding line is Manikkavacagar, perhaps of the fifth century A.D.[34] Śaiva Siddhānta tradition venerates him as among its hallowed founders and typifying the culminating phase of gnosis, presumably in the light of his allegorical love poem called *Tirukkovaiyar* (henceforth abbreviated as TK).

TK is the oldest among the poetical compositions of its genre in the Tamil language which are labeled to imply 'love lyrics arranged in thematic sequence spanning interconnected episodic themes.' The 'episodes' range from premarital 'clandestine' love to the marital, postnuptial life of love. At the end, without losing its effervescence, romantic love matures into domestic love and entails efforts to be widened and deepened through separation and reunion. Though its Tamil is typical of the medieval language of *bhakti* poetry, TK is a lineal descendent of the more ancient Tamil lyrics of the Sangam period (of the pre-Christian era). Unlike didactic and descriptive poetry relating to themes like war, exploits and other sundry things of life, a particular class of the Tamil lyrics relates expressly and exclusively to the theme of what is aptly translated as 'interior landscape' (*akam* poetry).[35]

The distinguishing feature of its 'interiority' is that it pertains to the 'inner world' and speaks of something 'non-objectifiable.' The class of literary writing expressly addressing the male-female relation in its non-objectifiable aspects stands apart from other types of literature. It is a discourse whose referent is not visibly present, 'flamelike,' to be perceived in terms of a configuration that stands out visibly etched but whose presence or reality nevertheless can be felt like the joy brought on by the awakening that 'she loves me.'[36] This is the tender, intimate love poetry, anonymous, stylized in accordance with strict grammatical convention comprising some of the greatest love poems ever composed in world literature.

The *akam* genre of classical poetry has for its *dramatis personae* anonymous types representing men and women *an sich,* irrespective of class, caste, clan or other kinds of distinction, who are participants in the common and total human experience of love in all its phases and aspects. There is, strictly, no personal love poetry in the sense the poet never expressly speaks about his or her individual erotic experience and yet it can be interiorized as personal by anyone (and no one in particular) through empathetic participation.

The divisions of the theme of *akam,* uniquely characteristic of Tamil literary convention, relate to courses of conduct (*'tiṇai'*) incident to love proper, i.e., well-matched love like union, separation, waiting, pining and sulking with one-sided and perverted forms of expression of it on the fringes. Proper expression of love also entails a peculiar affinity and propriety in a particular locale or landscape: union and consummation of lovers is idyllically set in the hills; domestic life and patient waiting of the wife is described ideally to take place in forest and pastures; impatient (and often fidgety) waiting fits on the seashore; infidelity of the man chimes in farmlands; and elopement and separation mesh with the wasteland. There are also the six seasons, six major times of the year—the rainy season, winter, early dew, late dew, the seasons of young warmth and of ripe heat—and six times of day and night—dawn, sunrise, midday, sunset, nightfall, dead of night—which are correlated with the different courses of conduct, thus providing the idealized space-time coordinates of an event of love. The several situations that call for lyrical expression in these modes of development of love are stereotyped in accord with later literary conventions, but the situations themselves are not late ex-post ratiocinations but point to a live bardic tradition which became a part of a classical past and passed into post-oral literature of the classical age.[37] Within these limitations the poet was free to prove how good was his power of improvisation.

TK, one may say, utilizes the literary convention relating to the theme of love and its non-objectifiability as the mode in and through which alone can the 'impartite' be experienced *(anubhūti).* In particular, it utilizes, for its discourse about the transcendent, one of the rare insights displayed in *akam* poetry pertaining to the differences in the psychology of the sexes. [There is a beautiful poem in one of the eight anthologies (*Naṟṟiṇai* 94) in which the girl, smitten with love for her clandestine lover, confesses to her girl friend that it is fitting for man to disclose his urge in words but her feminine reserve does not allow her to do so.][38] It is always the hero who is described as starting the discourse or monologue on love. As he accidentally meets the lass in the millet field or on the seashore, it is he that breaks the ice and seeks to make conversation. When the girl and her friend are reticent, he questions whether the silent form before him may not be a celestial nymph. The doubt, however, gets cleared on seeing her feet touch the ground, etc., when he breaks into an adoration of her beauty. He senses her responsive heart from her eyes. He then ventures to consummate the union, the mental longing itself, as the commentator says, being part and parcel of bodily union. Then follows the monologue feigning exchange of words on the felicity of their union. I translate a crucial verse (TK 7) here:

She is the sweet nectar, I am its sweet relish; thus determining, the good wholesome, destiny brought us together today. Who really can discern the mystery of the *unitas* wherein *I verily have become her,*[39] in this stealthy hide-out off the stone slabs on the Pothia hills of the Pure One of Tiger Shrine?

It may be noted that the lover who discourses here uses the first person singular for self-reference and the beloved is referred to as 'she that is close by,' a third person singular but indicated almost as if interchangeable with 'thou.' The recollected felicity of sexual union finds its spontaneous expression in the language of identity suggesting that the manifestation of bliss is contingent on an overcoming of separation or otherness, i.e., union.

The verse, like all other verses of the text, is also in conformity with the specific requirement of the composition of *kovai* in that it sings in each stanza of some patron or deity praising the natural beauty of his terrain, his high qualities, etc., and glorifies Naṭarāja, the dancing deity of Cidambaram—(the Pure One of Tiger Shrine). Cidambaram, it may incidentally be noted, is the 'subtle ether of the heart' *(cidākāśa),* which is the theme of the celebrated *dahara vidyā* of *Chāndogya* and other Upaniṣads.[40] The hero in whose honor the text of TK is sung and the 'hero,' or more properly the 'heroine' of the poem, the 'she' whom the lover courts, makes love to and feels identified, are, in a manner unique to this text, coincident—the *deitas* dancing in the sanctum of the little space in one's heart. The work contains 400 verses grouped under 25 headings, each having a thematic unity. What was stated above represents one such heading captioned as 'spontaneous sexual union,' figuring as the first of many that follow.

That is followed by a constellation of situations grouped under the rubrics of the lover seeking the help of his friend for effecting further meetings, seeking the support and sympathy of the confidant of the lady-love for further meetings; the lady-love hiding her intense feeling in extreme shyness and the confidant interceding with her on behalf of the lover and fixing the places of rendezvous during days and nights; the confidant urging the lover to elope with his lady-love even through dry tracts and woods to far-off terrains or alternatively to hasten the formal proposal of marriage; the lover starting to gather funds for marriage when the lady waits for his return and pines by the delay; the confidant announcing the beating of the bridal drum accompanying the visit of the lover; and, finally, the occasions for separation after marriage, as when the lover has to depart in further pursuit of learning or to attend assemblies of learned men or to go on warlike and political missions or commercial enterprises. Lastly, there is separation or estrangement on grounds of real or feigned extramarital 'harlotry.' The sulking mood is a kind of teasing of love which makes the succeeding mood of love of reconciliation a precious gain worthy of achievement by love. The experience of love should be always fresh like the morning breeze.

The love themes of TK, with its calculated impersonality, better yet, transpersonality, and oblique personal reference to the deity made with seeming casualness, but couched in terms which not only make for poetry of the most exquisite kind but also import great philosophic ideas,[41] naturally provoke one's hermeneutical imagination. The celebrated commentator prefaces his commentarial colophon with the words that the author of TK 'intended at once two meanings,' esoteric or hidden and exoteric or common meaning pertaining to worldly life'; he adds that he, the commentator, was not adequate to the task of addressing the first task and that, therefore, he is content to comment on the text as only a poem of worldly love.[42]

One way of understanding the esoteric meaning is to perceive the built-in esotericism of love, the phenomenon of love itself in its idealized form, viewing the 'he' and the 'she' of the poem as representatives of man and woman and the drama of their life of union and separation as themselves sacramental reenactments of an eternal truth reflecting the union of the two aspects of the deity. The beatitude of their sexual love-life, idealized in 400 verses, is an exemplification of the supernal bliss of *unitas* through union with Śiva.

The unity of the Godhead rests squarely on love. If God is love in essence, the world is the outpouring of his love and love is its bond of union with God and with its own members. The very essence of God is love, both within himself and in relation to created beings.

For the Śaiva theology, salvation means a gradual 'growing into God.'[43] The 'growing into God' takes place in four stages, each of which corresponds to some specific form of religious activity. Acts of external worship, caring for the temples and so on, show the love of the servant for his master and are rewarded by participation in the world of God *(sālokya)*. To perform the same acts, but with an inner conviction that Śiva is present in his images and symbols as pure wisdom and light, is to acknowledge him as father; this is the trusting love of a son for his parent and it brings the worshipper into proximity of God *(sāmīpya)*. Thirdly, when the devotee turns from acts of external worship to yogic meditation subduing his sense and fixing his mind on God alone, he wins fellowship with God, the love of friend for friend *(sārūpya)*. In the last phase, God and the soul are inextricably united in knowledge and love *(sāyujya)*, an 'interpenetration' which is not simple identity but a conscious realization of oneness, the consciousness paradoxically constituting the element of bliss. The essence of the experience is love saturated in knowledge and is symbolized by the union of bride with groom. It is a melting away into the divine being, a simile that Manikkavacakar in his *Tiruvācakam* uses time and again. It has been stated: "Naught else subsists save Thee! Of these thy nature true I thought with ceaseless thought; Approaching nearer and nearer and wearing off atom by atom, I become one with Thee. Thou, O Śiva, who dwelleth in Sacred Peruntarai Shrine, Thou are naught of these at all and naught subsists sans Thee Who is there. Who can know Thee at all?"[44]

There is also a respected but relatively later interpretative tradition which explores the esoterics of sexual love of TK in a more detailed and one-to-one manner,[45] demonstrating that the text with its 400 love episodes and 20 groupings under which the episodes are organized carries a sustained allegorical suggestion with the following equations: the beloved, as the silent *dramatis persona* of the text providing its center and hidden focus, is none other than Śivam (or more properly, Śiva): the lover is the spiritually ripe soul that hath entered into a life of illumination *(śuddha)* as against the preceding stages of twilight *(sakala)* and darkness *(kevala)* in its spiritual life. The meaning of the advent of a life of illumination *(śuddha avastha)* is the advent of gnosis as the culmination of earlier disciplines. As the source of gnosis is Śiva, gnosis means disclosure or unveiling of Śiva. Śiva reveals in forms appropriate to the spiritual development of the soul. To the ripe human soul who typifies the terrestrial class of beings under multiple bonds *(sakalas)* Śiva appears in the guise of the 'perceptor' and imparts gnosis through instruction, book and the resulting experience. The appearance of the guru at the 'right' time is the greatest event in the spiritual history of the ripe soul that is ready to receive inculcation of knowledge, and is apparently discontinuous with anything that preceded it in its life. The historic encounter of the lover with his beloved which sets the stage for the drama of love is described both in TK and also by the generality of the *akam* literary tradition as something having a fatal character about it, happening not in a contrived way, the meeting itself described as providential, as the chance coming-together of a raft of wood floating on the Northern Sea with its counterpart floating in a far-off southern sea.

I am not going to describe in detail all the correlation between the love episodes and the soul's life of gnosis, but let me barely mention the broad equations: the five terrains of love, the landscapes that provide the right setting for union, separation, waiting, pining and sulking, stand for the five locales of transcendent states *(sthānas)* ranging from pure wakefulness *(śuddha jāgram)* to the final state described as beyond even the beyond *(turīyātīta)*. The male companion of the lover, to whom the lover confesses his love and seeks his oral support and whom the latter tries often to dissuade from such 'unmanly' distractions, is self-knowledge. The feminine companion that acts as the beloved's confidant and her mouthpiece is grace that acts as the mediatrix; the foster mother of the beloved who displays undue sensitivity about her foster daughter's welfare and woe is *Tirodhānaśakti;* and the real mother, who figures in the same role but less prominently, is the *parā śakti.*[46]

That Manikkavacakar could well have intended this esotericism as a free implication of an otherwise straight poem on human love becomes plausible both from his eloquent silence about these details in TK and what he eloquently delineates in his other work. *Tiruvācakam* ('sacred utterance') presents a phenomenology of spiritual life providing both in language and in content the basis for the later philosophical elaboration and systematization of Tamil Śaivism in the Śaiva Siddhānta philosophy.

NOTES

1. *'bahvīm prajām janayantim sārupam,'* cited in Srikaṇṭha's Bhāṣya, *Brahma Sūtras,* 1, 1, 5.
2. The conjunctive 'and' of the original is here translated as 'bi-unity.' Schomerus uses the expression 'zweieinigkeit' (coined on the model of 'Dreieinigkeit' meaning Trinity, as when he writes in his colophon to his translation of this verse: 'Alles Sein ist eine Widerspiegelung des Hochsten in Seiner Zweieinigkeit,' *Arunanti's Sivajnanasiddhiyar* Band 1 (Wiesbaden: Franz Steiner Verlag, 1981).
3. The reference here is to the Tamil cardinal *'oruvar'* in which the first member of the compound *'oru'* is the stem indicative of singular number and the suffix *'ar,'* the final member, which denotes plural number, the dual number being still a case of plural according to Tamil grammar.
4. For a discussion of the 'theological' nuances of *aikṣata* (thought) *kāmayata* (desired/intended) used in apposition to *'tat'* (that), *'sah'* (he) in the Upaniṣads, see *Brahma Sūtras,* 4.1.1, 5–11, debated in the context of demonstrating the inadequacy of naturalism.
5. *Aitareya Up.* 3, 1, 2. Psychological expressions used appositionally to *sat, ātman, brahman* and their pronouns in the Upaniṣads are always understood in ontological terms. Cf. *maniṣā, hṛdayam, manas* (*Mahānārāyana Up.* 23, 1), *prasada* (*Kaṭha Up.* 2, 20), *prasāsana* (*Brahada. Up.* 5, 8, 9), *ādeśa* (*Kena Up.* 29).
6. *Śiva Ñāṅana Siddhi, Supakkam* 2, 27.
7. *'tavam taru ñānattot,' ibid.,* last line.
8. *Ṛg Veda* 10, 90, 3.
9. R. C. Zaehner, *Concordant Discord* (Oxford, 1970), p. 151.
10. *'brahmavid brahmaiva bhavati,' Muṇḍaka Up.* 3, 2, 9.
11. *'satyam jñānam anantam brahmā,' Taittirīya Up.* 2, 1.
12. *Chāndogya Up.* 7, 23, 25.
13. *Īśa Up.* 1.
14. *Śiva Ñāna Siddhi,* cited at the beginning of the article.
15. *The Dance of Śiva* (New York: Noonday Press, 1954).
16. *Chāndogya Up.* 7, 25, 2.
17. *Bṛhadāraṇyaka Up.* 3, 7, 15.
18. *Ibid.,* 4, 3, 21.
19. *Ibid.,* 1, 4, 1–4.
20. Genesis 1:25, 26.
21. *Coomaraswamy,* Selected Papers, Metaphysics, ed. by Roger Lipsey (New York: Bollingen Series, 1977), p. 234.
22. See footnote 18.
23. *Kaṭha Up.* 3, 2, 12, *'astīti brūvato'nyatra katham tad upalabhyate'?*

24. Cf. the verse of *Cidambara Seyyutkovai* cited at the title page.
25. Mircea Eliade, *Mephistopheles and the Androgyne,* p. 100.
26. *Satarudra samhitā, Śiva Purāṇa,* Vol. III (Delhi: Motilal Banarsidass, 1969), Chapter 3.
27. *Summa Theologica* 1.14.11 *ad* 3, cited in *Coomaraswamy,* p. 231. The essay on *The Tantric Doctrine of Divine Bi-Unity* is an able and plausible demonstration of the universality of divine 'bisexuality' in the Vedic Indian as well as in the Christian scripture and exegesis.
28. *Concordant Discord,* p. 54.
29. *Supakkam* 1, 47–54.
30. *Bṛhadāraṇyaka Up.* 2, 4, 4.
31. For a readable account of the early history of Tamil lyrical poetry, see Kamil Zvelebil, *The Smile of Murugan: On the Tamil Literature of South India* (Leiden: Brill, 1973).
32. See footnote 12.
33. *Tirukkovaiyar* (TK), Verse 8.
34. For a general introduction to the author and his *Tiruvācakam,* see Glen E. Yocum, *Hymns to the Dancing Śiva, A Study of Manikkavacakar's Tiruvācakam* (New Delhi: Heritage Publishers, 1982).
35. For a general orientation to Tamil Akam poetry with excellent translation of Sangam lyrics, see A. K. Ramanujan, *The Interior Landscape* (Bloomington: Indiana University Press, 1967).
36. *Iraiyanar Akapporul,* Nakkirar's Commentary on the first Sūtra.
37. *Zvelebil,* N.P., pp. 14–17.
38. V. Sp. Manickam, *The Tamil Concept of Love* (Madras: 1959), p. 276.
39. *'Nān ivaḷām pahutip poṛppu ār aṛivār,'* TK 7. The word *poṛppu* is here translated as signifying by extension 'unity.'
40. *Chāndogya Up.* 8, 1, 1; also *Bṛhadāraṇyaka Up.* 4, 4, 22.
41. Cf. TK 9, opening line: 'He who defies becoming aware by those very people who are aware.'
42. Perasiriyar's Uraippayiram (Preamble) to his Commentary on TK.
43. Zaehner, p. 170.
44. *Tirukkovaiyar* (TK), Verse 390.
45. First outlined byTandavarayar in his Anuputi Urai on *Tiruvācakam Tiruvaka Vyakhyanam* (Madras: Adayar, 1954), and later elaborated somewhat obscurely in *Tirukkovaiyar Unmaivilakkam* (Tiruvaduturai, 1965).
46. For a detailed interpretation of these concepts, see Sivaraman, *Śaivism in Philosophical Perspective* (Delhi: Motilal Banarsidass, 1974).

7

Polar Principles in Yoga and Tantra

THAIYAR M. SRINIVASAN

1. Introduction

The roles played by men and women have been defined and understood within the framework of each culture. Man strayed outside the settlement to hunt and to gather food, woman stayed at home and tended the young. Man came face to face with untamed nature and nurtured a cosmology that reflected his awe and wonder at the cyclic variations around him. Woman turned inwards and experienced cyclicity, growth, birth, and decay within and around her, being a receptacle of activity and reflection of reality. What man expressed, woman experienced. Thus, there is complementarity in the function and ability of expression in man and woman. Several systems of philosophies and practices for transcendence have recognized this complementarity and suggested the intertwining of these polar principles as a necessary requirement for holistic experience.

We shall specifically deal with the ideas expounded in yoga and tantra, regarding the polar principles observed in nature and contained in each individual, and the necessity of their merger within a larger single whole for the realization of the ultimate. We shall also summarize the current scientific understanding of these practices and propose methods of testing these ancient hypotheses within the framework of modern science.

2. Cosmology and Psychobiology of Yoga

The concept of polar principles and their interaction is a recurrent theme in yoga. To understand these concepts, however, it is necessary to review the cosmological principles of yoga wherein the interaction of these principles is enumerated. In the world view of yoga, matter and energy are introduced in much the same way as they are understood in modern cosmology, as postulated by the popular "Big Bang" theory. In yoga, all matter is represented by a primordial mass called *prakṛti*—material and eternal, cyclically evolving and involving, interacting in this process of evolution with nonmaterial energy. In contrast to this material principle is *puruṣa,* the nonmaterial principle of consciousness. Primordially, *puruṣa* is in a state of exalted isolation from *prakṛti* and it is this consciousness that every practitioner of yoga experiences as ultimate reality within himself/herself. In the process of evolution, *puruṣa* and *prakṛti* come together, consciousness and matter interact producing subtle and gross differentiations that manifest in the material world. It is interesting to note that this evolution involves higher specializations and differentiations of the world of matter into atoms and molecules as well as their aggregates giving rise to vegetable and animal kingdoms. Furthermore, the conative and cognitive senses, states of consciousness, mind and intelligence, are all stated to be products of the material world arising out of the evolution of *prakṛti.* Thus, ultimate reality, due to its involvement with matter, gets trapped in the material form and expresses itself through the modifications of the mind.[1]

The reason for this coming together of the nonmaterial, transcendental *puruṣa* with the material *prakṛti* is an unexplained paradigm of yoga philosophy.[2]

The only passing reason offered to this marriage predetermined to failure is that this alliance is necessary for the ultimate self-realization of consciousness itself. In other words, the conscious *puruṣa* needs a material substratum to periodically experience itself and then go into isolation. In this interaction between the two polar principles, the mind and its modifications play a vital role. The mind goes out to the external, material world and its modifications interpret the outer world as the ultimate reality. These modifications of the mind are brought about through its own various tendencies and afflictions which give rise to attachment to the material objects. These actions perpetuate the modifications of the mind and this feedback in turn precipitates and strengthens the vacillations of the mind. Finally, the mind equates the ultimate reality with the material world through ignorance. Hence, yoga recommends removal of ignorance through stilling of the mind, tying it, as it were, to one place and turning the gaze inwards to experience reality. Thus, the whole range of yoga literature starting from its earliest compiler, Patañjali, focuses attention upon the removal of ignorance through control of mental distractions. The cosmology, the emergence of the polar principles, their union and ultimate separation, form the thesis of yoga philosophy.

There are both experimental and experiential methods recommended in yoga to overcome ignorance. Since the distractions of the mind are the cause of ignorance, yoga literature analyzes these distractions and offers antidotes. The distractions are due to disease, languor, doubt, carelessness, laziness, worldly-mindedness, delusion, nonachievement and instability. The symptoms for these distractions are pain, despair, nervousness and irregular breathing. The mental attitude required to overcome these are friendliness, concern for the happiness of others, compassion for misery, gladness in response to virtue, and indifference to vice. Once the distractions are annulled through counteracting emotional responses, one can proceed deeper into establishing steadiness of the mind by realizing the unity in all through meditation. The stilling of the mind may also be achieved through modulating and controlling the *prāṇa* which is the vital energy flowing in the human body. Since breath is the manifest form of *prāṇa,* being aware of and controlling the breath implies controlling *prāṇa.*

The experimental methods of reaching the states of enstasis are dealt with in yoga, through the introduction of the eight-limbed yoga, which includes now-popular postures and breathing exercises. We shall not tarry with these well-known and more-than-necessarily popular methods of physical control on the way to ascendance to higher levels of awareness. Ultimately the experimental has to merge into and give place to the experiential states wherein the inward-directed consciousness descends into the various subtle bodies to experience the ultimate reality.

3. Tantra—Fields and Channels

Tantra is derived from the root word "tan", meaning to extend as well as to unfold. Again, the connotation is in extending the purely physical to the paraphysical and in unfolding the inner states of enstasis as the practitioner progresses along the path to realization. Tantrism was prevalent at the time of Buddha himself and Buddhists had accepted four tantric methods as relevant in the process of removing ignorance.[3] Since tantra deals with subtle fields at the psychobiological and cosmic levels, we now turn our attention to the ideological specificities of tantric lore.

There is a close parallel between the macrocosm of the outer universe and the microcosm of the human body. Like the mighty rivers that irrigate and rejuvenate the earth, energies flow in the body through seventy-two thousand *nādis* or channels. These channels carry vital energies necessary for the body to function. Two of the ten energies are very important: a) *prāṇa* (*prā* implies primary, and *aṇa,* force), which takes in the energy through the breath and b) *apāna,* which expels waste products. Two activities are required for the preservation of the self and that of the species: one is through breathing; the second is through the discharge of semen. Hence, both these fundamental functions channeling the macroscopic energies into microscopic, dissipate energy in a person. Thus, the *Yoga Aphorisms* recommend the 'fourth variety of *prāṇāyama* that goes beyond the sphere of internal and external'—wherein the breath is altogether suspended—as a prerequisite for enstasis. Similarly, stoppage of outflow of semen and its upward movement is recommended by yoga and by tantra. We shall return to these concepts shortly.

The body of a person may be categorized into physical and supraphysical entities. The subtle bodies may be classified as the sonorous, the architectonic, the cosmological and the hystico-physiological bodies as suggested by Mircea Eliade.[4] Both the physical and the subtle bodies are bathed by the *nādis* and have *cakras* (centres). The cosmic energy flows through the *nādis,* and the *cakras* are the centres at which the physical and the subtle bodies touch. Thus, the breath in the physical body regulates the energy flow in the subtle bodies and *cakras,* while having no precise physical equivalence, induce feeling states in the body tissues surrounding it when the *cakras* themselves are stimulated. Thus, there is a mutual interaction between the physical and the subtle bodies through the energy coursing in *nādis* and through *cakras* that overlap.

Three *nādis* and seven *cakras* are important in the quest for enstasis. The three *nādis* connect the seven *cakras* directly. The *nādis* are *iḍā* (variously interpreted as semen, essence of Śiva, sun, day, *prāṇa,* Rahu) to the right, and *piṅgalā* (ovum, *śakti,* moon, night, *apāna, kalagnī*) to the left. The "*ha*" and "*ta*" of *hata-yoga* are respectively *iḍā* and *piṅgalā.* Between these two *nādis,* is *suṣuṁnā* which is the symbolic middle path that Buddha was referring to. The theme of yoga and tantra is the merging of *iḍā* and *piṅgalā* into *suṣuṁnā* and the ascent of the vital energy, *kuṇḍalinī,* which reaches the highest *cakra* through *suṣuṁnā.*

Kuṇḍalinī is the mystical fire in the subtle body, whose upward movement and merging with the eternal Śiva confers freedom and immortality. It symbolizes *kuṇḍ* (to burn), *kuṇḍa* (hole or bowl), *kuṇḍali* (coil, spring) and signifies *śakti,* the feminine aspect of the creative force. This *śakti* is dormant in all individuals and once awake, it traverses through the six lower *cakras* arousing the physical body to suprasensory levels and ultimately reaching the Lord at the highest level.

Tantra has rich symbolism in describing the ascent and the merger of *śakti* with *śiva.* Normally, *kuṇḍalinī* lies coiled at the base of the physical spine at the lowest *cakra.* Its passage through the two lateral channels of *īḍā* and *piṇgalā* portends disaster to the practitioner and instant death. Its passage through the central channel, *suṣuṁnā* implies the holy union of *śakti* with *śiva,* representing the female and male principle in each individual.[5]

The primordial force of *kuṇḍalinī* lies dormant in the lowest *cakra* known as *mūlādhāra.* In this lowest level, *kuṇḍalinī* endows the person with self-awareness and normal consciousness. The second *cakra svādiṣṭana* is at the root of the genitals and as *kuṇḍalinī* reaches this point, sexual energy is aroused which is necessary for the preservation of the species. Unfortunately, for many, the vacillations of *kuṇḍalinī* within these two *cakras* and the awareness and function of such individuals is limited to those represented by these levels. The third *cakra* is *manipūra* at the solar plexus in the region of the navel, seat of feeling states. The fourth is called *anāhata,* in the heart region wherein love blossoms and *bhakti-yoga* originates spontaneously when the *kuṇḍalinī* power strikes this *cakra.* The fifth is *viśuddhi* at the throat region and with *kuṇḍalinī* striking this centre, the practitioner devotes himself to *karma-yoga.* The sixth is *ājñā,* between the eyebrows concentrating on which, the path of *jñāna-yoga* is ascended. The last reaches of *kuṇḍalinī* is the seventh *cakra* called *sahasrāra* or thousand-petaled lotus when the *śakti* reaches *śiva* and a complete merger of the two takes the yogi to states of enstasis and final independence.

4. Polarity and Merging for Emergence

The *kuṇḍalinī* force residing at the base of the spine thus represents the active, female force in contrast to the passive, male *śiva.* The arousal, ascent and merging of the female with the male is the theme of the tantric tradition. It is important to note that, in this tradition, the female is the active, and the male is the passive principle. The most immediate experience of an aroused *kuṇḍalinī* is the activation of the sexual energies, which undoubtedly, is the most intense awakening of feeling states in a person. The tantric lore recommends the arousal of this power through an exercise of esoteric sex wherein the female-male in an individual is reintegrated through a physical juxtaposition of the polar principles of female-male. Some corporal positions, constrictions, and antiperistaltic practices are recommended for conserving the semen. The movement of semen is dependent on the energy flow in the subtle body which, in its turn, is controlled by means of breath. The breath is also connected to the mind. Thus, the control of semen in the physical plane, of mind in the vital plan, and the vital energy in the cosmological plane constitute stages in transcendence. The downward movement of the semen, the in and out motion of the breath, and the constant modifications of the mind must all be arrested in this process.

5. Polarity in Brain Functioning

In the recent past, a new avenue of female-male interactions in an individual is being opened up through the study of the right and left hemispheres of the brain and localization of higher functions within them. The brain is composed structurally of two hemispheres which are connected between themselves, by means of nerve fibers which take information back and forth between the two halves. The cortical areas of the left hemisphere control the motor functions of the right side of the body and receive sensory information from the right side. Similarly, the right hemisphere receives information from and sends commands to the left side of the body. The two hemispheres are assumed to be representing two modes of consciousness, one tending to feminine and the other masculine.

The left hemisphere is basically analytical and logical, while the right one is intuitive. The left represents transactional, while the right, transcendental. The left is normally considered 'male', while the right is regarded as 'female'. Robert Ornstein at the Langley Porter Neuropsychiatric Institute has written in detail regarding the two modes of consciousness that a person is endowed with through the functioning of these hemispheres in an individual.[6] Experiments with brain damaged persons and those in whom the connecting link between the two halves is severed for therapeutic purposes exhibit an unusual confusion in their memory retrieval and ability to correlate sensations felt through one hand with speech located in one side of the brain. When the connections between the hemispheres are severed, a person can identify an object by touch only with his right hand, not with the left. In these cases, the sensory information passes to his opposite hemisphere and if his dominant hemisphere is left, as is mostly the case, he can correctly identify the object while feeling with his right hand. Here, both the sensory information and memory retrieval as well as the speech, function within the same hemisphere. However, if the sensory information goes to his right hemisphere (while he touches the object with his left hand), this input does not reach his left brain where the verbal detail regarding the object felt is located. Several other experiments conducted around the world have indicated the diverse role played by each half of the brain in interpreting and integrating the information converging on us every moment. Thus, there is a polarity and a bimodality of function between the two hemispheres.

It is not the intuitive alone, nor the logical alone that is useful and necessary in the road to transcendence. As in the case of the polarity of the primal forces, a symbiosis between the left and right brain functions is necessary, in order to strike a balance and synthesize the logical and the intuitional. The observation and codification—in mathematical and physical science language—of the external world reinforces our left brain function. The intuitional has little role to play in our daily lives and most schools do not concern themselves with intuitional approach in learning. This understanding of the need for intuitive capacity and the shortcomings of traditional school systems led to the development of mental imagery and meditation as a requirement in practices towards transcendence. We have a sophisticated symbolism in the tantric tradition that provides specifically for the enrichment of the right hemisphere and thus brings about a balance in left-right brain functioning that is usually overlooked in most learning environments.

6. Evolution, Involution, and Enlightenment

The evolutionary direction is in the expansion of awareness and experience of transcendence. In this process, involution and going towards the centre of one's own Being becomes an important intermediary stage. The experimental procedures and the stages of experience one goes through during involution and enstasis are the concern of both tantra and yoga.[7] The states of awareness become more subtle as one descends into the consciousness domain with an inward-directed meditative technique. The states of consciousness are initially polarized into the kinetic *śakti* and the immobile *śiva.* The symbolism of the coiled snake as the *kuṇḍalinī* energy occurs in almost all cultures. This coiled snake serves as a reclining bed on the ocean of milk for Visṇu, Śiva adores snakes on his limbs, nonrecognition of the primal cause and polarization of this into man and woman is symbolized in the story of Adam and Eve. The seven energy centres and awakening of awareness is also a recurrent theme among native American Indians, especially the Hopi. The shamanistic rituals, their concepts of immortality and transcendence, all portray a common desire of every culture to proceed in this direction of evolution through involution.

At the centre of discussions on this primal force, *kuṇḍalinī,* several specific questions remain needing elucidation. They are fundamental and difficult ones raised in this age of reductionism: Is *kuṇḍalinī* a measurable force in the way that many other—such as weak, electromagnetic, strong—forces are measured in a laboratory? What is the role of *kuṇḍalinī* in health and disease? Can *kuṇḍalinī* be roused at will for transactional and transcendental purposes? These questions imply that we are making several subtle and naive assumptions: a) *kuṇḍalinī* force could be postulated within the paradigms of present scientific knowledge; and b) its course and interaction is perceivable in quantities such as heart rate, brain function, hormonal function, etc. It is needless to say that such assumptions are naive, implying that we have reached the pinnacle of knowledge regarding ourselves and the physical world, while even the normal functions of the brain and its higher activities such as thought, memory consolidation and retrieval, etc. are not properly understood. This does not imply that *kuṇḍalinī* is a mystic experience whose occurrence is totally out of hand. Indeed, the entire tantric teaching is about controlling and chanelling this unknown force in practical terms.

Several attempts at understanding changes in consciousness and psychophysical functions during yoga and tantra practices are available from both highly competent scientists and yoga teachers.[8] The 'electrical bliss' of *kuṇḍalinī* vibrating throughout the body, which is also orgasmic in nature, has been described by several researchers.

Eugene Wigner, the renowned physicist and a Nobel laureate, writes regarding the directions in which the search in physics should proceed if scientific understanding of consciousness is attempted. He proposes new and as yet unknown, nonlinear quantum mechanical formulations and theories for defining consciousness. Itzhak Bentov, a freelancing scientist, speculated that microvibrations of the body and the brain during tantric practices might set up standing waves resonating in the skull producing all types of suprasensory experiences. Altered sensory perceptions take place along with reduced psychosomatic load, relieving the person of any diseased states. Kindling (sending minute electric currents at specific sites in the brain during surgery) and *kuṇḍalinī* effects seem to have some common traits in the global responses and behaviour, indicating an overlap in cause-effect criteria. Motayama, in Japan, has attempted to measure the *kuṇḍalinī* effect by placing antennae close to the spinal cord and computerizing the results in search of associated activities.

In conclusion, the psychophysical energy of *kuṇḍalinī* resides in all forms of life and it takes an ascendence in humans enabling individuals to reach heights of moral and spiritual states transcending the human condition. The recognition, fostering and deliberate channelling of this potent energy through the symbiosis of the polar principles is the concern not only of spiritual teachers, but of psychosomatic healers as well.

NOTES

1. See Swami Vivekananda, *Rāja-Yoga* (Calcutta: Advaita Ashram, 1962), pp. 117–124; and S. N. Das Gupta, *Yoga as Philosophy and Religion* (Calcutta: Kennikat Press, 1924), p. 124.
2. S. N. Das Gupta, *Yoga Philosophy* (Calcutta: University of Calcutta Press, 1930), p. 172.
3. M. P. Pundit, *Kuṇḍalinī Yoga* (Madras: Ganesh and Co., 1968), pp. 18–22.
4. Mircea Eliade, *Yoga, Immortality, and Freedom* (Princeton: Bollingen Series, 1958), pp. 85–97.
5. G. S. Arundale, *Kuṇḍalinī,* (Madras: Theosophical Press, 1938), p. 24.
6. R. E. Ornstein, *The Psychology of Consciousness* (California: Freeman and Co., 1972), pp. 50–72.

7. See T. M. Srinivasan, "Electrophysiological Correlates During Yogic Practices," *The Yoga Review,* Vol. 1 (1981), pp. 165–173; and Elmer and Alyce Green, *Beyond Biofeedback* (U.S.A.: Delacorte Press, 1972), pp. 244–260.
8. John White, *Kuṇḍalinī, Evolution and Enlightenment* (U.S.A.: Anchor Books, 1979), p. 72.

8

A Christian Speculation on the Divine Intention for the Man-Woman Relationship

RUTH TIFFANY BARNHOUSE

The Christian religion, like all others known to me, is full of paradoxes. When these are symbolic or theoretical, they do not impinge in any obvious way on the lives of ordinary people. But nearly every troublesome question about right conduct is linked to one or more of these paradoxes. The one which bears most pressingly on the topic of this paper is that Christians are urged to adhere to timeless principles ordained by God; but they are simultaneously urged to become more mature, both personally and collectively. The prophets of the Old Testament constantly urged the people to "sing a new song." The entire Bible is filled with admonitions to discard outworn or childish habits in favor of a better way. Sometimes that better way is in direct violation of what was previously understood to be God's clear commandment. One of the most famous examples is Peter's dream, in which he is urged to eat of the animals hitherto forbidden as unclean. And yet, the admonitions to adhere to established traditions are just as frequent.

Many "holy wars" between rival groups of Christians, some even involving bloodshed, have resulted when there was disagreement over whether a particular issue should be evaluated in terms of the new or the old understanding. Although such extreme persecution is less likely now than in the past, the current differences between various factions on the issue of sexuality are no less heated. These range from strident insistence, sometimes tinged with panic, on the eternal validity of the strict code of sexual behavior proclaimed in the past (usually including the idea that of all sins the sexual ones are the worst), all the way to extreme permissiveness proclaimed in the name of Christian freedom.

The discussion could be reduced to more manageable proportions were the distinction between principles and rules borne clearly in mind. Principles are eternal and do not change. Rules do change, since they are only the cultural clothes worn by a principle to suit a particular time and place. For example, in the Old Testament adultery was not only prohibited by the Ten Commandments, but offenders were to be stoned to death. In the New Testament, when the Pharisees were about to stone the woman taken in adultery, Jesus stopped them with the famous words: "Let him who is without sin amongst you cast the first stone." At the same time, he told the woman "Go, and sin no more." Thus he maintained the principle that the marriage covenant is inviolably sacred but changed the rule about how to deal with offenders.

We are free to change rules but not to alter basic principles. To affirm that, however, does not solve the current problems. It does help to eliminate the extremes. Mindless adherence to old rules, taking no account of the changed conditions of modern life or of the light shed on the nature of sexuality by psychology and sociology, is surely not right. If we *do* decide to keep some or all of the old rules, it must be because we have established that they express the underlying divine principles in terms which are applicable to contemporary life.

Abolition of all rules is equally likely to be wrong. There is no known culture without some limitations on sexual behavior, and this is nearly always expressed in religious terms. Ours is hardly likely to be the only exception, particularly since our own tradition has always had such limitations. These must express some underlying principles, and it is our duty to try to discern what these may be and to align with them any proposed changes in the rules.

Many developments during the last three centuries bear on our problem. Perhaps the most important is the gradual rise of the principle of individual liberty, with equal rights and justice for all. We are far from achieving any such goal, but that is certainly the direction in which all are struggling to move. The abolition of slavery and the decline of the colonial system are obvious results. The rise of feminism is another result. This inevitably entails the decline of the patriarchal system, which, so far as anthropologists can estimate, has prevailed all over the world for about eight thousand years. Although feminism has been stirring for about 150 years, serious inroads on patriarchy are only a generation old.

Other germane developments include the population explosion, modern obstetrics including reliable methods of birth control, and important contributions from the depth psychologies toward a better understanding of the nature of sexuality. No serious theological inquiry into the man/woman relationship can afford to ignore any of these factors, any more than it can afford simply to capitulate to the latest secular "wisdom." For reasons of space, they will not all be discussed in this paper, which is principally addressed to specifically theological issues as I perceive their pertinence to Western culture, especially in its American (U.S.) variant.

Christianity addresses the relation between humanity and God. Humanity comprises men *and* women, and we are all created in God's image. God is described as a trinity: Father, Son, and Holy Spirit, although the three are One. Through the incarnation of Christ the Son in the male human person of Jesus, including his life, death and resurrection, we are rescued from sin and reconciled to God.

That statement is deliberately general in an attempt to formulate the basic context in language acceptable to Christians of any denominational affiliation. How literally the statement is to be taken, the precise mechanics of atonement, theories of sin, justification, eschatology and other theological esoterica need not detain us here. Such topics have occupied theologians for many centuries, and I do not wish to belittle their importance. But excessive concentration on them has caused neglect of something which I believe is not only obvious but fundamental. Much of the actual language, the governing metaphors, used throughout Scripture to describe the relation between humanity and God is rooted in sexuality. A good deal has been written about this, but to my mind most of it has been in the service of explaining that fact *away* rather than helping us to understand its deep implications.

First of all, if humankind is created in the image of God and comprises both men and women, this not only enlightens us about ourselves but also about God. The passage in Genesis reads: "let us make Man in our own image, in the likeness of ourselves . . . in the image of God, male and female created He them." Note that God refers to himself in the plural. The infinite richness and diversity of God's nature is expressed by the many names for him used in the Old Testament. Significantly, the particular God-name used in this passage is Elohim, which in Hebrew is a feminine noun with a masculine plural ending. The Hebrew word for the "spirit of God" which "moved over the face of the waters" at creation is *ruach,* a feminine noun. Thus we see that there is something about the personalness of God which includes both masculine and feminine, whatever we may mean by those terms. We may presume that in God those qualities are fully integrated and indivisible but that in order to bring them into manifestation on the physical plane of distinct and separate particularities, it was necessary to create both sexes. Thus, in some high and important sense, God is androgynous. That statement is profoundly shocking to many people, and in fact, given the state of modern Western culture, it is easily open to misinterpretation.

The culture of the United States has an oversimplified and degraded concept of sexuality. It is the old Gnostic dualism turned upside down. The Gnostic heresies, in various forms, held that there was an unbridgeable gulf between spirit and matter and that matter was evil and spirit good. Our current culture is still heavily under the influence of 19th century scientific determinism. According to this theory, everything is ultimately reducible to its physical components, and only matter is real. Spirit is, for the most part, held to be a foolish illusion at best, and some consider it actively dangerous. This extends to the way in which we conceptualize sexuality. Masters and Johnson, Kinsey and others have claimed to tell us something about that. What they have actually told us is a great deal of frequently interesting and useful information about the physical components of it. But there is much evidence to show that the physical components are perhaps the least of sexuality and in any case do not constitute the most important part.

Nor are the scientists the only ones to make this reductionistic error. Our popular culture, heavily supported and informed by the media in general and the advertising industry in particular, has tended to sexualize practically everything in the crudest physical terms as a commercial attention-getting device. What is even more disturbing is that this is all done from a male point of view, and an immature one at that.

It is normal for the sexuality of adolescents to be dissociated from the rest of their personhood. It is still so new to them that they have not yet learned to integrate it with their other faculties. In young males, the dissociated awareness of sexuality is at first almost entirely physical, unconnected with any relationships, since those have not yet been formed. Instead of encouraging a mature and responsible integration, the culture tends to fixate boys at this immature level. What is worse, in many quarters young women (whose first experience of sexuality tends to be emotional, rather than physical) are urged to imitate this example!

We have a disgraceful mixture of mistakes, each reinforcing the other. There is a devaluation of the feminine in general and of women in particular. There is rampant immaturity. There is mounting inability of men and women to form lasting convenantal relationships with one another. There is a prevalent model of sexual behavior which is exploitative, obviously of women but in the long run also of men even though that is not often recognized. The time-honored connection between sex and love is dismissed in many quarters as sentimental mystique. Sexual activity is seen as a recreational end-in-itself, no longer either as a means to an end or as an expression of something enduring and profound. Immature masculine values of competition, swagger, conquest and toughness are glorified and, what is worse, seen as essential preconditions for success in what is tragically misnamed "the real world." Women are, understandably, objecting to all this—at least to the parts which they perceive as oppressive. Unfortunately, too often their objections are expressed only in a desire to get their share of the male power pie. Few realize that unless the very shape and texture of masculinity changes *from the inside,* the oppression will continue.[1]

Modern psychology, particularly that of the Jungian school, demonstrates that the psyche of every human person, whether male or female, carries elements of the other sex. Psychologically, every person is androgynous. Personal maturity consists importantly in coming to terms with the contrasexual portion of one's own psyche, integrating it into the total fabric of one's personality. This urgent maturational task is next to impossible in a culture which systematically devalues the feminine. Men are reluctant to admit to any of the devalued components in their own psyche and instead deal with these by projecting them onto women. They then despise women, consciously or unconsciously, for manifesting them. This is the case even when the characteristics are essential to the survival of the human community. Many women accept the negative valuation of the feminine and perceive themselves as inferior, acting out that role in various ways which often are outrightly masochistic. Still others, believing in the negative valuation, rebel against it by overdeveloping their own masculine side, identifying with male values and behavior, neglecting their own feminine, and often being contemptuous of other women.

The only solution to all this is a radical re-evaluation of the feminine. Women caught in this struggle will have an easier time if they think of themselves as engaged in the noble task of recovering the neglected half of the image of God. Furthermore, they must see themselves as doing this not only for their own sake as women but for the sake of the whole human family.[2]

Where is the Church in all this? Where has it been? Where is it now? And where should it be? The answers are not very encouraging. This is because the Church has never really faced up to the significance of the sexual language of Scripture. We are, men and women together, created in the image of God and therefore we reflect his androgyny. This can be expressed when men and women join together, but it is also expressed in the individual psyche of each person as she or he comes to full maturity. Furthermore, throughout the Old and New Testaments, the relation between God and his people is frequently described in marital language. The children of Israel are the spouse of God. The Church is the bride of Christ. We have heard those statements so often that we don't listen any more.

There is no barrier to truth so great as the overfamiliar word. We must try to think about these metaphors anew, to take them really seriously. The principle of wholeness, of at-one-ment, of union, is vividly conveyed by the images of sexuality. Nor are these biblical images in any way simplistic, reducible to the merely physically sexual. The intermingling of masculine and feminine can be seen at all levels. For instance, the Church is the bride of Christ, but the Church includes both men and women. Both, therefore, are to take a "feminine" posture vis-à-vis God. This is a posture of receptive trust. It has nothing to do with the devalued caricatures of passivity often currently associated with the feminine. But just as men are physically more powerful than women, and therefore at least potentially frightening to them, so God is more powerful than any person, hence the "fear of the Lord." How, then, can a true relationship be established? In each case, the attitude of the weaker one must be what I described, receptive trust. This comes about through love. When we are convinced we are loved, we can trust. This is how women overcome the fear of the physically powerful male; it is also how human persons of either sex overcome their fear of the powerful God: "We love him because he first loved us." The parallel is precise.

But there is an additional paradox. The Church is not only the bride of Christ, it is also the body of Christ. Like any sacred symbol, this has many levels of meaning (only some of which are accessible to us at any given time). Jesus, to be sure, was male. However, the Christ, incarnated in Jesus, part of the Godhead for all eternity, is not simply male. Yet we are his body! This is an astounding image. It subsumes within itself the androgyny of God, as well as the androgyny of human beings, both as individuals and also as men and women together, cohering as Christ's body. (Here it is important to remember that "androgyny" refers only to qualities of consciousness, not to anything sexual in the physical sense.)

The wonder is that given the prevasiveness and depth of these Scriptural images, anyone was ever seriously able to maintain belief in the inferiority of femininity. The idea of the inferiority of women is a little easier to understand. According to the best estimate of anthropologists, some form of patriarchy has been the prevailing pattern of social organization all over the world for about 8000 years. Thus patriarchy was in full sway when our Scriptures were written, and no matter what theory of inspiration one holds, the individual authors were persons whose consciousness was thoroughly conditioned by that patriarchy. The same circumstance applies to those portions which represent a cumulative oral tradition. There are therefore many passages, more in the Old than in the New Testament, which reflect the inferior and subordinated position of women in the prevailing culture. These are all familiar. They have been endlessly quoted, often misquoted or taken out of context, while those passages which reflect a different attitude have been glossed over, explained away, or simply ignored.

Recent careful scholarship has thrown a new light even on the passages which seem most antithetical to women. Jewett, the conservative Protestant scholar, coming as he does from a tradition which lays the heaviest possible emphasis on the actual wording of Scripture, is particularly persuasive when he concludes that there is no biblical basis for perpetuating any theory of female inferiority.[3] Furnish, in his recent book *The Moral Teachings of Paul,* has conclusively demonstrated that Paul believed mutuality to be the ideal relation between the sexes, in contrast to the prevailing pagan standards governing the place and treatment of women.[4] The most cursory reading of the Gospels shows that Our Lord treated women as full, individual, autonomous persons, often violating the customs of his day in order to do so.[5]

As the church historian McLaughlin has shown, "Christianity carried revolutionary egalitarian implications into the late classical world."[6] She also explains that when the early Fathers wrote abstract theology, they often expressed themselves in misogynist terms, blaming women for the Fall, and sometimes equating that with sexual activity. This is clearly hindsight—projecting the prejudices of later interpreters on the actual Genesis account. That does not even hint that sex was in any way responsible for the Fall. Such a view could only have been entertained when it was believed that Adam and Eve were two historical persons. Modern theology must take account of the scientific fact of evolution. Therefore, Adam and Eve must be understood as symbolic of our human ancestors at the dawn of consciousness with its accompanying faculty of moral choice. The usual reproductive mechanisms had obviously been present long before that stage of human development so perfectly and poignantly described in the Genesis account.

In their discussions, the Church Fathers were far from consistent. Their descriptions of their own marriages often present a different picture. Consider this passage from Tertullian:

> How beautiful, then, the marriage of two Christians, two who are one in hope, one in desire, one in the way of life they follow, one in the religion they practice. . . . Nothing divides them, either in flesh or in spirit. . . . They pray together, they worship together, they fast together; instructing one another, encouraging one another, strengthening one another . . . side by side they face difficulties and persecution, share their consolations. They have no secrets from one another; they never shun each other's company; they never bring sorrow to each other's hearts . . . Hearing and seeing this, Christ rejoices.[7]

Nevertheless, many early writers found it difficult to avoid "a deep theological misogyny." But in the institution of religious virginity, "a real mutuality between the sexes could be found. Jerome writes of his female companions in Christ, 'I only wish that men would follow the example that women have publicly given them.'"[8]

For a long time we have been accustomed to hypermasculine God-language, and the Christian woman has strayed from hearth and home with difficulty and peril. But it was not always so. McLaughlin has written about this in a number of articles, including one with the provocative title "Male and Female in Christian Tradition: Was There a Reformation in the 16th Century?"[9] Considered from the standpoint of possibilities for women and the meaningful presence of the feminine in the Church, the answer to that question is clearly no. Nor is it only that the cult of the Virgin Mary was abandoned along with that of other saints, more than half of whom were women. At the Reformation much more than that was lost. Prior to that time there was more than one religious hierarchy. The lowest level was the secular clergy, ranging from parish priest to Pope. This was open only to males. But these men were deeply involved in the affairs of the world and were therefore in many respects considered inferior to those in monastic life. Here both men and women were welcome. Higher still was the "category of holiness or sainthood, which cut across every [order], for there were kings and prostitutes, robbers and queens among the saints." Holiness was no respecter of sex or of one's station in life. If the Mass could only be celebrated by a celibate male, other more valued spiritual powers resided with Mary and the other saints or with the local holy man or woman. "Women stood beside men among the saints and the holy ones as models of Christian living."[10]

Even more startling is the language of popular piety during that period. The fundamental androgyny of God was taken for granted and was expressed in the most vivid images. Consider the passage written in the 14th century by Lady Julian of Norwich:

> The human mother will suckle her child with her own milk, but our beloved Mother, Jesus, feeds us with himself, and with most tender courtesy, does it by means of the Blessed Sacrament, the precious food of all true life. . . . The human mother may put her child tenderly to her breast, but our tender Mother Jesus simply leads us into his blessed breast through his open side, and there gives us a glimpse of the Godhead and heavenly joy, the inner certainty of eternal bliss.[11]

That passage cannot be explained simply by the fact that a woman wrote it. Medieval men spoke easily of both God and themselves in feminine as well as masculine terms. (In a shocking anachronism, reflecting the deteriorated attitudes to sexuality mentioned above, some modern authors interpret this fact as evidence of homosexuality!) In the 11th century, St. Anselm of Canterbury also referred to Jesus our Mother, seeing him as through his passion and death giving birth to Christian souls, as a caring mother comforting her children and feeding them. Thus not only is Mary seen as Mother of Mercy, but also the Lord Christ himself is seen that way. A 13th century prioress compared Christ's passion to woman's experience in these words:

Ah, who has seen a woman give birth thus! And when the hour of birth came, they placed You on the Bed of the Cross. And it is not astonishing that Your veins ruptured, as you gave birth in one single day to the whole world![12]

Both male and female mystics frequently described their deepest experiences of prayer in explicitly sexual images, perceiving themselves as the feminine partner in the intercourse with God. Such passages are rarely known to modern Protestants, but when they are, they seem peculiar at least—perhaps even perverse. But that says more about our view of sex than it does about the appropriateness of such experiences of God. And here, I think, is to be found the explanation of what, from the feminine point of view, can only be seen as the post-Reformation deterioration.

The physical sexual act and our attitude toward it is central. In fact, that attitude has remained constant throughout most of church history and has been one of nervous apprehension at best. We must not forget that the ability to experience the androgyny of God during the Middle Ages arose in a context of the ordered religious life, where the participants were vowed to perpetual chastity. Actual sexual experience was ruled out. The spontaneous and natural experience of the sexuality of God was therefore not threatening in any of its manifestations. Nor was the development of high, intimate, spiritually ennobling friendship between monastic men and women. The holy pairs were common: St. Theresa of Avila and St. John of the Cross; St. Francis and St. Clare; and many others. But neither our religious forebears from the earlier periods nor the Reformers ever made peace with the implications of physical sexuality. When the religious orders were abolished and clergy became free to marry, everything changed. The real, actual, physical—not just spiritual—feminine was brought too close for comfort. Full and equal relationships with real women in the context of the family, with all of the implications for the social and political system, were simply unthinkable.

The idea of questioning the traditional patriarchal system occurred to no one at that time. But the presence of women as equals in the daily world is completely incompatible with patriarchy.[13] And so we see the beginning of the gradual process of the hypermasculinization of God, of forgetting the feminine modes of experiencing and conceptualizing him. Not only that, but the process was hastened by the absence of holy women, religious writing and teaching from their honored positions in the convents. There, of course, their spiritual equality with men was not threatening since they had no direct hand in the conduct of society's daily affairs, which were all in the hands of the patriarchal bureaucracy. But now, even their advisory voice was lost.

And so, with the abolition of monasticism and the cult of the Virgin, the feminine face of the Church fell into deep shadow. The poetic references to Mother Church lost their liveliness and immediacy as the whole notion of motherhood itself gradually took on overtones of inferiority to the powerful human males, backed up by that great Macho God in the sky, Wholly Other, from time to time engaging in Mighty Acts in History, stern judge, and all the rest of it. It is impossible to read Scripture in this way without ignoring or distorting most of the record of how God actually exhibits the personal aspect of his Mysterious Being to us, who are both his children and his spouse.

Nevertheless, these one-sided views are what made possible the rampant hypermasculinization of post-Enlightenment culture, and the gradual deterioration of the position of women. In the narrowest sense of increasing legal and social and educational rights, significant progress has been made. But in the deeper sense there has been retrogression. Woman is confronted with an unloving God (in spite of lip service paid to the cliche that God is Love), who is characterized by a disembodied masculinity with which she not only cannot identify but which is often not even admirable. God is too often presented as a cruel, capricious heavenly Parent, one who, by ordinary humane standards, should be taken to court for Child abuse! Women don't want to be made in the image of that God and so can no longer truly ground their self-respect in their unalterable identity as loved and valued children of God, who reflect an indispensable part of his holy image. No wonder so many women want to change the God-language and can no longer understand themselves as included in Man. But we need to change much more than the language. In fact, changing the language alone will not do very much.

Let me give an example. I teach a course in Marriage and Family to students nearly all of whom are in their last year of Seminary. There are more men than women in the class, but even so they have been very well trained. None of them would think of using any "sexist" language. But recently we did a role-play in class. A woman, played by a woman student, was taking a problem to her pastor, played by a male student. She was concerned about her 15-year-old son whom she perceived as on the road to juvenile delinquency. But her husband said she was turning him into a sissy and insisted that there was nothing wrong with the boy's outbreaks of violence, dangerous games, vandalism and so forth. This was causing serious trouble not only between herself and her son, but also with her husband. She was coming to her pastor for advice about how to handle the problem.

The way that role-play went in the classroom, supplemented by the discussion afterward, made it clear that nearly all the men in the room felt in their gut that the hypothetical husband was right. Boys will be boys, to grow into men they must toughen up, be rough, competitive, fight, dominate others, and at least go through a period of showing contempt for women. Many of the men students knew intellectually that such ideas needed to be modified, but they had no idea that there could be any other way to bring up a male child so that he would turn out to be a "real man." These men had been well indoctrinated into the outer need to use inclusive language, but that had made no dent in their view of what constitutes appropriate masculinity. If only the language is changed, all we have is a sort of spiritual transvestism, in itself pathological, which can only confuse the issue and prevent the discovery of a new and better-grounded view of masculine identity. Reform of language *only* will merely have the effect of superficially including women in the preexisting male mindset. But it is *that* mindset which needs changing.

This problem ultimately depends on the fact that the Church does not have and never has had an adequate theology of sex. As long as sex is viewed as an inferior activity, shameful if not actually sinful, things cannot change. The general secular consensus is that sex is fun, period. The church in some quarters concedes that it is fun but is seldom able to get over the view that it is not quite nice. Why does this problem persist?

I believe that the secular and traditional religious attitudes to sex are only superficially different. At bottom they both have as their ultimate unconscious object the perpetuation of female inferiority. If sex is only a recreational activity, then one does not have to take the other player seriously. One is free to control or dominate, to play as long as one pleases and then leave, all without having to take into account the full humanity of the partner. Usually it is men who treat women this way, and that has caused an enormous amount of emotional suffering. In some places, however, "sexually liberated" young women are taking the aggressive role in casual sexual relationships, giving the men a taste of their own medicine. In such circles the immediate result has been a dramatic rise in the incidence of healthy young men suffering from impotence! Men are not used to being sexually exploited in that way, and of course they cannot tolerate it, not even as well as women can, and God knows they have suffered much.

The Church's attitude that there is something inferior about sex itself, leading to such things as calling it "dirty" (and some of that has permeated secular culture too), is also exploitative. But sex is essential, a powerful drive the exercise of which is fundamental in human experience. If it is "not nice," what feelings will the patriarchal perpetrators have about the objects of their sexual attentions? Contempt and revulsion. This was much more obvious in the old days when men expected to gratify their lustier impulses with "bad girls"—and the bad girls were the ones who (supposedly) had fun at it. But they were ostracized, inferior, exploited, nothing more. "Good girls" were beyond and above all that, and in some quarters the really nice ones were said not to enjoy sex, merely to tolerate it for the sake of the holy joys of motherhood and the secure position of the wife in patriarchal society.

If sex is degraded either to mere pleasure or to something nasty, the end result is that the woman does not have to be taken seriously as a full and equal partner. (If she notices how she is being used, her private opinion of men will not be high, no matter what public deference she may pay them.) Perhaps still more tragic is that such degradation of sex stunts the man's growth as well. This is part of what makes it so difficult for men to face their own feminine side and to integrate it in that growth which is essential to full human maturity. Immature men, uncomfortable with their own feminine component, are just the ones who will perpetuate and even worsen the exploitation of women in order to keep their fragile hold on their own adolescent two-dimensional masculinity.

This is why it is important for us to reconsider the sexuality of God and to understand deeply that being made in His image includes our sexuality. Like every other aspect of our personhood, that runs the risk of being contaminated by sin. But the way to deal with that is to reconsider God, to see the example which he sets, to discern how we should use the gift of sexuality. It is perhaps the most difficult lesson, but to handle this by repression and denial is a dangerous, pathology-producing failure of nerve. And the pathology is not only the sort that psychiatrists see every day but is deep and severe spiritual pathology as well. To the extent that the Church is widely perceived in secular culture as a dying institution, our attitude to sex is an important cause, especially as it results in a suppression of the feminine.

This must be distinguished from the suppression of women. If enough women make enough noise, they may well be admitted into formerly all-male bastions. But that will do absolutely no good if the price they must pay is to play the game according to the established rules and take care not to challenge the male assumptions. This is true both in and out of the Church. It makes possible the continued dominance of men no matter how many women enter a field. Since men made the rules in the first place, they can always play the game better than women. And the rules include the notion that the feminine is inferior and must be kept out of all important loci of decision-making and policy. (In my capacity as a psychiatrist, I am seeing an increasing number of business and professional women suffering from the disillusioning realization that in order to get ahead they must do violence to their own specifically feminine values.)

Because of the inherent sexuality of God and the ineradicable existence of the feminine as part of the very ground of being, even the most patriarchal Church structures cannot entirely do away with the feminine. It is at least necessary to preach sermons about love, about caring for one another, about the virtues of submission and humility and so forth. One cannot talk about the majestic mighty acts and divine transcendence all the time. What is the result of this? The problem with secular culture is that it is ruthlessly and pathologically hypermasculinized, much more than the Church. It does not have to pay lip service to love and humility and other "sissy" qualities which have no application in what it mistakenly calls "the real world." The Church, especially in its more liberal modes, is therefore perceived as a relatively feminine institution which can be ignored, used, flattered or pacified when it threatens to be troublesome. In short, it can be treated just as women are treated. It does not have to be taken seriously. Ultraconservative parts of the Church which develop some political clout, such as the Moral Majority, are correctly seen as annoying rivals for patriarchal supremacy. But that just deteriorates into the usual spectacle of men fighting over the loot and has nothing to do with real religion at any level. As long as the true feminine face of the Church remains in shadow, it will be treated by the secular culture with tolerance at best.

But what happens in those parts of Christianity where Roman Catholicism is the strongest religious thread in the culture? In a recent book Harvey Cox has argued that the Latin American revolutionary fervor to right the wrongs of the oppressed is directly traceable to the cult of the Virgin. True liberation always includes the feminine, both as inspiration and as that which must be liberated. As one might expect, this provokes severe patriarchal backlash when traditional power structures are threatened. I suggest that here is a deep meaning of Our Lord's assertion in the Sermon on the Mount that "Happy are those who are persecuted in the cause of right: theirs is the kingdom of heaven. Happy are you when people abuse you and persecute you . . . on my account."[14] That is not an exhortation to masochism, as detractors of the passage have ignorantly suggested. Rather, it tells us that blessedness and happiness are to be found in resisting exploitation. And what is exploitation? It is the substitution of our own authority and power over others for God's, because only God should have that. The only power and authority we have any right to exert over our fellow humans is that which God may exercise through us as we try to live the exemplary life of Love. Contemplation of the life and work of Martin Luther King, Jr. or Mother Teresa of Calcutta makes the point absolutely clear.

We desperately need the feminine to be restored to its position of balancing force harmonizing the masculine so that it can find appropriate rather than destructive expression. This is why interest in the cult of the Virgin Mary is rising. North Americans studying this and other features of Latin American life have often been bizarrely mistaken in their interpretations. As the sociologist Norah Kinzer has said, "North American researchers working in Latin America are most often Protestant North American white males who see Latin America through a Calvinist glass darkened by male supremacy."[15]

The cult of Mary has taken many forms over the centuries, ranging from seeing her as a kind of divine goddess all the way to seeing her as an unimportant figure except (what male arrogance lies in that word "except"!) as the mother of Jesus. But now there is a growing view of her as a real woman, "answering Yes to life, Yes to humanity, Yes to God's invitation. A new Mary is emerging . . .

who is the personification and prototype of the Christian mission—a woman who humanizes the world by being present where needed."[16]

Nevertheless, I believe that both Protestants and Roman Catholics are guilty of serious heresies about Mary. The Protestant heresy has been to ignore, sometimes even to despise her. This contributes heavily to Protestant problems with the feminine. But the Roman heresy has been to desexualize her, by insisting that she remained virgin all her life and that she and Joseph did not have marital relations. In view of the clear biblical references to Jesus' siblings and the constant reference to Joseph as her husband, such an idea is not reasonable. The idea of the semignostic "spiritual marriage" is a very late development in practical Christianity. Mary and Joseph were good Jews, in a Jewish culture, and given the Jewish views of sex and marriage it simply does not make sense to claim that she remained virgin all her life. That claim did not appear until the 3rd century, and is not part of the earliest tradition.

If Mary is to be a real person, to say Yes to life and Yes to humanity, how can she be asexual? Such a concept arises from the male attitude which devalues sex in order to keep women under patriarchal control. And yet, one certainly cannot devalue the Mother of God. This problem has been "solved" by desexualizing her which removes the threat to the established patriarchy. This "solution" disempowers Mary's symbolic value as saying "yes" either to life or to humanity, and makes her "yes" to God mere submission to the super-patriarch. Men are then free to deal with Mary in one of two ways. They can exercise the astonishing male faculty of compartmentalization and revere her as a nice holy lady who has nothing to do with the "real male world," or else they can dismiss her cult as a sentimental necessity for female worshippers and perhaps a good submissive role model for them too. But this is not her message!

The real Mary is a real woman who must be taken seriously in every way. This means accepting not only her impregnating encounter with the Holy Spirit but also her sexuality and her real life on earth with Joseph. To desexualize her negates her feminine reality and once more leaves men free for phallic domination of woman and nature, with contempt for them because they permit it. Men then attribute to the male God their own unbalanced (and therefore immature) masculinity, producing the current image of God against which women are now in totally justified rebellion.

In the new *Book of Common Prayer,* recently adopted by the Episcopal Church after more than fifteen years of intense study by good, devout and learned men, there are several new eucharistic prayers. One of the most beautiful is designed to acknowledge modern understanding of our creation and development. Unlike the more traditional eucharistic prayers, it includes congregational responses. I quote part of it:

At your command all things came to be: the vast expanse of interstellar space, galaxies, suns, the planets in their courses, and this fragile earth, our island home. *By your will they were created and have their being.* From the primal elements you brought forth the human race, and blessed us with memory, reason and skill. You made us the rulers of creation. But we turned against you, and betrayed your trust; and we turned against one another. *Have mercy, Lord, for we are sinners in your sight.*[17]

Nowhere in that service is there any "sexist language." But even so, that prayer is tragically, I even say sinfully, incomplete. "Memory, reason and skill" are not enough. They are essential, to be sure, but they are derivatives of the masculine principle only. When using that prayer, I always add "the capacity to love and the gift of tears." The good men who composed that prayer are no doubt loving persons, able to weep over their own pain and that of our troubled world. Nevertheless, they did not realize that those faculties are essential to their very humanity. It is by thus constricting our understanding of what it is to be human that we have betrayed God's trust, and have brought ourselves and Mother Earth, our island home, to the brink of both physical and spiritual destruction.

What may we conclude is the divine intention for the man/woman relationship? The very question is too limited. First we should ask what is the divine intention for the relationship between masculine and feminine, wherever those qualities may surface? The answer is obvious—balance and harmony.

Rightly understood, the trinitarian concept of God is a model of balance and harmony. We speak of God in personal terms but must never forget that our emphasis on this aspect of the Mystery has to do with the limitations of our understanding. Whatever qualities exist anywhere in the universe must reflect something about God's nature. We can never say God is this and not that but must always say God is this *and* that.[18] Some fearfully claim that this must mean that God is good *and* evil. C. G. Jung came to that conclusion in his monograph, "Answer to Job."[19] But this obviously depends on how one defines evil. The definition which I find most enlightening is that *evil is unbalanced force.* There is no form of energy, personal or impersonal, and no form of matter which is intrinsically evil. Evil enters only when there is imbalance, including misdirection of energy, being in the wrong place and/or bad timing. The energy or matter itself cannot be evil, since all were created by God. God himself did not introduce the imbalance. On the cosmic scale, the symbolic figure of Lucifer introduced the first imbalance, from which all others eventually depend.

How was the evil of imbalance brought to humanity? As we saw earlier, the image of God contains elements which, though unified on the divine plane, are divided into two sexes on the human plane. The Genesis account, divinely symbolic of human pre-history, is instructive. Eve was to be Adam's partner. The imbalance between the sexes is a consequence of the Fall, directly attributable to Adam's refusal to take responsibility for eating the forbidden fruit. Instead, he pointed at Eve and said "she did it." Eve refused to take the responsibility for having offered it to him, instead saying "no—the snake did it." They failed to stand together before God and say "We did it." This behavior broke the original perfect intimacy which God had given them and set the pattern of wary mistrust of one sex toward the other. And this in turn led to the dissociation of the sexual instinct from its natural context of faithful, heterosexual intimacy, reducing it too often to its physical components.

Some now claim that the man/woman relationship is not part of God's plan, is not the divinely given social basis for human community. They say that heterosexuality has to be learned, is not innate. They seem not to know that sexuality is one of God's gifts, and the heterosexual form is not only what God gave to Adam and Eve, but he also made it instinctive throughout the animal kingdom. (Just as with humans, only unusual and unnatural environments ever produce anything approaching homosexuality, and in humans this includes the many failures of trusting, mature intimacy between male and female.[20]) It is to emphasize this point that throughout Scripture sexual metaphors are used to describe God's relations with his people: Israel is the spouse of God, and the Church the bride of Christ. When we are separate from God, we are not truly whole, and that fact is emphasized by such metaphors.

Western culture is heavily influenced by Freud, who was a product of the 19th century's scientific deterministic reductionism. He believed that every manifestation of the human psyche was to be explained in terms of its primitive instinctual components. Further, he thought that eventually these instincts would yield the secrets of their intrinsically chemical nature to further research. There is therefore nothing in classical Freudian theory which throws any light on the goals of human sexuality beyond the ultimately physical issues of pleasure and reproduction.

Jung offers a very different perspective, one far more consonant with the theological views I have been expounding. The following quotation expresses the difference succinctly:

> Freud undoubtedly attributed supreme value to the orgastic release of sex, whereas Jung found supreme value in the unifying experience of religion. Hence Freud tended to interpret all numinous and emotionally significant experiences as derived from, or a substitute for, sex; whereas Jung tended to interpret even sexuality itself as symbolic, possessing 'numinous' significance in that it represented an irrational union of opposites and was thus a symbol of wholeness.[21]

The goal of Christian sexuality is not satisfaction but completeness. Without this goal of completeness, satisfaction pursued as an end-in-itself deteriorates into lust. The definition of lust which I find most compelling is that it substitutes the part for the whole—part of the body for the whole body, or the body for the whole person. (By this definition, all lusts are not sexual, in the usual meaning of that word.) Thus sex is a holy symbol of union and reconciliation against which sacrilege is perilously easy to commit. No other phenomenon of human existence can symbolize the vision of the sacramental universe in which all things are harmoniously connected, and at the same time manifest the tragic discontinuities which were inflicted on us and our world through the Fall. No other human activity so lends itself to subtle, as well as obvious, exploitation both of self and of others.

As suggested earlier, the Fall is constituted by the refusal to take appropriate responsibility and by resorting to projection and patterns of mutual blame and distrust. This is why men and women fear or resent their differences from one another instead of experiencing them as an opportunity for complementarity leading to wholeness. This is why they exploit either themselves or one another, often both at once.

I do not believe that it is accidental in the general evolutionary pattern that we are now simultaneously emerging from the patriarchal era and realizing that the human family cannot continue to expand indefinitely. If we examine the history of human culture, it is evident that the creative possibilities of the uniting of the opposites of the masculine and feminine principles have never been widely understood or implemented except at the biological level. Here men and women unite, and the third, or child, that arises out of their union shares the nature of both. But at the level of consciousness we have always, except in individual blessed matings (whether only spiritual or including the physical), been in a different situation. Men and women have not united as equal opposites, and so real psychological union has seldom occurred. But another possibility exists. Many now yearn for a truer, richer union, of mind, heart and spirit, rather than only of body and social convenience. The third which will arise from such unions will no longer necessarily be a child, however desired and welcome such a child may be under appropriate circumstances, but a new consciousness, a new spirit, a new approach to the sacred order. No human activity may stand outside of the sacred order with impunity, and therefore all human activity must ultimately be religious.

The sacraments of the Christian religion translate the participants into the sacred order of eternity by means of the symbols of a time-bound event, namely, the outward and visible occasion of each particular celebration. It is for this reason (and not merely in support of patriarchy, as some misguided feminist reformers claim) that marriage is numbered among the sacraments. The divinely inspired author of the Song of Songs heads the list of those who, throughout the centuries, have understood that sexuality itself is a symbol of wholeness, of the reconciliation of opposites, of the loving at-one-ment between God and Creation. In the words of the great contemporary composer Olivier Messaien (a devout Roman Catholic), " . . . the union of true lovers is for them a transformation on the cosmic scale."[22]

This is the principle which must be kept in mind as we consider changing some of the rules governing sexual behavior. If we do that, it becomes immediately obvious that some of the ancient rules must be kept. Promiscuity and adultery (defined as breaking the marriage covenant) continue to be unacceptable. Though many responsible people disagree with me, I believe homosexuality also departs from the principle.[23] There is room for discussion in some other situations. At present it is sometimes difficult to discern the influence of patriarchy on many of the old rules. We must ask: do they really serve to uphold the eternal principle? Or are they concealing under a religious vocabulary a real motive of maintaining women's subservience to men?

We must also understand that marriage is only one possible vocation. Some are called to celibacy in religious orders. Some are called to secular celibacy. Whether all persons who, either by choice or circumstance, remain single are called to celibacy is one of the issues which urgently requires serious theological inquiry. But I cannot emphasize too strongly that those who do not mate are not deprived of the possibilities of wholeness. When we get over the error of conceiving of sexuality in exclusively physical terms, this will be easier to grasp. After all, a crucial component of real maturity is the integration of the contrasexual part of one's own psyche rather than repression, denial or projection of it onto members of the other sex. This is true for all, whether mated or not. Enduring friendships between men and women can assist this process and contribute to the harmonizing of the masculine and feminine principles in the world. The cases of spiritual friendship between saints cited earlier can be inspiring models. On psychological as well as theological grounds I believe it is important for everyone to be celibate not only through adolescence but also during at least part of adult life. Only thus, especially in a culture like ours, can people learn that they have sex, it doesn't have them. Too many people have believed the distorted popular views of Freudian theory which present sexual activity as a sort of psychological vitamin without regular doses of which one is prey to the twin dangers of repression and madness. Nothing could be further from the truth!

I take for granted that those who fail to live up to the sacred standards should not be ostracized or scapegoated in any way. In the sight of God all sin is the same—it is all a result of our misdirection of one or more of the energies with which he endowed us. All can stand before God only as forgiven sinners, and to point the finger of shame or blame at the sins of others is to repeat the original sin of the Fall. It is enough to deal with our own failures, as Jesus so often said in so many ways, most succinctly when he exhorted us to take the beam out of our own eye before trying to take the mote out of our brother's, adding that it was rank hypocrisy to do otherwise. If the Christian religion had spent less time telling us not to sin and more time telling us to try as hard as possible never to commit the same sin twice, following our Lord's instructions in these matters would be much easier and more likely to promote spiritual growth.

NOTES

1. Mark Gerzon, *A Choice of Heroes, The Changing Face of American Masculinity* (New York: Houghton Mifflin, 1982).
2. Ruth Tiffany Barnhouse, *Identity* (Philadelphia: Westminster Press, 1984).
3. Paul K. Jewett, *Man as Male and Female* (Grand Rapids: William B. Eerdmans Publishing Co., 1975).
4. Victor Paul Furnish, *The Moral Teachings of Paul* (Nashville: Abingdon Press, 1979).
5. Alicia Craig Faxon, *Women and Jesus* (Philadelphia: United Church Press, 1973).
6. Eleanor L. McLaughlin, "The Christian Past: Does It Hold a Future for Women?" *Anglican Theological Review,* LVII (Jan., 1975), p. 41.
7. *Ibid.,* p. 41.
8. *Ibid.,* p. 42.
9. Eleanor L. McLaughlin, "Male and Female in Christian Tradition: Was There a Reformation in the Sixteenth Century?", *Male and Female: Christian Approaches to Sexuality,* ed. Ruth Tiffany Barnhouse and Urban T. Holmes III (New York: Seabury Press, 1976), pp. 39–52.
10. Eleanor L. McLaughlin, *ATR,* p. 54.
11. *Ibid,* p. 49.
12. Eleanor L. McLaughlin, *Male and Female.*
13. Ruth Tiffany Barnhouse, "Is Patriarchy Obsolete?", *Male and Female: Christian Approaches to Sexuality,* ed. Ruth Tiffany Barnhouse and Urban T. Holmes III (New York: Seabury Press, 1976), pp. 223–235. Also: "Patriarchy and the Ordination of Women," *Nashotah Review,* vol. 15 (Fall, 1975), pp. 161–324 and *St. Luke's Journal of Theology,* vol. 18 (Sept., 1975), pp. 299–462 (Joint Issue).
14. Matthew 5:10–11 (Jerusalem Bible).
15. Norah Scott Kinzer, "Sexist Sociology," *The Center Magazine* (May/June, 1974).
16. John O'Connor, "The Liberation of the Virgin Mary," *Ladies' Home Journal* (December, 1972), pp. 75 and 126–127.
17. *The Book of Common Prayer,* (New York: The Church Hymnal Corporation and The Seabury Press, 1977), p. 370.
18. John MacQuarrie, Gifford Lectures (1984) (unpublished).
19. C. G. Jung, "Answer to Job," *Collected Works of C. G. Jung,* Bollingen Series XX, Vol. 11 (Princeton: Princeton University Press, 1969).
20. Ruth Tiffany Barnhouse, *Homosexuality: A Symbolic Confusion* (New York: The Seabury Press, 1979).
21. Anthony C. Storr, *C. G. Jung* (New York: Viking Press, 1973), p. 13.

22. Olivier Messaien, "Turangalila Symphony," notes by the composer on record jacket (New York: RCA LSC-7051, 1968).
23. Ruth Tiffany Barnhouse, *Homosexuality: A Symbolic Confusion* (New York: Seabury Press, 1979).

9

The Role of the Spiritual Director and the Divine Intention for the Male-Female Relationship

EVELYN S. NEWMAN

Created in God's Image

The primitive religious intuition that God created man in his own image, in the image of God he created him; male and female he created them (Genesis 1:27), may well be seen to be the most profound awareness achieved by the human species. It is both humbling and disturbing to realize that this insight has been around so long and is still so little understood. Perhaps, its brilliance has been hidden by familiarity. At any rate we know that truth can be apprehended at different levels. Moses Maimonides addressed himself to this phenomenon in *The Guide for the Perplexed,* saying:

> Know that for the human mind there are certain objects of perception which are within the scope of its nature and capacity; on the other hand, there are, amongst things which actually exist, certain objects which the mind can in no way and by no means grasp: the gates of perception are closed against it. Further, there are things of which the mind understands one part, but remains ignorant of the other; and when man is able to comprehend certain things, it does not follow that he must be able to comprehend everything.[1]

The notion that "God created man in his own image, male and female he created them" is a precocious spiritual insight whose full meaning awaits the maturing evolution of our thought. There have, however, been religious geniuses for whom this truth has come alive and through whom our understanding of what it means to be human has been nourished.

Let us examine, for example, John Wesley's thought about being created in God's image. Wesley defined religion as the "recovery of the image of God."[2] (Later we shall see how the male-female relationship can aid us in recovering the image of God.) The importance of this notion is illustrated by looking at the historical examination for admission into full membership of an annual conference of the United Methodist Church. In preparation for this examination, those who are seeking ordination as Elders are encouraged to engage in serious self-examination and prayer before presenting themselves before the conference. The first five questions are revealing:

1. Have you faith in Christ?
2. Are you going on to perfection?
3. Do you expect to be made perfect in love in this life?
4. Are you earnestly striving after it?
5. Are you resolved to devote yourself wholly to God and His work?[3]

Every Methodist minister from the beginning has had to answer these questions. They have remained virtually unchanged throughout the years. When Wesley formulated these questions, he was setting forth what he believed to be the essential living core of the faith. He could be remarkably free from doctrinal constraint, firmly insisting upon the integrity of Christian truth even while allowing some degree of latitude in the interpretation of that truth. This attitude is expressed in his oft-quoted words: "As to all opinions which do not strike at the root of Christianity, we think and let think."[4] Therefore, Wesley's insistence upon having the ministers examined with regard to the questions cited above gives clear and unmistakable evidence that "going on to perfection" held a pivotal position in his thought. Frank Whaling writes:

> The Wesley's spirituality of Christian Perfection contained a cluster of interlocking ideas. Perfect love was at the center, purity of heart was important, the possibility of obtaining a character free from known sin was there, purity of intention was central, the fruits of the Spirit were paramount, the possibility of an inner experience of perfect love was present, and above all a lived conviction that *there were no limits to what God could do with a human life if it was fully given into His hands. . . .* For them, perfect love was the fulfillment of faith. It amounted to holiness. It, like faith, was the product of God's grace, which was not given all at once but from moment to moment. Yet it was real holiness within the life of the Christian. . . . Perfect love was both inward and outward holiness. It was possible for all men. *It was the point of human life.*[5] [Emphasis added]

With this in mind, let us now turn back to John Wesley's definition of religion in order to draw the connection between the "recovery of the image of God" and "going on to perfection." Wesley succinctly says: "But I still think that *perfection is only another term for holiness, or the image of God in man.* God made man perfect, I think, is just the same as He made him holy, or in His own image."[6] [Emphasis added]

Wesley clearly urges the understanding that the purpose of life is to bring forth the image of God in our souls and that this is helped to happen by a disciplined, guided striving to be made perfect in love. The thesis, then, is that the divine intention for human life is for each person, male and female, to become a contemporary expression of Christ. Our highest privilege, greatest fulfillment, and deepest joy should be to make Christ present to this terrible/wonderful world of ours through the living of our ordinary lives.

It is interesting to see the scriptural background in which this thought is rooted. Tracing the use of the word "image" in scriptural passages offers an intriguing picture of the developing thought about images and the conflicting notions which grew up around them. Humankind, unable or unwilling to assimilate the meaning and moral demand of being created in the image of God, instead fashioned images external to itself which could be worshipped. The image was projected outward instead of being revealed inwardly. The Book of Genesis offers the first instance of the word "image":

> Then God said, 'Let us make man in our image and likeness to rule the fish in the sea, the birds of heaven, the cattle, all wild animals on earth, and all reptiles that crawl upon the earth.' So God created man in his own image; in the image of God he created him; male and female he created them (Genesis 1:26,27).

The Lord spoke to Moses, saying: "Speak to the Israelites in these words: You will soon be crossing the Jordan to enter Canaan. You must drive out all its inhabitants as you advance, destroy all their carved figures and their images of cast metal, and lay their hill-shrines in ruins," (Numbers 33:50–52).

Soon the Lord was to have a word against the Israelites: "Their beautiful ornament they used for vain-glory and they made their abominable images and their detestable things of it; therefore I will make it an unclean thing to them" (Ezekiel 7:20). Yet not all succumbed to the worship of graven images. Shadrach, Meshach, and

Abednego answered the king: "We will not serve your gods or worship the golden image which you have set up," (Daniel 3:18). But it is in the New Testament that the full import of the understanding of what it means to be formed "in the image of God" takes hold: "He is the image of the invisible God, the first-born of creation," (Colossians 1:15).

Again in II Corinthians we read: "But we all, with open face beholding as in a glass the glory of the Lord, are changed into the same image from glory to glory, even as by the Spirit of the Lord," (II Corinthians 3:18). And in Romans we find: "For those whom he foreknew he also predestined to be conformed to the image of his son, in order that he might be the first-born among many brethren," (Romans 8:29).

St. Paul takes this truth through to its ultimate meaning when he exclaims: "I have been crucified with Christ; it is no longer I who live, but Christ who lives in me; and the life I now live in the flesh I live by faith in the son of God, who loved me and gave himself for me," (Galatians 2:20). Then he opens the meaning of that truth to us for our own lives: "Examine yourselves, to see whether you are holding to your faith. Test yourselves. Do you not realize that Jesus Christ is in you? —Unless indeed you fail to meet the test?" (II Corinthians 13:5). The divine intention for every man and woman is shown to be: " . . . the mystery hid for generations and now made known," " . . . Christ in you, the hope of glory," (Colossians 1:26–28).

The awesomeness of that revolutionary concept is not easily comprehended. When Peter blurted out, "You are the Christ, the Son of the living God," Jesus answered him saying, "Flesh and blood has not revealed this to you, but my Father who is in heaven." We, too, must receive this knowledge as life-changing revelation. It is one thing to possess a secure knowledge about God; it is another thing to find oneself suddenly possessed by God. It is one thing to have a secure religion about Jesus; it is another thing to find one's life upended by the realization that God asks of us the incredible permission to make us over "into other Christs." All our murmurings about inadequacy count for nothing because nothing depends upon our adequacy. "Do not be conformed to this world but be transformed by the renewal of your mind, that you may prove what is the will of God, what is good and acceptable and perfect," (Romans 12:2). "He who calls us is faithful and he will do it," (II Thessalonians 5:24).

William McNamara, in a superb little book entitled *The Art of Being Human,* tells us that the purpose of life must never be seen in terms of "getting" anything. Not even moral improvement, perfection, or salvation. He would have us look at it only in terms of giving—giving honor and glory to God. Perfection, holiness, and salvation are the by-products of zest and zeal for God's glory. McNamara says:

> Giving honor and glory to God is the purpose of all life—vegetable and animal as well as human. Trees give glory to God by being good, decent trees. Dogs give glory to God by being as doggy as possible. Humans give glory to God by being human—as human as possible.
>
> On that day that we become as perfectly human as we can in this world, then we shall be saints. . . . *If, here and now we are not saints, it is only because we are not human enough.* I think the best definition of a saint is a whole man—holy. That is why it is true to say that if a man does not become a saint he is a failure.[7] [Emphasis added]

We have paid a high price for our isolation of the saints to the far-flung edges of our societal structure. While our intention may have been veneration, the end result is that the "holy person" is viewed as not being one of us. Deeming the saint unique spares us the necessity of being like him or her. Indeed, the aspiration to sainthood in our society seems like an anachronistic notion. The saint would be chronologically out of place. If McNamara is correct in his judgment that the saint is a "whole man" then we might deduce that the ill-fit of the saint into our society is not a reflection upon the saint but a reflection upon the inability of our culture to recognize/nourish mature spirituality.

It is interesting to note that at the time when the revival movement swept over this country, men and women were being challenged forthrightly to repent, sin no more, and even to "go on to perfection." A description written for that day remains apt for ours: The poor unawakened sinner has no knowledge of himself. He knows not that he is a fallen spirit. Full of diseases as he is, he fancies himself in perfect health.[8] Wesley certainly knew that the folk to whom he preached repentance would not achieve perfection overnight. Still, by holding up that high ideal for them he offered them a catalyst for growth and a measure for sinfulness which demanded repentance and cried out for forgiveness. And, quite simply, that message got results.

There is some truth in the old cliché that instead of "being made over into God's image we want to make God over in our image." It is time that we took seriously the driving force for transformation which is the Gospel of Jesus Christ. We can no longer afford to look the other way. We have outdone ourselves at the foolishness of seeking to make the Gospel acceptable through "relevance." We ought never to have departed from the precept given to Abraham: "Walk before me and be thou perfect."[9] Realizing that the heart of Christian perfection lies in the intention to aim at perfection, we must once again hold up the goal of perfection and press on toward it. We can do no less and be faithful.

The Spiritual Director

Christian perfection has been defined as normally being the culmination of a long process of giving one's whole self and one's whole possibilities to God. It is necessary or even preferable to have a spiritual director if we feel called to strive after perfection?

In one of the great classics of the devotional life, *A Manual for Interior Souls,* Abbe Grou writes:

> It is necessary to have a director, because the greatest wish of all is to guide ourselves, and the greatest delusion we can fall into is to think we are in a fit state to guide ourselves. Even the most clever man, and he who is in the best of dispositions, is blind as to his interior conduct; and even if he were a saint, and capable of directing others, he is not capable of directing himself; and if he thinks he can, it is through presumption. . . . The way of perfection is full of darkness and obscurities, of temptations and precipices; and our wish to walk alone in it is to expose ourselves to our own ruin.[10]

John of the Cross comments on the need for spiritual directors in these words:

> Even though these souls have begun to walk along the road to virtue, and our Lord desires to place them in the dark night so that they may move on to the divine union, they do not advance. Sometimes, the reason is, they do not want to enter the dark night or allow themselves and are without suitable and alert directors who will show them the way to the summit. . . . So, it is sad to see them continue in their lowly method of com-

munion with God because they do not want to know how to advance, or because they receive no direction in breaking away from the methods of beginners.[11]

A word of caution must be inserted here. Perhaps, nowhere is our ignorance of the complexities of the whole subject of spiritual formation more in evidence than in this matter of spiritual direction. The term itself is unfamiliar to most Protestants. Some branches of Protestantism, having all but severed their link to the tradition which bore them through pre-Reformation years, remain to this day virtually unaware of the highly respected and revered tradition of spiritual direction which formed and nourished the saints.

The current resurgence of interest in spiritual formation must be welcomed and yet one detects a "faddish" element in it. Naturally, the temptation is to go for quick results in order to compensate for years of neglect. Courses on spiritual direction are springing up all over. Degrees in spirituality are granted with as little as two years of preparation, the assumption being that one can read "x" number of books and gain the comprehension needed to qualify as a spiritual director. At the very least it is a case of "fools rushing in where angels fear to tread. . . ." As S. C. Hughson comments:

> It is not from books, however, that the priest will best learn how to discern the state of the soul, valuable as books may be in showing him how through the ages the Holy Ghost has taught those who were called to this ministry. *He is to acquire his skill on his knees.* His own life of prayer and meditation, of Communion and walking with God, will give him the spiritual prescience which will enable him to judge souls rightly. He will indeed need to sit at the feet of saintly guides who have transmitted to us in their writings what the Holy Spirit has taught them, but he will not be able to interpret and apply their teaching unless he has drawn in some measure from the same source from which they drew their wisdom. He who would guide others along the way of holiness must have learned something of the geography of the way by walking in it himself.[12]

As Henri Nouwen states: "[This is] the central mystery of the spiritual life: The director, guide, counselor, comforter, healer is not the well-trained human person, but God himself."[13]

Spiritual direction is the science of the soul. It seeks to discern the workings of grace in the heart in order to prepare the soul for the sharing of God's very life, for partaking of the divine nature. Union with God is the goal of all earnest spiritual direction. This necessarily implies the "putting off of the old man" and the "putting on of Christ." This is a lifelong process of transformation.

Spiritual direction involves the systematic guidance of the soul in interior activities in such manner as to remove all obstacles to God's action. The aim is the spiritualizing and divinizing of the whole life. The work of the director is to lead the soul in the ways of God, teaching it to listen for divine inspiration and to respond gladly to every movement perceived of the divine will. The director takes the responsibility for guiding the soul to the degree of sanctity which God has destined for it, giving instruction in virtue appropriate to the soul's progress and position in life and encouragement to advance in perfection.[14] The director is obliged to work under the guideline that "God has called no soul to take a mediocre position in His Kingdom."[15]

The confessor should be the instrument of divine grace, cooperating with the work of the Holy Spirit to such a degree that he is the "voice of God." He must be well versed in spiritual things as much by his own experience as by study and reading. Above all, he must be a prayerful person who considers only the glory of God and the good of souls with no motives of self-interest.[16] Grou says: "He should never act according to the leadings of his own spirit, but he should judge of the things of God by the spirit of God. From all this it is easy to conclude that true directors are very rare."[17]

Francis de Sales reminds us that Teresa of Avila considered only one out of a thousand as being capable of the task of spiritual direction. He takes an even more strict view of it for himself, saying that he considers only one in ten thousand capable of the task of spiritual direction. De Sales further warns that the spiritual director "must be full of charity, knowledge, and prudence, and if any one of these qualities is lacking there is danger."[18]

Spiritual Formation and the Male-Female Relationship

The term " spiritual formation" traces back to Paul's letter to the Galatians in which he writes, "My little children, with whom I am again in travail until Christ be formed in you!" (Galatians 4:19). The *forming of Christ* in us is the long, slow process of sanctification. It is the maturing of the mystical awareness through the "love of God unfolding, flowering, and bearing fruit in the human soul."[19] John Wesley sums it up in this manner:

Christ liveth in me. This is the fulfilling of the law, the last stage of Christian holiness: This maketh the man of God perfect. He that being dead to the world is alive to God; the desire of whose soul is unto his name; who has given Him his whole heart; who delights in Him, and in nothing else but what tends to Him; who, for his sake, burns with love to all mankind; who neither thinks, speaks, nor acts, but to fulfill his will, is on the last round of the ladder to heaven: Grace hath had its full work upon his soul: The next step he takes is into Glory.[20]

Christ in us, the hope of glory! The human soul in love with God, lured on by God, progresses toward divine union through the stages of awakening, purgation, illumination, dark night of the soul, and finally arrives at union. At this point the human personality has undergone a radical transformation. The self has attained a glorious freedom.

The human personality remains limited, of course, but the secret place of the soul, its fine point and inner fortress, has been built up and integrated with the rest of the personality so that the whole human being is now joined to infinite love. The union goes on developing, and though this may never be felt, it can deepen in quality without, however, changing in kind. This is as far as union can go here on earth or at least, as far as it can be apprehended and described.[21]

The self is detached from all which held it back from God. It has been re-made, transformed, and unified. One way in which this transformation of the personality manifests itself is through the integration of the unconscious feminine or masculine components of the personality. Those components are no longer denied or repressed but now are welcomed as enriching faculties for the personality, *anima* and *animus* are united.[22] The person has moved toward completeness or wholeness, toward a deeper and richer humanity which has realized its destiny in God.

The marks of the unitive life are as follows:[23]

1. a complete absorption in the interests of the Infinite, under whatever mode it is apprehended by the self
2. a consciousness of sharing its strength, acting by its authority, which results in a complete sense of freedom, an invulnerable serenity, and usually urges the self to some form of heroic effort or creative action
3. the establishment of the self as a 'power for life,' a center of energy, an actual parent of spiritual vitality in other persons.[24]

Rufus Jones makes this claim for the power of the unitive life:

> . . . when the powers of the mind are fused and unified, over-brimmed and revitalized by intense mystical concentration and unification *the whole interior self becomes an immensely heightened organ of spiritual apprehension in correspondence with the real world to which it belongs.* . . . Something like that, in my judgment, has sparked the contribution of the mystics through the ages. They have not had secret messages from sociable angels. They have not been granted special communications as favored ambassadors to the heavenly court. They have been men and women like the rest of us, only they succeeded, better than most persons do, in accumulating the spiritual gains of the past, in building the truths of life into the permanent fibre of the soul, in forming a passionate *intent* for God, and then, through the fusing and concentrating of all the strata of the interior life, becoming a sensitive organ for the interpretation of realities that lay beyond the former frontiers of spiritual truth.[25]

The soul, at this point, has been called the "mother of souls" as it goes about its work of bringing other souls into the same kind of vital relationship with God which it enjoys. In the words of the old phrase, "one loving soul sets another soul afire. . . ." Some might ask, "What is the evidence of this new life? Can it be measured? How can it be recognized?" Rufus Jones, in the book *Pathways to the Reality of God,* puts forth this answer for those who are skeptical of the validity of the religious experience: "St. Paul, writing to his Corinthian friends, talks of the 'demonstration of the Spirit.' He does not tell in any systematic way how the 'demonstration' is to be recognized. . . ."[26]

> The 'demonstration' for him is revealed in the heightened *power* of the life. It is what he often calls 'a new creation.' The new fruits of the Spirit for him are 'love, joy, peace, longsuffering, kindness, goodness, faithfulness, meekness, self-control,' what we today call *values.* These things are not spectacular nor startling. They are not 'psychic phenomena.' But they are laboratory evidences of something spiritual and not of something animal. There is a 'new creation' within; 'old things have passed away, and behold, all things are made new.'[27]

Every human being is gifted by God with a profound experience of the Holy, though few know how to claim this experience, much less articulate it. Therefore, it is of great value to study the lives of the saints in order to familiarize ourselves with the way in which God acted upon their lives. We are fortunate to have the original writings from some profound spirits who charted for us their path toward union. Knowledge of the peaks and pitfalls which they encountered can help us to recognize the clues to God's presence which surround each one of us at every moment of our lives. Their experience cannot be identical to ours for God respects the individuality given to us at birth and comes to each man and woman in a unique way. As one seminary professor commented to his class, "This, then, is Ignatius of Loyola's way to God. Thank God it is not the only way!"

Evelyn Underhill points out that it is a peculiarity of the unitive life that it is often lived, in its highest and most perfect forms, in the world where it exhibits its works before men.[28] Elizabeth Stopp supports this view saying that "unitive love, having simplified all the powers of the soul and subjected them to one overriding purpose, can only show itself here on earth in the humble practice of elementary virtues." Looking back over the course of history we see certain vital figures who stand out like beacons against the backdrop of humanity. Their lives defy explanation in ordinary, prosaic terms. We recognize them as saints by the quality of the lives they lived in our midst. It is interesting to note that the male-female relationship seems to have played a significant role in the spiritual development of some of these greatest saints and spiritual geniuses. A few names which come immediately to mind are: Teresa of Avila and John of the Cross, Francis of Assisi and Lady Clare, François Fenelon and Madame de Guyon, Francis de Sales and Madame de Chantal, and Evelyn Underhill and Baron von Hugel. It is interesting to note the mutuality of creative guidance and wisdom involved in these special relationships. It seems clear that in the process of spiritual direction, the interaction between the man and the woman works to complete the humanity of both in an extraordinary way. Due to the cultural taboos of the centuries in which these great Christian mystics lived, the male is most often found in the role of the director while the woman is in the role of the one receiving direction. It is not, as one might expect, only the person who "receives direction" who grows, but also the one charged with the responsibility for direction. The process of interaction between male and female works to deepen the spiritual awareness and vitality of both people involved. This is well illustrated in the relationship of Francis de Sales and Madame de Chantal where God used the male-female relationship to strengthen each of them in their vocation to sainthood.

Francis de Sales (1567–1622) was the eldest son of a noble family. From childhood it was apparent that he possessed brilliant gifts. At an early age he was marked out for the priesthood and he was ordained a priest in 1593. Not surprisingly, he rose quickly through the ranks and was consecrated Bishop of Geneva in 1602. Jane de Chantal (1572–1641) was born the second daughter of the President of the Parliament at Dijon. Her ancestors traced back to the family of Burgundy's greatest saint, Bernard of Clairvaux. There was no evidence of precocious spirituality when she was younger, but when her husband died of a gunshot wound from a hunting accident, she pledged her life to God, vowing to love and serve him in the same spirit she had loved her husband. She was twenty-eight years old and had responsibility for their three little children. It was a few years later that Francis de Sales and Madame de Chantal were destined to meet in Dijon. That meeting was to make the beginning of a relationship which transformed her life and profoundly affected his life. Shortly after their first meeting he sent her a note which said: "It seems to me that God has intended me for you, and every hour I become more convinced of this. This is all I can say to you now."[29] A week later he wrote again, "The further I am from you in space the more strongly do I feel the link between us."[30] For her part, she was convinced from the very moment that she saw him step into the pulpit in Sainte Chapelle that this was the priest whom God meant to give her guidance. The bond between them deepened and grew stronger throughout the years that followed.

Before Jane de Chantal made her life confession before Francis de Sales he cautioned her to prepare carefully for it: "Bring it before our Lord in prayer. Search into every fold and crevice of your soul and consider everything that needs to be re-arranged or banished. But above all, avoid any anxiety over your preparation, make it quietly and without strain."[31] When Francis became her spiritual director they exchanged formal documents, for this was considered a binding contract before God. She wrote: "All powerful lord . . . graciously receive this offering of myself; and as you have freely given me grace to want it, so too may you give me all the grace I need to carry it through. Amen." He answered: "I accept, in God's name, responsibility for your spiritual guidance and shall carry it out as carefully and as faithfully as I can, and in so far as my office and my previously contracted duties allow."[32]

Jane de Chantal's motive in seeking spiritual direction from Francis de Sales was to learn how to give herself more completely to God than she was already doing. When she thought of the cloister, he responded by asking her what could possibly prevent her from giving herself to God even more fully in her ordinary life in this world? He prodded her, saying: "Was she prepared to do this, to hold the world as nothing even while playing her full part in it?" She responded by saying that she would "pray for God to consume her and change her into himself; henceforth the world itself would be her cloister and her enclosure invisible."[33]

This was a male-female relationship of unusual depth and intimacy. There was to be nothing hidden behind artifice of any sort. Francis sensed in her an almost inexhaustible spiritual capacity to learn, understand and respond to his teaching, and then an extraordinary eagerness to translate into action all that she had learned. For his part, he grew in grace though trying to meet her needs. Under his careful guidance, she persevered through the next years in her nursing work, household management tasks, care of the children, and difficult personal relations in her father-in-law's home. This provided her with a training in the exercise of patience and humility which were of a kind to make the strictest religious novitiate appear plain sailing.[34] This ordinary and unassuming work quietly done to the glory of God constituted exactly the kind of atmosphere in which holiness could take root. De Sales aimed at relaxing her, "getting her out into the sunshine to see the wide horizons of a life of true devotion instead of brooding housebound, over imaginary failings or even very real temptations. He wanted her henceforth to enjoy the liberty of a child that knows it is beloved by the best of all Fathers."[35]

He wanted to control her impulsive vehemence, to teach her to learn patience and the real meaning of the offering of her will to God. She continually professed a desire for complete withdrawal from the world. He discerned the immaturity which was present in that desire, and rather than encourage such wishes, suggested to her the simple sanity of accepting the trials and difficulties given by God in the course of normal living as being superior to any self-chosen martyrdoms. He taught her how to gather up all the strands of her inner and outer life and offer them back to God from whom they came. He was extremely gentle and yet that gentleness masked an iron-clad determination. He did not waiver in his demands or expectations. He made his aims clear to her: "There must be no more of the woman in you, you must have the courage of a man."[36] But all the while in giving guidance to her, he learned from her: "Capacities in him, dormant till then woke in response to her soaring aspiration. He had been greatly gifted, and the blessings of Heaven seemed to rest on all his work. He may have been in danger of contentment, but that danger ceased when he and she were in unity of mind and spirit."[37]

While he had the training, skill and spiritual depth necessary to understand her, at the same time he found in her a personality equal in calibre to his own. Once he had written: "Ah, my daughter, how I long that we should be altogether dead to ourselves that we may live altogether for God, and that our life be hid with Christ in God. Oh, when shall we ourselves live, yet not we ourselves, and when will it be that Jesus Christ is all our life?"[38]

Their last conversation, shortly before his death, reveals the integrity with which they both approached their relationship, always subordinating their personal desires to the supreme goal toward which they aimed together:

> 'Now which of us is to begin?' asked the bishop as he sat down in front of the convent grille which divided them.
>
> 'May I please, Father?' she at once replied. 'My heart badly needs looking over by you.'
>
> 'How is this, my dear Mother? Still an eager desire? Still a personal choice?' he asked gently but very insistently. 'I thought by this time you would be quite angelic.'
>
> He knew her so well; he could not have expected her to succeed altogether in being as detached as the angels. But he wanted her to be perfect; so she just had to go on trying, and he had to go on helping her even to his own cost. She expected his help in one way, he gave it in another, knowing what she now needed: a last lesson in detachment and humility that only he could give.[39]

From the beginning their relationship had at its center the shared aspiration toward sainthood and they never deviated from that high goal. In all they did and all they said, in all the labor they undertook together for God, they called out the image of God in each other. Thomas Kelly, in the contemporary Christian devotional classic, *A Testament of Devotion,* holds up for us that divine intention, that same high level of interaction for all our relationships:

> The final grounds of holy Fellowship are in God. Lives immersed and drowned in God are drowned in love, and know one another in Him and know one another in love. God is the medium, the matrix, the focus, the solvent. . . . Such lives have a common meeting point; they live in a common joyous enslavement. They go back into a single Center where they are at home with Him and with one another.[40] All friendships short of this are incomplete. All personal relationships which lie only in time are

open-ended and unfinished, to the soul who walks in holy obedience. Can we make *all* our relations relations which pass *through Him?* Our relations to the conductor on a trolley? Our relations to the clerk who serves us in a store? How far is the world from such an ideal? . . . Yet we, from our end of the relationship can send out the Eternal Love in silent, searching hope, and meet each person with a background of eternal expectation and a silent, wordless prayer of love.[41]

Perhaps a few in our day would care to embrace the discipline which served as the foundation for the spiritual formation of these two saints. A superficial glance calls it life-denying. Is it not the highest fulfillment of the divine intention for all those created in the image of God?

> All which I took from thee I did but take,
>   Not for thy harms,
> But just that thou might'st seek it in My arms.
>   All which thy child's mistake
> Fancies as lost, I have stored for thee at home:
>   Rise, clasp My hand, and come![42]

NOTES

1. Moses Maimonides, *The Guide for the Perplexed* (New York: Dover Publications, Inc., 1956), p. 40.
2. John and Charles Wesley, *John and Charles Wesley, Selected Writings and Hymns,* The Classics of Western Spirituality, ed. Frank Whaling (New York: Paulist Press, 1981), p. 86.
3. *The Book of Discipline of the United Methodist Church 1980* (Tennessee: The United Methodist Publishing House, 1980), p. 203.
4. *The Book of Discipline,* p. 40.
5. John and Charles Wesley, pp. 49–50.
6. John Wesley, *Selections from the Letters of John Wesley,* Living Selections from Great Devotional Classics, ed. J. Manning Potts (Tennessee: The Upper Room, 1951), p. 6.
7. William McNamara, *The Art of Being Human* (New York: The Bruce Publishing Company, 1962), p. 16.
8. Steve Harper, *John Wesley's Message for Today* (Michigan: Zondervan Corporation, 1983), p. 33.
9. Genesis 17:1.

10. Jean Grou, *Manual for Interior Souls* (London: Burns Oates and Washbourne Ltd., 1892), p. 130.

11. St. John of the Cross, *The Collected Works of St. John of the Cross,* trans. Kieran Kavanaugh and Otilio Rodriguez (Washington, D.C.: ICS Publications, 1979), p. 70.

12. S. C. Hughson, *Spiritual Guidance* (New York: Holy Cross Press, 1948), pp. 42–43.

13. Francis W. Vanderwall, *Spiritual Direction: An Invitation to Abundant Life,* Foreword by Henri J. M. Nouwen (New York: Paulist Press, 1981), x.

14. Grou, p. 128.

15. Hughson, p. 19

16. Grou, pp. 128–129.

17. Grou, p. 129.

18. St. Francis de Sales, *Introduction to the Devout Life* (New York: Image Books, 1972), p. 47.

19. Elisabeth Stopp, *Madame de Chantal, Portrait of a Saint* (London: Faber and Faber, 1962), p. 156.

20. John and Charles Wesley, p. 78.

21. Stopp, p. 159.

22. Evelyn Underhill, *Mysticism* (New York: The World Publishing Company, 1967), pp. 415–416.

23. Underhill, p. 416.

24. Rufus M. Jones, *Pathways to the Reality of God* (New York: The Macmillan Company, 1931), p. 41.

25. Jones, p. 44.

26. Jones, p. 213.

27. Jones, p. 214.

28. Underhill, p. 414.

29. E. K. Sanders, *Sainte Chantal* (London: Society for Promoting Christian Knowledge, 1928), p. 33.

30. Sanders, p. 31.

31. Sanders, p. 39.

32. Stopp, p. 63.

33. Stopp, p. 80.

34. Stopp, p. 49

35. Stopp, p. 71.

36. Stopp, p. 40.

37. Sanders, p. 43.

38. Sanders, p. 270.

39. Stopp, p. 185.

40. Thomas R. Kelly, *A Testament of Devotion* (London: Harper and Brothers Publishers, 1941), pp. 82–83.
41. Kelly, pp. 87–88.
42. Francis Thompson, *Poetical Works* (London: Oxford University Press, 1969), p. 94.

10

Cooperative Contributions to Community

HENRY O. THOMPSON

Introduction

Is there a divine intention for female-male relationships? In the Judeo-Christian tradition, one might turn to several sources for an answer to this question. In the United Methodist Church in the United States, of which I am a member, authority is vested in four sources: scripture, tradition, experience and reason.[1] Scripture is primary. Categories other than these can be made and indeed, must be made, such as the distinction between theory and practice. Within organized religion, one cannot help but be aware of the power and influence of current organizational structures. Power might be wielded by a bishop or a rabbi or a group of them. Power might be vested in organizational rules, such as canon law or the United Methodist Book of Discipline.

If the authority of the four sources is questioned, one may claim that it rests on the earlier source of scripture or tradition or that it is derived from scripture in some way, as the Pope is the vicar of Christ. Thus we see an interweaving of the sources which may vary from group to group, an interweaving that may not be acceptable to all.

The same issue of acceptance may apply to scripture, whether a group considers it primary or secondary. Scripture is interpretation, and interpretation varies from one group to another. A given interpretation may not be acceptable to all; a Muslim may choose the Qur'an, while a Jew would choose the Hebrew scriptures. The choice is interpretation and has already begun to answer my opening question. That is true for Christians as well and, in fact, the choice begins even earlier, as indicated in United Methodism's four sources. Non-Protestant groups, for example, might turn first to tradition. The primacy of scripture was the watchword or the war cry of the Reformation. However, even within Protestantism there are those who turn first to experience. Experiential religion has been a hallmark of pietism, Pentecostalism, charismatic movements, Wesleyanism, and so on. To be sure, this does not preclude the use of scripture. Indeed, there are those who would say that without the experience the scriptural word is a dead letter, while the experience of faith makes the scripture come alive. It may not be an accident that women play a more prominent role in experiential traditions. I will come back to the experiential. As a Protestant, I begin with scripture.

Even here, one must begin with the issue of interpretation. The very definition of something as scripture means it has some special quality. In this case, it is related to the initial question in terms of an earlier one. How do we know if there is a divine intention about anything? Imbedded in this question is an even earlier one. How do we know there is a divine? Both questions would carry us far afield from the theme of this paper. Briefly, as an agnostic I would answer the epistemological issue by saying that we do not in fact know anything at all in an absolute sense, including this sentence. We live and speak by faith, whether we speak of God or female-male relationships or the so-called data of scientific research or anything else. By faith, we accept the axioms of science. By faith, we agree and even proclaim that there is a God. By faith, we claim to know God's intentions. These faith claims are made with the awareness that not everyone accepts scientific laws, and with good reason. The historical road of science is littered with the bones of dead theories. Ruth M. Tappen reminds us: "Although we laugh now at the use of leeches . . . , some of our current practices may seem just as irrational and unfounded 100 years from now." There are those who do not agree that there is a God, and among those who agree, not everyone agrees that we can know God's intentions. For those who do acknowledge the knowability of the divine intentions, however, a common starting point is scripture. In some sense it contains a revelation or the word of God that reveals the divine intention. In the Judeo-Christian tradition, that scripture is the Bible.[2]

The Hebrew Scriptures

"In the beginning God created the heavens and the earth." The book of Genesis goes on to describe the creation in terms reminiscent of modern evolutionary theory. Here is a sequence of light and darkness, the waters being gathered together so the dry land might appear, the beginnings of vegetation and animal life in the air, in the sea, and on the land. In Chapter 1, verses 26–31 read in part:

> Then God (elohim) said, "Let us make people (adam) in our likeness. . . ." So God created people in God's own image, in the image of God . . . male and female God created them. . . . And God saw everything that he had made, and behold, it was very good.[3]

The interpretation begun by choosing the Bible rather than another scripture continues in my choice of the Hebrew scriptures rather than the Greek New Testament. The interpretation continues in my choice of the above passage rather than an earlier or later one. Genesis 1:1–2:4a is considered part of the P or Priestly Code, for those who accept the Graf-Wellhausen documentary hypothesis. The P document is usually dated to c. 550 B.C.E.[4] That makes the passage above rather remarkable. There is some consensus that the Hebrew-Jews came out of the exile as monotheists. Some would argue that the monotheism begins with Amos or with Moses and even Abraham. But while these earlier designations are debated, there is far less debate about the exilic and post-exilic periods. The people who wrote and preserved the above were monotheists, in all probability. The Hebrew term "elohim" is plural in form, but it is usually seen as singular in intent. However, the plurality continues with the "Let *us* make people in *our* image, after *our* likeness." Bernhard W. Anderson explains the plural, repeated in 3:22 and 11:7, as probably the divine beings who surround God in his heavenly court (I Kings 22:19; Job 1:6; Isaiah 6:8; Psalm 29:1) and in whose image people were made. Alternatively, one might interpret the plural as the so-called royal "we": Queen Victoria said, "We are not amused"; by "we" she meant herself. It might be an editorial "we," as in the newspapers. It is perhaps more common to interpret the plural as God and to interpret the verse to mean that God created people in God's image, not in the image of divine beings. To reverse the interpretation, God is both female and male.[5]

Parenthetically, we note that the Hebrew language has feminine and masculine gender but no neutral. God is not an "it" but a "thou," to borrow from Martin Buber. To be accurate, God should be referred to as "s/he" or some other euphemism that denotes both genders. It is not surprising, however, that this was not followed in this or in subsequent portions of scripture. To the ancient mind and many modern ones in the concrete-operations stage of intellectual development, such dual designation would mean duotheism rather than monotheism. Given the opposition to the ancient Near Eastern fertility cults, one can understand why the female aspect of God should go largely unacknowledged in the biblical text. It is not ignored. Here I note the gender of those priestly writers. As males, they might have a personal predilection to God as male, though males have served female deities from time immemorial and continue to do so, as women have served male deities.[6]

The point in this context is that God is female and male. That divine relationship could be taken as indicative of the divine intention for female-male relationships among human beings. Stanley S. Harakas suggests that the revelation of God as a trinity of divine persons in perfect loving interrelationship provides the clue for the ethical life. One would like to think that the divine intention for female-male relationships is for an ethical life so that Harakas' thought can apply to this concern. The interpretation is restricted here to people. It may be that God also has intentions for female-male relationships among the so-called lower animals. That would be a topic for another paper. Here the context is woman-man relationships.[7]

The reference to lower animals, however, is deliberate. We could probably find general agreement (a rare thing in academia) that sex and reproduction are a part of female-male relationships, at least for those forms of life which reproduce sexually rather than asexually. The gods and goddesses of the ancient Near Eastern world, the context of the biblical world, were certainly seen in sexual terms. That included reproduction with both divine and human partners. The condemnations of the prophets suggest that the Hebrews participated in the fertility cults, but the "official" religion was against them (Hosea; Jeremiah 2:20; Isaiah 57:5). This may have led to a refusal to see God in sexual terms. What happened was that power over reproduction was ascribed to Yahweh, the God of Israel who grants or withholds fertility of crops, flocks and people rather than the Baal of the Canaanites (Hosea 2:16–22). But the biblical writers continued to describe God in anthropomorphic terms. God has feet and eyes and hands and even a backside—he sits on a throne in heaven and the earth is his footstool (Isaiah 66:1). While concrete operational thinking is tempted to take this literally, God was eventually described in terms of spirit rather than flesh (Isaiah 21:3).

The spiritual nature of God would not necessarily preclude the sexual relationship on a human level, celibates to the contrary. At the same time, that spiritual relationship of the female-male in God the spirit suggests a spiritual dimension in the human pair's relationship as well. I am reminded here of the *Imago Dei* and interminable discussions on just what is the "image of God." In times past it has been equated with spirit, with life or breath, with reason, with love, with the divine spark of immortality, with the human capacity for relationship, etc. The concern here is not to enter into that discussion but only to note that whatever the *Imago Dei* is, females have it or are part of it, as are males. Females and males relate to each other, or ought to relate, as mutually in or within the image of God, as mutually divine, spiritual, reasoning, living, loving, etc. Some Christian thinkers have held that the *Imago Dei* is or can be lost or is partially lost, while others have claimed people still have it, in whole or in part. Whether lost or retained, in whole or in part, females as well as males have retained or lost, in whole or in part, without distinction between the sexes. This "lost" issue forms part of the second creation story in Genesis, that of the so-called J writer or the "Yahwist" writer of Judah, c. 950 B.C.E.[8]

Genesis 2:4b begins a new story, or at least a different one: "In the day that the lord God made the earth and the heavens. . . ." It is a dry creation. God makes it rain and then, verse 7: "The Lord God formed man of dust from the ground, and breathed into his nostrils the breath of life; and man became a living being." In this other creation story, the sequence of events is different. After the creation of man come the plants of the garden in Eden and then the animals on the land and in the air. Finally, as the epitome of his creative acts, God created woman from one of the man's ribs. To quote an old friend, God saved the best until last. In the story, we read in verse 23 that the man said: "This at last is bone of my bones and flesh of my flesh; she shall be called woman, because she was taken out of man."

A modern poster notes that woman was not made from man's head that she should be over him, nor from his feet that she should be under him. Woman was made from man's side, that she might be beside him. I would alter the last phrase to say that "they might be beside each other," or "that they might be together." Trible notes that "man discovered a partner in woman rather than a creature to dominate." Brueggemann says "bone of my bones, flesh of my flesh" is a covenant formula (II Samuel 5:1, 19:13–14; Judges

9:2; Genesis 29:14). The partnership is not sex but mutual concern and loyalty. While God, in creating the human female, saved the best and the finest of his creative energies for the last creative act, the earlier (in the text) or later (in time of writing) story puts female and male together in the godhead without distinction.

The J writer does not end his story with the rib. He continues, to say in verse 24: "Therefore a man leaves his father and his mother and cleaves to his wife, and they become one flesh." This stands in contrast to the patriarchal norm which prevails in the Old Testament and many societies in which the woman is expected to leave her parents and cleave to her husband. That human switch on what the biblical writer thought was the divine intention should not obscure the intended relationship. It is often a sexual relationship, but common sense knows that two people remain two people. Centuries later, the apostle Paul called this a great mystery. He saw it as symbolic of the union between Christ and the church (Ephesians 5:31–32). Genesis 2:24 is far more than physical sex, which is obviously not part of the union of Christ and church. It is a spiritual relationship. Brueggemann extends the covenant language of verse 23 to verse 24. "One flesh" means mutual concern.[9]

The story continues with that which part of the Christian tradition has called "the Fall," but which Carol L. Meyers sees as a continuation of the "far more than physical sex." In Genesis 2:17, God tells the man not to eat of the tree of the knowledge of good and evil. This was before the creation of the woman, in 2:22. The J writer continues in what is now Chapter 3. Here the serpent speaks to the woman: "Did God say, 'You shall not eat of any tree . . . ?'" The woman answers, "We may eat of the fruit . . . but God said, 'You will not eat the fruit of the tree in the middle of the garden. . . .'" Either it must be understood that God spoke again to both the female and the male, or that the man told the woman about the command and that she, or they, understood that the command applied to her also. There is nothing in the text which says this. We interpret that the divine intention conveyed to Adam (man in the generic sense) applied to female and male together.

The story is often cited as the beginning of sin, though the Hebrew word for sin is not used until the story of Cain. The garden story is often told with an emphasis on the woman, called Eve later in 3:20. The serpent tempted her to eat the forbidden fruit. She responded negatively by quoting God (verse 3). But the snake (masculine) said in effect that God was a liar and was trying to keep the fruit for himself. In the face of this contrary opinion, the woman made some empirical, scientific observations. On the basis of her pondering of this scientific data, she proceeded to eat the fruit. Then she offered some to her husband. Without resistance, without quibble, without scientific investigation, without reason, he ate. So much for the stereotype that says the male is scientific and the female is not.[10]

When God appeared on the scene, he asked what happened.[11] The male blamed the female, who blamed the serpent. So much for human responsibility in both of them. Subsequently, the snake is said to have blamed it on God and the etiology of sin is found in God, until the pious rebelled against such a thought. Perhaps by 400 B.C.E., the angel Satan became identified with the devil as the source of evil. Perhaps by 100 B.C.E., the devil became identified with the snake in the garden.[12]

No matter what the interpretation of the snake's role, misogynist interpretations have blamed women for the problems of the human race. However, the standard translations show both as disobedient and as punished, though in different ways. While both were created in the image of God (story one) and woman was created from man (story two), neither is a carbon copy of the other. The woman will have pain in childbirth and her husband (note well—not males in general) will rule over her, while the man must earn his living with sweat.

In contrast to this standard interpretation, Carol Meyers translates 3:16b and c as: "I will greatly increase your work and your pregnancies; (along) with toil you shall give birth to children. To your man is your desire, and he shall predominate over you." She goes on to interpret this as a reflection of the actual state of affairs in Israel in the Early Iron Age (1200–900 B.C.E.) as the pioneer Israelites settled the hill country of Canaan. Women tended the gardens and orchards near the homestead while producing the children to help work the farm. The males went out to the fields and cultivated the cereal crops. By staying closer to the home, the women could care for the children, which meant that about forty percent of the food production was in the hands of women, while sixty percent was covered by males who thus did indeed "predominate."

She notes, in support of her interpretation, that while the rest of the Hebrew scriptures are full of concerns with sin and judgment, the Adam and Eve story is not cited in any way, let alone as a prototype of sin and judgment, which they might well have done, given the usual interpretation of "the Fall."[13]

The usual interpretation is that here we have divine judgments which indicate the divine intention for female-male relationships. Thus women were expected to have pain in childbirth. The verse was quoted as a reason for not using anesthesia or any pain-relieving drug during childbirth until Queen Victoria broke the taboo. These verses have been taken as a divine decree to explain why women *must* be subordinate to males in society, though the divine judgment is only for the husband and wife and not for males in general over females in general. Interestingly enough, the "sweat of your face" of verse 19 has never been taken to mean that male rulers or rich males should have to work. Nor has it stopped the creation of labor-saving devices for males, whether they be the use of an animal to pull a plow or the modern elevator that saves walking up the stairs. The verse has been used to perpetuate the oppression of the poor and the powerless male. Interpretation has been selective—against women and powerless males, which may give some clue as to why the traditional interpretation developed.

In contrast, the rabbis responded to the anesthesia controversy with the observation that we are not called to perpetuate the results of sin. They allowed the anesthesia.[14] That stands in contrast, in turn, to their own continued insistence on the inferiority of the female in female-male relationships as indicated by the Orthodox awakening prayer, "Thank you God that I was not born a woman, a slave or a goy." That continued insistence on the inferiority of women also stands in contrast to the actions of God, who made clothes for Adam and Eve before he drove them out of the garden. Both were punished. But even in punishment, he continued to care for them both. If human beings are in the image of God, they might consider the need to continue to care for one another. That holds true even as male is to care for male, as exemplified in Genesis 4:9. God's question to Cain is, "Where is thy brother?" Cain responded, "Am I my brother's keeper?" The answer is an obvious, "Yes, you are." The implication for the female-male relationship is obvious. The patriarchy perpetuated throughout much of the Judeo-Christian tradition is a violation of the divine intention. In Trible's words, it "is a perversion of creation." It perpetuates the results of sin rather than what God intended for female-male relationships and, for that matter, for all human relationships. Harakas thinks people "realize the image and likeness of God by avoiding evil and doing good, both as individuals and in community with others."[15]

I am interpreting, of course. That interpretation is selective, as just noted for both Jewish and Christian cultures which perpetuate females leaving parents and for the male willingness to avoid the "sweat of his face" whenever he can find alternatives and has the power to do otherwise. The selectivity includes perpetuating the results of sin for women and powerless males, rather than seeking the good that God intended. That God himself tried, is trying, to perpetuate good is part of the history of redemption and salvation, which extends to both female and male. Before moving on to the Christian New Testament with its proposal of salvation in the Jew, Joshua or Yeshua of Nazareth, it is worth noting other selective and hence interpretive points in scripture.

The feminine dimension of the divine appears at a number of points. "In the beginning, the Spirit [feminine] of God was moving over the face of the waters" (Genesis 1:1–2). The wisdom of God is represented by the feminine noun, "hokmah." Wisdom is described as a woman in the wisdom literature of Proverbs. Proverbs 8:22–30 denotes wisdom as beside God in the creation, "like a master work man" or a "little child." In time, wisdom became identified with the sacred Torah, the law of God, and is the wisdom of Solomon as an emanation of God. While the normative term for God is masculine, feminine imagery appears as well (Deuteronomy 32:18; Jeremiah 31:15–22; Isaiah 49:15, 66:13). In either case, God is not an "it" but a personal "thou."[16]

If this masculine-feminine God is personal, one could argue that human females and males in the image of God are called to personal relationship. Neither one is to treat the other as an object. In a later time, Immanuel Kant (1724–1804) claimed that human beings are an end in themselves.[17] They are not to be treated as means to an end. They are not objects. One of the present-day charges of the anti-pornographers is that pornography treats women as sex objects rather than as persons. One could hardly say that treating others as objects is limited to males, but one might say they have been the predominant offenders, treating women and children and even other males as objects to be manipulated for gain. This would seem to perpetuate the sin which the rabbis say we are not to do, the sin which the prophets denounced in the strongest terms.

In Christian tradition, sin is related to the human person's fallen nature. Some would say it is humanity's real nature or natural way.

Others would say that we are always free to choose not to sin. The debate over free will and determinism is beyond the scope of this paper. Here the point is that whichever way the debate leans, it leans on women and men alike. If the *Imago Dei* has been lost, or partially so, it has been lost by both sexes. If it has been retained, it is retained by both. That women and men have sinned against each other, and against other women and other men and children, is a part of the historical record. One is tempted to suggest that the greater sinners have been the males, but one notes in this regard that males are more normally in positions of power. There is little if any evidence to suggest that women would differ in any substantial way if they had the power. We do not actually know that, however. In research for his moral-development theories, Lawrence Kohlberg began with males. The epitome of this development in the early theory is stage six, the stage of justice. He has since partially retracted his belief in this stage, or rather, recognized that the evidence is not yet all in.

In contrast, Carol Gilligann, working with females, has suggested that the epitome of moral development is caring for others and the self to avoid harm. At this writing, her evidence is not clear. Perhaps her current research will clarify the matter. Alternately, however, one can note that in the civil rights movement and in the feminist movement, women are often concerned with justice. Justice itself might be considered in terms of the Hippocratic Oath to do good, or at least to do no harm. The justice is "good and no harm" for all people, women and men alike. Historically, however, there are numerous examples of women doing harm to themselves and to others. The same must be said for males and children as well. Thus, it seems doubtful that, whether the *Imago Dei* is lost or retained or partially so, there is any distinction in the female-male relationship. The divine commands against sin and for good apply to both sexes alike. The divine intention for female-male relationships is for good, not evil. While woman as the epitome of God's creative genius might seem to give her a superior position to the male, this stands in contrast to the imagery of creation from the man's side. It is balanced further by Genesis 1:26, where female and male are mutually created in the image of God. For good or ill, women and men are in life together.[18]

One more example is worth citing in terms of J. Cheryl Exum's study of Exodus 1:8–2:10. The pharaoh tried to stem the growth of the Israelites but failed. Two of the three stories here turn on defiance by women—midwives, Moses' mother, the pharaoh's own daughter. The liberation of Israel from bondage began with women. This may be of interest to the liberation theologies that lean heavily on the Exodus tradition. The mutuality in this tradition is in the recognition that without Moses there may not have been an exodus or a liberation, but without the women, there would have been no Moses![19]

The patriarchism of the Hebrew scriptures is too well attested to need documentation here. Lloyd R. Bailey notes that "we do not know, in many cases, who the biblical authors and editors were, and thus cannot be certain of their gender." In an absolute sense, he is quite right. I do not know of any serious contenders, however, for female authorship of the officially anonymous materials, nor for the pseudepigrapha. Phyllis Trible notes the more common understanding that the Bible was written by males. We could say with some reasonable confidence that the so-called priestly school which collected or wrote and preserved the P document of the Wellhausen theory, and perhaps other materials as well, were males. This and the presumed male authorship of other biblical texts makes it all the more intriguing that the female of the species was recorded as created in the image of God, on the one hand, and as the epitome of God's creative activity, on the other. It makes it even more remarkable that there are as many positive references to women as there are in the biblical tradition. These comments hold for the Greek scriptures as well as the Hebrew. While the quantity recorded is far less for women than for men, women are represented in an otherwise largely male record. The roles of Eve, Sarah, Miriam, Deborah, Ruth, the wise woman from Tekoah, Hulda, Esther, Judith, the good wife of Proverbs 31 and the courageous mother of II Maccabbees 7, could be considered the "tip of the iceberg" if we chose to so interpret these fleeting glimpses. Miriam led her people in worship (Exodus 15:20), while Hulda (II Kings 22:14–20) held the prophetic authority. Wisdom was with the woman of Tekoah (II Samuel 14:1–20), while military inspiration and action was given through Deborah (Judges 4–5) and Judith. Esther was the savior of her people. While the reports are limited, the individuals represent significant words and deeds. If the records had been kept by females, one might readily suspect that many more would have been recorded. The point for female-male relationships is hopefully clear. Women as well as men may represent God in human affairs.

The divine intention is that women and men together can carry leadership roles.[20]

The sexual relationship was noted earlier. One hesitates to enter an arena that is related to wars and murders, to human creativity, not only in the arts but in all dimensions of life, and to more words in print than most subjects known to the human mind. It was touched on in my reference to pornography that it makes women and frequently children (and in the view of some, men as well) into objects rather than persons. Ascetics have been known to deny human sexuality, at least to some extent. Genesis 1:28 quotes God as saying to the newly created female and male, "Be fruitful and multiply and fill the earth." St. John Chrysostom (327–407) and St. Augustine of Hippo (354–430), among others, have suggested that the earth was filled and the commandment fulfilled, so it was time to stop. Their comments are echoed by modern proponents of zero population growth. Reproduction may be normal, but it is not required. Even if humans are required to multiply and fill the earth, thoughtful people have suggested that no one couple is expected to do the whole job itself. Jewish law says a woman is not required to build the world by destroying herself. In the Swedenborgian tradition, Bishop William Pendleton noted that while, on the one hand, contraception was not officially approved, it would not be advisable for the health of a woman to produce as many children as she could physically produce in a lifetime. Therefore he left it up to the conscience of the couples themselves. Emanuel Swedenborg himself (1688–1772) was not married. Pendleton's humane change contrasts with the attitude of the Protestant reformer Martin Luther who calmly declared that if having too many children killed a woman, never mind. That's what women are here for.[21]

At one time, it was thought that sexual activity in the lower animals was strictly for reproduction. Proponents of natural law who opposed contraception were quick to note this as evidence that human sexual intercourse was for reproduction and reproduction alone. More recent observations are that animals engage in a variety of nonreproductive sexual activities. The complexity and variety increase as one moves up the phylogenetic scale from lower to higher animals. Thus natural law, so far as it is interpreted to be expressed in animal life, points to the permissibility of nonreproductive sexual activity. Sexual activity has nonreproductive purposes as well as reproductive.[22]

It is widely conceded that in the Hebrew tradition, sexuality is not evil. "Do not call what God has created common or unclean," to paraphrase Acts 10:15. Sexuality is a normal part of human existence rather than something to be suppressed and banned as ascetics then and now tend to do. But within the Hebrew tradition, sexuality was seen as something other than a mere wave of the hand or some mere biological function. The *Imago Dei* suggests that humans are something other than animals, even as they are also both female and male. The divine intention for female-male relationships includes sexuality. It does not require genital sex and does not require reproduction but within limits allows for both. In modern terminology, one could say that intention is for healthy relationships.[23]

The Greek Scriptures

The misogynism that has plagued the Jewish tradition is repeated in the Christian tradition. One is tempted to say that it is repeated geometrically rather than linearly. The biblical tradition, however, suggests a different perspective rather than this sinful one. One verse that is often quoted for the divine intention for female-male relationships is Ephesians 5:22–23: "Wives, be subject to your husbands, as to the Lord. For the husband is the head of the wife as Christ is the head of the church." As in Genesis 3:16b, quoters rarely distinguish between husbands and men in general. Even in its most literalistic interpretation, the most diehard fundamentalist cannot say this verse gives all males the authority of God to lord it over all females. It does not, in fact, warrant anyone to lord it over another.[24]

Those who quote the text for the divine intention for male-female relationships do not normally (never in my experience) go on to quote verse 25 with its injunction: "Husbands, love your wives, as Christ loved the church and gave himself up for her." There may be some husbands who would die for their wives, but few do it on a regular basis. If husbands were to take seriously even the humanistic suggestion of verse 28, we would not have an international problem called wife-beating that is becoming endemic in America.

> Even so, husbands should love their wives as their own bodies. He who loves his wife loves himself. For no man ever hates his own flesh, but nourishes and cherishes it, as Christ does the church (Ephesians 5:28–29).

I will pass over here the sadomasochist tradition which suggests that, for accuracy's sake, the author of Ephesians should have said "most men" instead of "no man."

But neither for accuracy's sake should one overlook the mutuality represented in these verses. Chapter 5 closes with verse 33: "Let each one of you love his wife as himself, and let the wife see that she respects her husband." Ephesians 6 opens with the words, "Children, obey your parents. . . ." Susan Brooks Thistlewaite takes note of "the lectionary newly developed by the North American Committee on Calendar and Lection" which she calls "the most commonly accepted lectionary now in use in North America." That lectionary leaves out Ephesians 6:5–9 with its injunction, "Slaves, be obedient to . . . your . . . masters. . . ." That is understandable. We no longer have slavery in North America. Or, to put it more accurately, we no longer have official slavery in North America, nor in most of the world. That lectionary also leaves out Ephesians 6:1–4 with the commandment quoted above for children to obey their parents. In the North American context, and perhaps in others as well, that is understandable. In today's extended babyhood the "children" may be 16 or 36. They are not interested in obeying parents. Parents as often as not obey their children, in today's *laissez faire* attitudes toward child-raising. Thistlewaite notes, however, that Ephesians 5:22–23 is included in this lectionary with its commandment for "Wives, be subject to your husbands. . . ."[25]

She speaks in the context of a dialogue in print with James Luther Mays who claims the canon of scripture is fixed in unchanging consistency. If there is truth in his statement, it is stretched beyond the breaking point. He is responding to the *Inclusive Language Lectionary* (Westminster, 1983) by claiming that the committee has produced a different Bible. The charge, of course, is in the same category as those who charged the translators of the Revised Standard Version (RSV) with being tools of the devil and evil purveyors of heresy for daring to tamper with the real Bible. The charge was made earlier against the translators of the King James Version and even earlier, against Jerome for his translation known as the Vulgate. The ignorance here is more appropriate to Desiderius Erasmus' (1465–1536) *The Praise of Folly* than to serious discourse. But it hardly differs from the misogynism that would warp the divine intention for female-male relationships from good to evil, from mutual cooperation to an oppression more appropriate to the evil one than to the holy one of Israel who offers salvation to all.[26]

Another *locus classicus* for the woman-man relationship in the New Testament is I Corinthians 11:3. While scholars quibble and many hold the non-Pauline authorship of Ephesians, there is general agreement that Paul is the author of I Corinthians.[27] It's a moot point, since the New Testament is authoritative for those who believe in it, whether one is quoting the gospels or Revelation. However, for non-Fundamentalists, some portions of scripture carry more authority than others. Neither position, however, stops the translators from translating.

Elizabeth Schussler Fiorenza compares translations of verse 3 and notes the variety. The RSV reads "the head of every man is Christ, the head of the woman is her husband . . ." while the New English Bible reads " . . . woman's head is man. . . ." Living Letters uses husband, as does Good News for Modern Man, which declares "the husband is supreme over his wife." Fiorenza claims "the translators have smoothed out the text theologically while interpreting it in terms of patriarchal hierarchy." A word-for-word literal translation reads ". . . the head of every man is the Christ, however, a head of woman is the man, however, head of the Christ is the God." "Head" in this passage translates the Greek *kephale* which Scroggs interprets as "source" here. Paul is reflecting on the creation narrative of Genesis 2. The early Christians associate Christ with the creation, as in John 1. Christ comes from God. Man comes from Christ, or at least the "new man" does. In the creation story, the woman was made from the rib of the man, but since then, men have been born of women. In the Lord, they are not independent of each other. All things come from God (verse 12). In context (verse 5), women continue to pray and to prophesy.[28]

It is one thing to say that the man or the husband, who is the head of the wife or the woman, is supposed to die for her as Christ died for the church. That most men do not, in fact, die for either the women of the world or even their own wives is self-evident. Rather, they use these verses as an excuse to hold authority over and oppress either their own wives or the women of the world in general. One can understand this in terms of the human sin discussed earlier. To use Christ as an excuse for sin is blasphemy. This is hardly so for those who do not believe in Christ. They will continue their oppression on other grounds. But for those who do believe in Christ, lording it over women is not merely blasphemy;

it is a travesty on the faith that violates every shred of integrity to raw hypocrisy.

Rabbi Hillel said, "Do not do unto others that which is hurtful to thyself. That is the whole of the Law. The rest is commentary." If he is right, those who seek deliberately or who in carelessness hurt others in the same way they have been hurt, violate the whole of the law, violate the whole of the Torah. In Judaism, they violate the whole of Judaism and stand as the real anti-Semites of today.

In Christianity, those who thus hurt others violate the Torah which is identified with wisdom, which is identified with Christ, and they stand as the real anti-Christs of today. Such absolute total violation of the Judeo-Christian tradition should be sufficient to expose the violation of the divine intention for female-male relationships. In Christian terms, the Christ is identified with Jesus of Nazareth. In the gospels, this Jesus refers to himself as the son of man. In Luke, the story is told in general terms (22:24–27) while in Mark, James and John seek a place of special favor (10:35–45). In Matthew 20:20–28, it is their mother who seeks favor on their behalf. Responding to the dispute that arose among the disciples over this or over "which of them was to be regarded as the greatest" (Luke 22:24), Jesus points out that the rulers of the Gentiles love to lord it over them.

> It will not be so among you; but whoever would be great among you must be your slave; even as the Son of man came not to be served but to serve, and to give his life as a ransom for many (Matthew 20:26–28).

The followers of Jesus, then, are quite deliberately called away from the position of boss over others. It is not just a refusal to perpetuate the so-called results of sin in Genesis 3:16b. Here is a positive commandment to do something quite opposite. The Christian male who is the head of his wife or the head of women as Christ is the head of the church is the servant of his wife or of all women. Instead of being served, the Christian man will do the serving. One is reminded of Dietrich Bonhoeffer's (1906–1945) Christ as the "man for others" and Martin Luther's belief that we are called to be a Christ unto our neighbors.[29]

We are called individually as servants, even as suffering servants, as in the Isaianic servant songs (Isaiah 42:1–40, 49:1–6, 50:4–11, 52:13–53:12). In 41:8 and 49:3, Israel is called "my servant." Some would say the servant is Israel, using the device of corporate personality to translate the references to the servant as an individual into the whole people. That in turn could, and perhaps should, lead Christians to see themselves, the new Israel, as the servant and even as the suffering servant, living for others.[30]

For the Christian male, the others are women and children and non-Christian males. The whole people of God, however, draw us back to the earlier notations on the divine intention for female-male relationships. We are in this together.

The mutuality expressed in Ephesians, in contrast to the more usual misogynist misuse of the text, along with earlier tradition, such as female and male both created in the image of God, suggests that women, too, are called to serve. The divine commandment comes to both female and male. Note, however, that we come to this from a quite opposite direction than the usual male perspective which agrees rather too quickly that females are called to serve—them. If anything, the primary call to be a servant is to the human male. "Headship" means service. In the ancient Near Eastern world, whether in the eastern or western quarter of the Fertile Crescent, a good king was one who cared for the widow and the orphan, the poor and the downtrodden.[31] Dominion is not lordship for the sake of privilege. Any male who seeks privilege or exercises it, violates the service to which he is called. He violates the Christ of the gospels.

The call to women to serve rather than to be served comes as they are called to be Christ-like. The call to service is not in fact to women as women or because the female is inferior. It is the call to the *Imago Dei,* the image of God in which they were created. It is a call to service that is carried out mutually with males, rather than as subservient to male or even to an individual husband. To claim privilege in the name of Christ is to spit on the one that one is claiming to follow. It is to hold in contempt the one that Christianity has traditionally called the savior of the world. Here is the anti-Christ indeed. The divine intention for female-male relationships continues to be mutual service under God. Christianity throughout its almost 2,000 years of history has been more concerned with perpetuating sin than the divine intention.

Before turning to tradition, experience and reason, we can include several footnotes in the New Testament text that are worthy considerations. It is well known that Jesus accepted women who were to a degree largely unacceptable in the male culture of his day. He allowed sinners to touch him (Luke 7:36–50). That included males, but it became an issue only when a woman touched him. He was touched by a woman who, through her faith, was healed (Matthew 9:20). He had women followers as traveling companions (Mark 15:41, Luke 8:2–3) and in Bethany he turned to the home of Mary and Martha and their brother Lazarus whom he later raised from the dead. Mary was allowed and encouraged to listen to his teachings at a time when women were not so encouraged (Luke 10:38–42). In all four gospels, women were the first witnesses, and continued among the witnesses of his resurrection (Mark 16:1–8; Matthew 28:1–10; Luke 24:1–11, 22–24; John 20:11–18). Jesus was a feminist. If his followers have been gentiles lording it over women, they have betrayed their lord.

Christian misogynism is one of the weirder phenomena of history. The Sikhs ask, "How can you discriminate against women when women are the mothers of kings?" How can Christians discriminate against women when it was a woman who gave birth to the baby Jesus? Joan Engelsman, in her text *The Feminine Dimension of the Divine,* notes Mary and the continuing veneration of Mary as a part of that feminine dimension. What the church has tried to suppress in one direction has become expressed in another. Female witnesses to Jesus as the Messiah are not limited to the gospels and the lifetime of Jesus. They have continued throughout history. Though the witness of a woman may have been disdained by males, ancient and modern, the biblical text and church history have a goodly share of female witnesses, indicative of the role intended by the divine. In fact, one could make a case for female witnesses as a deliberate choice by God. Elsewhere, as in I Samuel 16:1–13, God chooses one who is least or less or an unexpected choice in human, or at least male, eyes.[32]

In contrast to Jesus, the apostle Paul has often been seen as a misogynist and even the epitome of that twisted attitude toward half the human race.[33] Part of this refers to such passages as I Corinthians 11:3 and, for those who ascribe to a Pauline authorship, Ephesians 5:22–23. As noted earlier, those using Ephesians ignore the context of mutuality, as do those who misuse I Corinthians 11. As noted earlier, the context has women continuing as liturgists, while verse 11 clearly notes that women and men are not independent but in mutual relation, a point made earlier in I Corinthians 7:4. The social customs that he outlines in I Corinthians 11 are seen by some as permanent injunctions. It is a curious interpretation, for the same people do not insist on riding a donkey downtown to their work, nor do they refuse to use labor-saving devices.

The same concern for social customs might be noted in I Corinthians 14:34 where women are to keep silent in church. The context is social order. However, David W. Odell-Scott has pointed out that Paul's use of the enclitic "what!" in verse 36, as in I Corinthians 11:22, marks a contrast that has been overlooked throughout the centuries. Perhaps it was to the advantage of misogynist males to misinterpret the passage. Odell-Scott notes that the audience to whom Paul writes is male. Paul is saying, "You males think women should keep silent in church. . . . WHAT! Did the word of God originate with you, or are you men the only ones it has reached?" In contrast to the usual interpretation, women are here declared equal to males.[34]

The traditional interpretation continued to prevail in the days of John Wesley. But when he translated the New Testament, Wesley put in exegetical and commentary-like notes. At the point of women keeping silent in church, he added the note, "unless they be moved by an extraordinary impulse of the Holy Spirit." He recognized the call that God can make on women and men. One might be permitted the personal observation that Wesley might have added that men should keep quiet unless moved by an extraordinary impulse of the holy spirit, but that would expose my doubt that some may not have even an ordinary impulse of the spirit.[35]

Also in contrast to what is often interpreted as Paul's misogynism, one can note Paul's famous statement in Galatians 3:28: "There is neither Jew nor Greek, there is neither slave nor free, there is neither male nor female; for you are all one in Christ Jesus." Bruce sees this threefold formula as the direct antithesis of the Greek, Zoroastrian and Jewish traditions noted earlier in which a male is thankful he was not born a woman, a slave, or a barbarian/gentile (the irony of males' being thankful they were not born like other males is usually lost in interpretation). Robin Scroggs sees parallel structures in I Corinthians 12:12–13 and Colossians 3:9–11. Scroggs goes on to say:

> To enter the Christian community thus meant to join a society in which male-female roles and valuations based on such roles had been discarded. The community was powerless to alter role-valuations in the outside culture, but within the church, behavior patterns and interrelationships were to be based on this affirmation of equality.

Scroggs points out that the practice of Paul and his churches was congruent with this perspective (Romans 16:1, 3, 6, 12, 15; Philippians 4:2–3; Acts 18:2, 18, 26; I Corinthians 11:2–16, 16:19). In addition to the life of the church, I Corinthians 7 expects women and men to be mutually responsible in family life.[36]

Paul associated with women as his lord did before him. Among the women noted in Acts and the letters, with whom he worked and to whom he sent greetings, one can note especially several mentioned in Romans 16. Phoebe is a presiding minister (*diakonos*—compare II Corinthians 6:4—and *prostatis,* ruler, I Thessalonians 5:12). Priscilla is a co-worker like Timothy, Titus and Luke. Julia (not Junias) is an apostle.

One can also note the apocryphal acts of Paul, with the story of Thecla, a Greek girl in Iconium. She was converted by Paul's preaching, baptized herself and visited Paul in prison. She went to Myra to work with him, but he sent her back to Iconium to preach. Before her death, she "enlightened many with the word of God." Morton Enslin notes that it is uncertain to what extent this legend was produced as a direct correction of Paul's views on women as teachers. Rosemary Radford Ruether says: "The figure of Thecla remained the authority for women's right to preach and to claim a religious vocation independent of the demands of the family and public authority" well into the Middle Ages. Earlier, Tertullian disapproved of the story's encouraging women to preach. He claimed its author was a presbyter from Asia who wrote it out of love for Paul. The written version of the story dates to about 160 C.E., while the oral tradition may go back to the first century. Thus there were Christians who continued to recognize women's right to preach and teach. This is also clear in 112 C.E. from the letter of Pliny. He told the Emperor Trajan that he had tortured two Christian women whom the Christians call ministers *(ministrae)*.[37]

Tradition

Women did in fact continue to teach and preach, to serve as priests and even bishops, if current evidence is correct, up to the 8th century C.E. Monasticism was well under way by this time. It is said to have begun with individual hermits, perhaps people who fled into the desert to escape persecution. The first monastic community was started in Egypt by Pachomius c. 320 C.E. Before his death, he established communities for women as well. St. Jerome (342–420) is well known for his translation of the Bible, the Vulgate version. He is less known as the leader of a monastery, while his friend Paula established three convents. My concern here is not to review the history of convents and monasteries but to note that if the monastic tradition was appropriate for males, a similar commitment or spiritual way of life was appropriate for women as well.

Similarly, through church history one can note such movements or traditions as that of mysticism. Teresa of Avila (1515–1582) is but one example. Her mysticism was not the stereotyped hiding-in-a-cave type. She started a reformed convent and marched up and down Spain, reforming both convents and monasteries. Her concern was justice and right living, rather than the solitary meditation of Simeon Stylites. She was assisted by her devoted follower, John of the Cross. The related roles and partnerships of women and men are well known in the history of missionary movements. That history does not need to be repeated either. The point continues that both women and men, singularly or together in parallel activities, have served God and humanity throughout history.[38]

The role of women in other traditions might also be traced. With frequent resistance from males, they have continued to serve. The modern Hindu reformer, Mohandas K. Gandhi, recognized the important role of women. The attitude of the Sikhs was cited earlier. Initially, Gautama Buddha resisted women as nuns but recognized his mistake and welcomed them as part of the Buddhist tradition. While throughout history Indian women have often been oppressed as in the Judeo-Christian tradition, they have stepped forward in numbers and quality of service when males allowed them to do so. As Prime Minister, Indira Gandhi served India carrying the heavy responsibilities of political office. In Sri Lanka, Sirimavo Bandaranaike picked up the burden of government from her assassinated husband, S. W. R. D. Bandaranaike, and led the island nation through two terms and turbulent times. Women serve in major ways in the social service movement called Sarvodaya, primarily Buddhist but ecumenically including other religious traditions as well. In Judaism, the traditional patriarchism has not stopped women from major roles through such groups as Hadassah. In the nation of Israel, Golda Meir was one of its outstanding Prime Ministers.

While Islam has not been noted for equality among men and women, there are some notable exceptions and developments. It has been suggested that Muhammad the prophet had a higher view of women than did his followers. The Persian poet, Rumi, wrote:

The Prophet said that women totally dominate men of intellect and Possessors of Hearts. But ignorant men dominate women, for they are shackled by the ferocity of animals. They have no kindness, gentleness, or love, since animality dominates their nature. Love and kindness are human attributes, anger and sensuality belong to the animals. She is the radiance of God, she is not your beloved. She is the creator—you could say that she is not created.

As with Judaism and Christianity, the tradition and scripture involve interpretation and a careful choosing of emphasis.[39]

Experiential

Sheila D. Collins notes that "the starting point for feminist theology is experience. . . ." [40] Earlier, I noted United Methodism's four sources of authority: scripture, tradition, experience and reason. Wesley's note about women and the impulse of the holy spirit was cited in relation to women preachers and teachers. They were the exception for well over a century, though that did not stop their on-going contribution to the whole life of the church. They were accepted as lay speakers before ordination became official in 1958. The election of Margorie Swank Matthews as bishop (1980) was a milestone in overcoming the resistance of misogynism, but it was a long overdue acknowledgement of the mutual role women and men can and must have in both the secular and the sacred realms. In 1984, the United Methodist Jurisdictional Conferences elected two more women as bishops. Earlier, Mollie Alma Bridwell White (1862–1946) was a Methodist Episcopal minister's wife. Her success and enthusiasm disturbed Methodist officials as Wesley's disturbed the Anglicans. She sought ordination and was refused, so she started her own movement, the Methodist Pentecostal Union (1901–1917), renamed The Pillar of Fire at Denver and later at Zarephath, New Jersey. She was ordained and in 1918 was elected a bishop.[41]

There are those who would object because she did not have the apostolic succession, that supposedly continuous line in history of the laying on of hands of the apostles of Jesus, on the next generation of preachers, and the next and so on. Wesley himself noted that apostolic success is more important than apostolic succession. Women have had that success as have men. Many of the early converts to Methodism were women. Wesley's acceptance of them may have been related to the strong role his own mother had in his life. After his strange heart-warming experience at Aldersgate, Wesley went out to preach with a new assurance that he himself was accepted by God, that he himself was saved. That experiential religion became a part of the Wesleyan tradition. Women received the gift, the charisma of the holy spirit. They were given the gifts of tongues, of healing, of wisdom, of preaching and teaching. The gifts have continued to this day. Women have been prominent in both the Pentecostal movement which began in 1905 and in the neo-Pentecostal movement of today. To quote Acts again, God is no respecter of persons (Acts 10:34). Women and men both participate in experiential religion.

Reason

My final note is on reason. Throughout history, women have often been put down by males. Thomas Aquinas thought females were genetic defects for males. Women have often been proclaimed emotional while men were rational. When one looks at mobs of males lynching a Black or rioting with massive destruction, one wonders how any sighted person could claim that males are rational. The elite male would distinguish between the masses and the educated. As a longtime resident of the academic world, I would offer a personal testimony about the numbers of males with doctoral degrees and sometimes several of them who have exhibited enormous amounts of emotionality. This is not necessarily bad. A human being without feelings is sick; the technical term is psychopath or sociopath. No one wants a male around who is unable to love, who has never had a warm feeling for a child. But time and time again, male rationality has been used to serve the emotions of fear and anger. Vengeance is not limited to the masses. While a male-dominated society has proclaimed its ethics as one of truth-telling, doing good and doing no harm, fair play and justice for all, others have observed that the *real* values of our society are greed, status, power and technology. In government, business, labor, academia, religion, health care and any field of human endeavor, one can cite example after example in which the rational was absent from the male or the reason was merely used to further those real values.[42]

Lawrence Kohlberg was noted earlier for his work in moral development. His standards have been challenged as being male-oriented rather than being inclusive of human beings. Evidence has been cited which shows that there are fewer women in the higher stages of moral development than males. However, Kohlberg has found the development consistent in both Western and Eastern, both Northern and Southern cultures. The one variable that consistently affects this development is education. It is a social fact that there are fewer women than males in higher education. Where women and men of similar educational background are compared, their moral development is the same. It should be noted that Kohlberg's concepts of moral development are cognitive rather than affective, though he claims that the affective development is similar to the cognitive. While there is enormous variability in development among males, there is enormous variability among females. There is variability among individuals, but the reasoning power of women in general is equivalent to that of males in general. Where social opportunity has been allowed, women have shown their ability in all walks of life, including those where reasoning power was most significant.[43]

By way of summary, men and women together can build a better world. Together they can serve God and humanity. The divine intention for female-male relationships is one of partnership. This partnership may be expressed in marriage or in parallel situations in both secular and sacred realms of activity. This partnership may be close working relationships or people "doing their own thing" as people under God. Neither females nor males are to be confined to a given vocation or lifestyle. Women athletes and male parents are found throughout history where the human social situation allowed them to function in these patterns. All this is not to say there are not differences of any kind between females and males. Of course there are differences. Beyond the immediate biological differences of reproduction, the real differences, however, are not clear. A female weight lifter, Bev Francis, can power-lift 497 pounds, far more than the average male can lift; so even that biological difference is suspect, though one might say that on the average, males are physically stronger.[44] For years, psychologists have been trying to find real, i.e., not culturally conditioned, differences with little success. The primary emphasis in this paper has been on the spiritual, but the role of the rational and the will are significant as well. Whatever the differences, as women and men cooperate for God and humanity, we can complement each other for a better world, perhaps even the kingdom of God on earth.

NOTES

1. *The Book of Discipline of the United Methodist Church 1984* (Nashville: The United Methodist Publishing House, 1984), pp. 78–81.

2. Tappen, *Nursing Leadership: Concepts and Practice* (Philadelphia: F. A. Davis, 1983), pp. 74–75. One hesitates to start citing examples of these dead scientific bones because they are virtually infinite in number. However, I beg the reader's indulgence for at least one more for its longevity. The Ptolemaic geocentric theory of the universe was widely accepted for 1400 years. It was named after Claudius Ptolemeus, or simply Ptolemy, the Greco-Egyptian astronomer of the 2nd century C.E. "It dominated astronomy until the advent of the heliocentric Copernican system in the 16th century" [William H. Harris and Judith S. Levy, eds., *The New Columbia Encyclopedia* (New York: Columbia University Press, 1975), pp. 2237–2238]. While the theory of male dominance of females has been around for thousands of years, its longevity is not an indicator of its correctness.

   William J. Abraham, *The Divine Inspiration of Holy Scripture* (New York: Oxford, 1981). Paul Ricoeur, *Essays on Biblical Interpretation* (Philadelphia: Fortress, 1980). G. Ernest Wright, "Historical Knowledge and Revelation," in *Translating and Understanding the Old Testament,* Harry Thomas Frank and William L. Reed, eds. (New York: Abingdon, 1970), pp. 279–303.

3. Gerhard von Rad, *Genesis: A Commentary* (Philadelphia: Westminster, 1961). "Adam" is singular in form but plural in its meaning of mankind. Phyllis A. Bird, "'Male and Female He Created Them': Genesis 1:27b in the Context of the Priestly Account of Creation," *Harvard Theological Review* 74 (1981), pp. 129–159.

4. Julius Wellhausen, *Prolegomena to the History of Ancient Israel* (New York: World, 1965; original 1878). Edwin C. Bissell, *Genesis Printed in Colors* (Hartford, CT: Belknap and Warfield, 1872). Von Rad, pp. 43–65. Bernhard W. Anderson, *The Living World of the Old Testament* (London: Longmans, 1958), pp. 381–383.

5. Anderson, notes to Genesis, in *The Oxford Annotated Bible with the Apocrypha* (RSV), Herbert G. May and Bruce M. Metzger, eds. (New York: Oxford, 1965), pp. 1–66. Von Rad, p. 57. Ephraim A. Speiser, *Genesis* (Garden City, NY: Doubleday, 1964), p. 7. John Dart, "Balancing Out the Trinity: The Genders of the Godhead," *The Christian Century* 100, No. 5 (February 16–23, 1983), pp. 147–150. Rosemary Radford Ruether, "The Female Nature of God: A Problem in Contemporary Religious Life," in *God as Father?,* Johannes-Baptist Metz and Edward Schillebeeckx, eds. (New York: Seabury, 1981). Marjorie Suchoki, "The Un-male God: Reconsidering the Trinity," *Quarterly Review* 3, No. 1 (Spring, 1983), pp. 34–49.

6. Martin Buber, *I and Thou* (New York: Scribners, 1970; original 1923). Maurice Friedman, ed., *Meetings* (LaSalle, IL: Open Court, 1973). Jean Piaget and Barbell Inhelder, *The Psychology of the Child* (New York: Basic Books, 1969). R. Harris, "Woman in the Ancient Near East," in *The Interpreter's Dictionary*

of the Bible, Supplementary Volume (IDBS), Keith Crim, ed. (Nashville: Abingdon, 1976), pp. 960–963. Phyllis Trible, "Woman in the Old Testament," *IDBS,* pp. 963–966. Robin Scroggs, "Woman in the New Testament," *IDBS,* pp. 966–968. Paul D. Hanson, "Masculine Metaphors for God and Sex-discrimination in the Old Testament," *The Ecumenical Review* XXVII, No. 4 (October, 1975), pp. 316–324.

7. Harakas, *Toward Transfigured Life: The "Theoria" of Eastern Orthodox Ethics* (Light and Life, 1983). Reviewed by Jerry K. Robbins in *The Christian Century* 101, No. 16 (May 9, 1984), pp. 493–494. Von Rad, pp. 58–59.
8. Beverly Wildung Harrison, *Our Right to Choose: Toward a New Ethic of Abortion* (Boston: Beacon, 1983), pp. 73–74 notes these varied opinions. The capacity for relationship was noted by Karl Barth, *The Humanity of God* (Richmond: John Knox, 1960).
9. Trible, p. 965. Cf. also her, "Depatriarchalizing in Biblical Interpretation," *Journal of the American Academy of Religion* XLI, No. 1 (March, 1973), pp. 30–48. She also interprets the creation of the woman as the epitome of God's creation. In contrast to the patriarchal perversion of "for this cause shall a man leave father and mother," she notes (p. 45) that in the Song of Songs 3:4 and 8:2, the woman leads the man to the home of her mother. Walter Brueggemann, "Of the Same Flesh and Bone (Genesis 2:23a)," *Catholic Biblical Quarterly* XXXII (1970), pp. 532–542.
10. Trible, "Depatriarchalizing," p. 40 for similar observations. Jean M. Higgins details the way in which males throughout the centuries have blatantly added their misogynism to the text. Genesis 3b says nothing at all about any temptation of Adam by Eve. The plain sense of the text is that he stood right there throughout the entire conversation. "The Myth of Eve: The Temptress," *Journal of the American Academy of Religion* 44, No. 4 (1976), pp. 639–647.
11. What this says about the doctrine of the omniscience of God is interesting. The plain sense of the words is that God did not know what happened. God is not omniscient. Some, however, suggest God's question was rhetorical. The point in the context of this paper is that the divine intention for female-male relationships may not be foreordained. It may be in process. See pantheism and process theology for a similar thought.
12. For a similar process in the identification of snake and devil, see Egyptian religion. Set or Sutekh, the god of Upper Egypt, was the god of destruction. He became a kind of devil and was later identified with Apophis, the evil serpent. Meyers suggests the snake was reduced from a symbol of fertility and wisdom to a mere creature crawling on its belly. God is the source of both wisdom and fertility. "Gender Roles and Genesis 3:16 Revisited," in *The Word of the Lord Shall Go Forth,* Meyers and M. O'Connor, eds. (Winona Lake, IN: Eisenbrauns, 1983), pp. 337–351.
13. Meyers; Trible, p. 41 claims also that the verse describes rather than prescribes. It protests rather than condones. It condemns this pattern rather than approves it.
14. Immanuel Jakobovits, "Judaism," *Encyclopedia of Bioethics* 2 (1978), pp. 791–802. David M. Feldman, *Marital Relations, Birth Control and Abortion in Jewish*

Law (New York: Schocken, 1978), pp. 64, 293–294, 302. Helen B. Holmes, et al., eds., *Birth Control and Controlling Birth* (Clifton, NJ: Humana, 1980), p. 155.

15. David Baken, *And They Took Themselves Wives: The Emergence of Patriarchy in Western Civilization* (San Francisco: Harper and Row, 1979). Trible, *IDBS,* p. 965, and "Depatriarchalizing," p. 41. Harakas, cf. Robbins, p. 492. F. F. Bruce cites parallels to the orthodox Jewish male's prayer, back to 150 C.E. in the Jewish tradition, to Socrates and Thales (6th century B.C.E.), and to Zoroastrianism. Cf. Bruce, *The Epistle to the Galatians* (Grand Rapids: Eerdmans, 1982), p. 187.

16. Joan C. Engelsman, *The Feminine Dimension of the Divine* (Philadelphia: Westminster, 1979). Roland E. Murphy, *Wisdom Literature and Psalms* (Nashville: Abingdon, 1983). R. J. Williams, "Wisdom in the Ancient Near East," *IDBS,* pp. 940–952. J. L. Crenshaw, "Wisdom in the Old Testament," *IDBS,* pp. 952–956. Metz and Schillebeekx, *God as Father?* (New York: Seabury, 1981). For the feminine dimension of the divine in another tradition, cf. C. Mackenzie Brown, *God as Mother: A Feminine Theology in India—An Historical and Theological Study of the Brahmavaivarta Purana* (Hartford, CT: Claude Star, 1974).

17. Kant, *Foundations of the Metaphysics of Morals* (Indianapolis: Bobbs-Merrill, 1959; original 1785).

18. Lawrence Kohlberg, *The Philosophy of Moral Development. Volume 1, Moral Stages and the Idea of Justice* (San Francisco: Harper and Row, 1981), and *Vol. 2, the Psychology of Moral Development* (San Francisco: Harper and Row, 1984). Carol Gilligan, *In a Different Voice* (Cambridge: Harvard, 1982).

19. Exum, "'You Shall Let Every Daughter Live': A Study of Exodus 1:8–2:10," *Semeia* 28 (1983), pp. 63–82.

20. For instructive comments on this patriarchism, see Mary Ann Tolbert, "Defining the Problem: The Bible and Feminist Hermeneutics," *Semeia* 28(1983), pp. 113–126. Bailey, "Tough Questions for Us All: *An Inclusive Language Lectionary: Readings for Year A . . . ,*" *The Review of Books and Religion* 12, No. 6 (March, 1984), pp. 1, 9. Trible, *IDBS,* p. 695. C. V. Camp, "The Wise Women of II Samuel: A Role Model for Women in Early Israel," *Catholic Biblical Quarterly* 43 (1981), pp. 14–29. William J. Holladay, "Jeremiah and Women's Liberation," *Andover Newton Quarterly* XII (1972), pp. 213–223. J. H. Otwell, *And Sarah Laughed: The Status of Women in the Old Testament* (Philadelphia: Westminster, 1977). Leonard Swidler, *Biblical Affirmations of Woman* (Philadelphia: Westminster, 1979). C. J. Vos, *Women in Old Testament Worship* (Delft: V. J. Judels and Brinkerman, 1968). James G. Williams, *Women Recounted: Narrative Thinking and the God of Israel* (London: Almond Press, 1982).

21. Feldman, p. 242. George Trobridge, *Swedenborg: Life and Teaching,* 4th ed. (New York: Swedenborg Foundation, 1962). Mary Ann Meyers, *A New World Jerusalem: The Swedenborgian Experience in Community Construction* (Westport, CT: Greenwood, 1983), p. 66.

22. Anthony Kosnik, et al., *Human Sexuality: New Directions in American Catholic Thought* (New York: Paulist, 1977).

23. Feldman, *Marital Relations.* J. A. Sanders, *The Old Testament in the Cross* (New York: Harper and Brothers, 1961), p. 49. Trible, "Depatriarchalizing," p. 45, notes that neither the Eden story prior to the disobedience nor the Song of Songs includes procreation. She sees (p. 47) the Song as a midrash on Genesis 2–3.

24. For a full exegesis and commentary, see Markus Barth, *Ephesians 4–6* (Garden City, NY: Doubleday, 1974). See also the instructive comments of William E. Phipps, *Influential Theologians on Wo/man* (Washington, DC: University Press of America, 1980), pp. 19–24.

25. Thistlewaite, "Opening the Mail Which Did Not Tick," *The Review of Books and Religion* 12, No. 6 (March, 1984), pp. 6–8.

26. Mays, "Confused Interpretation and Translation," *Presbyterian Outlook* (November 14, 1983). David Ewert, *From Ancient Tablets to Modern Translations* (Grand Rapids: Zondervan, 1983). Wright, pp. 279–281.

27. For a full exegesis and commentary, see William F. Orr and James A. Walther, *I Corinthians* (Garden City, NY: Doubleday, 1976).

28. Fiorenza, *In Memory of Her* (New York: Crossroad, 1983), and "The Power of the Word," *The Review of Books and Religion* 12, No. 6 (March, 1984), p. 5. Scroggs, "Paul and the Eschatological Woman," *Journal of the American Academy of Religion* XL, No. 3 (September, 1972), pp. 282–303.

29. The reasoning here about the Christian man as servant to women was derived independently, but note a similar comment by Markus Barth, p. 618. Cf. Thompson, "Religious Feminist in the Spot-light," *The Christian Century* XCVII, No. 1 (March, 1973), pp. 1161–1162. Ruth Zerner, "Dietrich Bonhoeffer," in *Eerdman's Handbook to the History of Christianity,* Tim Dooley, et al., eds. (Grand Rapids: Eerdmans, 1977), p. 603. Anthony C. Thiselton, "An Age of Anxiety," in *Eerdman's Handbook,* pp. 594–611. Martin E. Marty, "Martin Luther's Reckless Grasp of Grace," *The Christian Century* 100, No. 31 (October 26, 1983), pp. 962–965.

30. Sanders, pp. 67–109. H. Wheeler Robinson, *The Cross in the Old Testament* (London: SCM, 1960; original 1926), pp. 55–114. Walther Zimmerli and Joachim Jeremias, *The Servant of God* (London: SCM, 1957).

31. Roland de Vaux, *Ancient Israel: Its Life and Institutions* (New York: McGraw-Hill, 1961), pp. 100–114. Henri Frankfort, *Kingship and the Gods* (Chicago: University of Chicago, 1948). John Gray, "Canaanite Kingship in Theory and Practice," *Vetus Testamentum* II (1952), pp. 193–220. George Widengren, *The King and the Tree of Life in Ancient Near Eastern Religion* (Uppsala: Lundequietska, 1951). Stephen Szikszai, "King, Kingship," *Interpreter's Dictionary of the Bible* (IDB) 3 (1962), pp. 11–17.

32. Engelsman, *Feminine Dimension.* Alicia C. Faxon, *Women and Jesus* (Philadelphia: United Church Press, 1973). Leonard Swidler, "Jesus Was a Feminist," *New Catholic World* (January, 1977), pp. 177–183, and "Jesus Was a Femin-

ist," *New York Times* (December 18, 1971), 29:4. Rachel Conrad Wahlberg, *Jesus According to a Woman* (New York: Paulist, 1975). Phipps, pp. 1–3, echoes the concept but Jesus was not just a feminist, but a radical feminist.

33. See Markus Barth, and Orr and Walther, for detailed data. Paul is a mutualist rather than a misogynist and indeed, the misinterpretation of Paul as one either promoting male superiority or baptizing the status quo into the Christian tradition is a betrayal of Pauline theology. William O. Walker, Jr., "The 'Theology of Woman's Place' and the 'Paulinist' Tradition," *Semeia* 28 (1983), pp. 101–112, suggests that 7 passages supporting male dominance are post-Pauline additions to the text. These include I Corinthians 11:3–16; 14:34–35; Colossians 3:18–19; Ephesians 5:22–33; I Timothy 2:8–15; Titus 2:4–5; and I Peter 3:1–7. He exempts I Corinthians 7 on the basis of Robin Scroggs' exegesis in "Paul and the Eschatological Woman," pp. 294–297. Walker sees the objectionable verses as part of the so-called "Rules for the Household" adopted from Hellenistic sources by Hellenistic Judaism and later Christianity which deny the egalitarianism of Paul. He may be right, but newer interpretations suggest these verses do not in fact promote male dominance at all. They have been cited that way in the past to promote such dominance as a perversion of Paul. Scroggs (p. 284) suggests that Ephesians, Colossians, the pastorals, and I Corinthians 14:33b–36 are to be discarded as post-Pauline. He sees (p. 302) Paul as asserting the freedom and equality of women.

34. Odell-Scott, "Let the Women Speak in Church: An Egalitarian Interpretation of I Corinthians 14:33b–36," *Biblical Theology Bulletin* XIII, No. 3 (July, 1983), pp. 90–93.

35. Wesley, *Explanatory Notes on the New Testament* (London: Epworth, 1954; original, 1754). Hilah F. Thomas and Rosemary Skinner Keller, *Women in New Worlds: Historical Perspectives on the Wesleyan Tradition* (Nashville: Abingdon, 1981).

36. Bruce, pp. 187–191. Scroggs, *IDBS,* p. 966. Darrell J. Doughty, "Women and Liberation in the Churches of Paul and the Pauline Tradition," *The Drew Gateway* 50, No. 2 (Winter, 1979), pp. 1–21. Donna Jackson, "St. Paul's View on Women," unpublished manuscript. Catholic Biblical Association Task Force, "Women and Priestly Ministry: The New Testament Evidence," *Bulletin of the Council on the Study of Religion* 11, No. 2 (April, 1980), pp. 44–46. Letty M. Russell, *Women's Liberation in a Biblical Perspective* (New York: United Presbyterian Church, 1971).

37. Phipps, pp. 14–19. Morton S. Enslin, "Paul, Acts of," *IDB* 3 (1962), pp. 678–680. Rosemary Radford Ruether, "An Unrealized Revolution," *Christianity and Crisis* 43, No. 17 (October 31, 1983), pp. 399–404. Dennis R. McDonald, *The Legend of Paul and the Apostle: The Battle for Paul in Story and Canon* (Philadelphia: Westminster, 1983).

38. Ruether, "Unrealized Revolution," p. 403. Michael A. Smith, "Christian Ascetics and Monks," *Eerdmans' Handbook,* pp. 204–210. Robert D. Linder, "Rome Responds," *Eerdmans' Handbook,* pp. 404–422. Caroline Marshall, "Teresa of Avila," *Eerdmans' Handbook,* pp. 417–418. Ursula King, "Mys-

ticism and Feminism: Why Look at Women Mystics?" *World Faiths Insight,* New Series 5 (Summer, 1982), pp. 13–19. Michael Bruce and G. E. Duffield, eds., *Why Not? Priesthood and the Ministry of Women* (Appleford, England: Marcham, 1972). Patricia A. Kendall, compiler, *Women and the Priesthood: A Selected and Annotated Bibliography* (Philadelphia: Episcopal Diocese of Pennsylvania, 1976). Eric L. Mascall, *Women Priests?* (Westminster, England: The Church Literature Association, 1972). Peter Moore, ed., *Man, Woman and Priesthood* (London: SPCK, 1978). Leonard Swidler and Arlene Swidler, eds., *Women Priests* (New York: Paulist, 1977). George Tavard, *Woman in Christian Tradition* (Notre Dame: 1973).

39. The Rumi selection is from *The Mathnawi of Jalalu'ddin Rumi,* 8 vols., R. A. Nicholson, ed. and tr. (London: Luzac, 1925–1940), I:2421–2437, quoted by William C. Chittick, *The Sufi Path of Love: The Spiritual Teachings of Rumi* (Albany: State University of New York, 1983), p. 1669. Nabia Abbott, *Aishah, The Beloved of Muhammed* (New York: Arno Press, 1973; original 1942). Denise Carmody, *Women in World Religions* (Nashville: Abingdon, 1979). Swami Ghanananda, *Women Saints of East and West* (Hollywood, CA: Vedanta Press, 1972). Nancy Falk and Rita M. Gross, eds., *Unspoken Worlds: Women's Religious Lives in Non-Western Cultures* (New York: Harper and Row, 1980). Elizabeth W. Fernea and Basima Q. Begirgen, eds., *Middle Eastern Muslim Women Speak* (Austin: University of Texas, 1977). Carolyn Fleuhr-Lobban, "Challenging Some Myths: Women in Sharia'a (Islamic) Law in the Sudan," *Expedition* 25, No. 3 (Spring, 1983), pp. 32–39. Diana Mary Paul, *The Buddhist Feminine Idea: Queen Srimala and the Tathagatagarbha* (Missoula, MT: Scholars Press, 1980). K. L. Seshagiri Rao, "Gandhi and Women's Liberation," in *The Search for Hinduism,* forthcoming. Jane I. Smith, "Women in Islam: Equity, Equality, and the Search for the Natural Order," *Journal of the American Academy of Religion* XLVII, No. 4 (December, 1979), pp. 517–537. Leonard Swidler, *Women in Judaism: The Status of Women in Formative Judaism* (Metuchen, NJ: Scarecrow Press, 1976). Walther Wiebke, *Woman in Islam* (Montclair, NJ: Abner Schram, 1981).

40. Collins, "Feminist Theology at the Crossroads," *Christianity and Crisis* 41, No. 20 (December 14, 1981), pp. 342–347. Exum, p. 119, agrees with the point on women and experience but adds that male theology is *also* based on experience. Males, however, say they are being objective. Judith Ochshorn, *The Female Experience and the Nature of the Divine* (Bloomington: Indiana University Press, 1981). The experiential is, of course, not limited to feminist theology. It is an important element in many movements and traditions, as noted earlier in the text. It appears in a variety of places. Cf. Richard W. Rousseau, ed., *Interreligious Dialogue: Facing the Next Frontier* (Scranton, PA: Ridge Row Press, 1981). It holds a crucial place in liberation theology. Harrison, pp. 91–118. The problem with experience for both women and the Latin American and other liberation movements is that it cannot be controlled by denominational hierarchies. The holy spirit does not come and go at the bidding of bishops or church councils. Thus, experience is opposed and put down as irrational or subversive, whether it be the experience of women or anyone else.

"Truth" becomes a euphemism to control others. This is a well-known phenomenon in academia. See Thompson, "Deception: The American Way of Life," forthcoming. Robert McAfee Brown, "Drinking from Our Own Wells," *The Christian Century* 101, No. 16 (May 9, 1984), pp. 483–486. This is a review of Gustavo Gutiérrez's *We Drink from Our Own Wells: The Spiritual Journey of a People* (New York: Orbis, 1984).

41. "Women in Ordained Ministry," Division of Ordained Ministry, Board of Higher Education and Ministry, The United Methodist Church, n.d. Anna Howard Shaw (1847–1915) was the first woman ordained in the Methodist Protestant Church, in 1880. The MPC became part of the Methodist Church in 1939. Amanda Berry Smith (1837–1915) was not ordained but preached at camp meetings, as did Alma White. The successor body, the United Methodist Church (formed in 1968) now has over 2,500 women clergy, the largest number of any Protestant denomination, but still a small percentage of that body's over 40,000 clergy. Of these, 1,232 service parish churches. Roy Howard Beck, "Gains by UMC Women Called 'Extraordinary,'" *United Methodist Reporter* 131, No. 12 (August 24, 1984), p. 3. The extraordinary appears when one sees that no clergywoman was accepted as a delegate to jurisdictional conferences (which elect the bishops) until 1964 when one was a delegate. In 1984, there were 970 clergywomen delegates. J. Gordon Melton, *Encyclopedia of American Religions* (Wilmington, NC: McGrath, 1978), I:231. Vergilius Ferm, *An Encyclopedia of Religion* (New York: Philosophical Library, 1945), p. 585. Henry Warner Bowden, *Dictionary of American Religious Biography* (Westport, CT: Greenwood Press, 1977), pp. 500–501.

42. Helen B. Holmes, et al., eds., *The Custom-Made Child* (Clifton, NJ: Humana, 1981).

43. Kohlberg, both volumes. James R. Rest, *Development in Judging Moral Issues* (Minneapolis, MN: University of Minnesota, 1979). Joyce E. Thompson and Henry O. Thompson, *Bioethical Decision Making for Nurses* (Norwalk, CT: Appleton-Century-Crofts, 1985).

44. "Newsmakers," *Newsweek* CIII, No. 19 (May 7, 1984), p. 71. Thomas Boslooper, *The Image of Woman* (New York: Rose of Sharon, 1980), and "Physical Fitness and Femininity," report to the American Association for the Advancement of Science, December, 1968, in Dallas, Texas.

11

A Unification Perspective on the Female-Male Relationship

PATRICIA E. GLEASON

Introduction

Any person who has been a member of the Unification Church for some time, and who has heard or read the Reverend Moon's speeches and experienced the dynamic of a Unification engagement and marriage, will affirm that the male-female love relationship is a fundamental concern of Unification theology and lifestyle. The *Divine Principle* (DP),[1] which functions as the official doctrinal text of the Unification movement, provides glimpses of the centrality of this issue, particularly in the chapters on creation and the fall. However, since it was written at a time in which marriage and family were only theoretical realities for the movement's members, I will supplement it with more recent literature from the Unification movement. In laying out what I would consider a Unification theology of female-male relationships, I will also refer to Rev. Moon's speeches,[2] to *Explaining Unification Thought* (EUT),[3] written by Dr. San Hun Lee, to Dr. Young Oon Kim's *Unification Theology,*[4] and to the *Outline of the Principle, Level 4,*[5] written by Rev. Chung Hwan Kwak.

This paper presupposes the self-definition of the Unification Church as a movement built on the foundation of Christianity. The discussion will therefore begin with a Unification interpretation of the traditional categories of Christian dogmatics, i.e., creation, sin, salvation. Where appropriate, I will bring in observations from disciplines other than theology, and I will also attempt to integrate an analysis of Unification practice in light of its theory.

Creation: The God-Human Relationship

Why do men and women need each other? It is not for their mutual satisfaction primarily—they need each other in order to be able to resemble

God in their unity. Together they exist in the total image of God and that is the reason they need each other.[6]

Christians have at times made use of the Genesis 1:27 affirmation, "So God created man in his own image, in the image of God he created him; male and female he created them" (RSV), to comment on the relation between God and human beings. The potential for this passage to undermine a patriarchal culture[7] has been recognized and often watered down in the Christian tradition, either by a reworking of it in light of I Corinthians 11:7–8 ("Man is made in the image of God, woman in the image of man") or by a subordination of the marriage relationship suggested by the Genesis text to a notion of relationality in general, making marriage one metaphor for the idea that "God is love."[8]

Rev. Moon's interpretation of this passage is generally quite literal. He would insist that a full manifestation of God is not possible without the unity of a female and a male human being. For a more nuanced understanding of this general stance, however, it is important to consider the fundamental ontological construct of Unification theology, the "four-position foundation," and its development in terms of the growth process through the "three blessings."

According to Unification theology, God created the world in order to experience joy. Unificationists, following many other religious people, speak of God's unconditional, unbounded love, but make a distinction between compassionate love and joyful love. Joy, which is the eschatological promise and hope, is thought to be most complete when the basis for a relationship is not one partner's weakness but both partners' strength. In the creation chapter of DP, it is held that God should have experienced the greatest joy through human beings, who are said to have been created to have a special love relationship with God as God's children. The possibilities for a mutual relationship between God and human beings would naturally expand with the growth of the human capacity to reflect, express, and extend God's infinite love and creativity. Unification theology describes the growth process as the "fulfillment of the three great blessings on the foundation of four positions."[9]

The "three blessings" get their name from the Genesis injunction to be fruitful, multiply, and have dominion over the creation.[10] The fulfillment of each blessing requires a relationship: the first blessing calls for development to maturity through give-and-take between one's internal character (mind) and external form (body) centered on the heart and will of God. The second calls for a mature woman and a mature man to unite and establish a God-centered family and society, and the third is accomplished with the unity of humanity with the rest of the created order, also in accordance with God's love and purpose. In each case, DP speaks of four positions: with God at the center (first position), the uniting beings (second and third positions) give rise to a fourth position—their point of unity.[11]

Divine Principle presents the unity of mind and body (first blessing) and additionally that of male and female (second blessing) as a prerequisite for a full reflection of God. To explain this requires a closer investigation of the Unification doctrine of God.

Affirming a creator God whose characteristics are expressed in the created order, DP employs a circular method of investigating and describing God and the creation.[12] It speaks of two sets of dual characteristics, or polarities, which are fundamental to all beings, and which have their origin in God. The most basic polarity is that of internal character and external form, referred to in Unification texts by the Korean terms *sung sang* and *hyung sang.*[13] God's internal character ("original *sung sang*") is manifested to varying degrees in created entities. In an atom, the *sung sang* would be the directing force which causes the electrons to orbit the nucleus, whereas in human beings, *sung sang* aspects include not only principles and laws of growth, but intellectual, emotional, and volitional functions. Most importantly, as beings created with the potential to express God's nature, humans' *sung sang* includes the capacity to give and receive love: "The core of God is Heart, and Heart lies in the very depth of *Sung Sang.*"[14]

God's *hyung sang* ("original *hyung sang*") is described in *Explaining Unification Thought* as "pre-energy"—"the attribute of God that constitutes the fundamental cause of the material aspect of all existing beings (i.e., their mass, shape, structure and so on)."[15] EUT further discusses how it can be called pre-matter, inasmuch as energy is convertible into mass. Original *hyung sang* is considered the cause of the visible aspects of matter, structure, and shape. EUT takes great pains to insure both that spirit and matter not be considered essentially different from each other and that they are each recognized as having their origin in God:

> . . . *Sung Sang* and *Hyung Sang* have something in common and are not essentially different elements in the world of ultimate cause. Thus, the

Unification principle says that God is the united body (harmonious body) of dual characteristics of *Sung Sang* and *Hyung Sang,* which means, first, that they are essentially of the same nature, and second, that they are united in God.[16]

The second set of dual characteristics to which DP refers is that of positivity and negativity, or the active (masculine) and responsive (feminine) poles of God.[17] These dualities are considered direct attributes of God's internal character and external form, thus prohibiting an exclusive alliance of activity with spirit, and responsivity with matter. (One can speak, therefore, of the "masculinity" and "femininity" of God's character and the "masculinity" and "femininity" of God's form, or energy.) Since all creation is said to reflect God, every individual being expresses a harmony of masculine and feminine elements. However, as individuals relate to other individuals, they take positions of relative activity and relative responsivity for the purpose of achieving harmonious and creative unions of ever greater intensity and scope.

Despite the technicality of presentation, the interpretation of these polarities has direct consequences for Unification theology and practice. The masculine/feminine polarity of God has received various interpretations within the Unification movement. While masculinity is not exclusively associated with males, nor femininity with females, in either EUT or DP, it is commonly assumed that whatever these terms mean (and they mean different things to different people), women would tend to express God's femininity more perfectly than men, and likewise men would more fully express God's masculinity. Thus the dynamics of the female-male relationship is significantly affected by the understanding of how the terms "masculinity" and "femininity" are related to God.

EUT makes more explicit than DP the notion that both femininity and masculinity are manifested in God's internal character as well as in God's external form. The DP, while separating the discussion of the two sets of dual characteristics initially, almost immediately conflates them such that masculinity is said to represent God's essential character and femininity, God's essential form.[18] The medium by which it creates this confusion is the "subject-object relationship," or the initiating-responding relationship. Since both women and matter are seen to be relatively more responsive than men and mind (all the while assuming that men and mind also take positions of response in mutual interaction with women and matter, respectively), femininity and external form (matter) get associated with each other in a way which is irreconcilable with other discussions of the human polarities in EUT and DP. (More importantly, however, this association is irreconcilable with anything but the male's fantasy of being disembodied, or at least more spiritual than the female.)

I would argue that it is more in line with the development of Unification theology, particularly as unfolded in Rev. Moon's speeches, to insist on feminine and masculine aspects of both God's character and God's form or energy. However, it is obvious from observing relationships between women and men in groups which revere female deities, that ascribing feminine aspects to God does not, of itself, guarantee a change in the status of women. This is particularly true if it is a patriarchal view of women which feeds into the construction of the God-symbol. For example, according to EUT, "obtuseness, dullness, unimaginativeness, and poor memory" are among the feminine characteristics of the intellect, as opposed to masculine characteristics of "perspicacity, keen perceptiveness, imaginativeness, and good memory"; and "unpleasantness, melancholy, and gloominess" describe the feminine aspects of emotion, compared with masculine "pleasantness, cheerfulness, and brightness."[19] Since Dr. Lee's patriarchal view of women feeds into his description of "femininity," it is understandable that the feminine aspects of the character of God have not been stressed in his system.[20]

A distinctively different attitude characterizes Dr. Young Oon Kim's works. In *Unification Theology,* she begins her chapter on the Unification creation doctrine with an affirmation of the feminine as well as the masculine nature of God. She points to parallels of this teaching in other religious and philosophical systems, including those of Mother Ann Lee, Mary Baker Eddy, Confucianism, Taoism, Jung, Mary Daly, and several others.[21] Since she does not clearly distinguish her own views from those which she investigates, it is difficult to ascertain precisely her own understanding of masculinity and femininity. This may be a wise strategy on her part, for until women and men are *present* in all spheres of life, it is of little help to make dogmatic statements regarding their natures.

Dr. Kim does forthrightly insist on the concrete presence of women as well as men for the full experience of God. She refers to Karl Barth's discussion of the *Imago Dei,* according to which the biblical claim that God created women and men in God's likeness indicates "our need to fulfill ourselves through love."[22] She claims that DP agrees with but goes further than Barth, because according to the DP,

> . . . the Adam and Eve story shows that their creation as a pair actually represents the external and objective manifestation of the polarity of God. Adam alone did not and could not be the complete divine image. Eve was needed to reflect God's total likeness.[23]

In her comparison of DP with Barth, Dr. Kim isolates two ways in which Unificationists understand the female-male relationship to be a reflection of God. The first is that the unity of women and men most fully expresses the love and creativity of God. The second implies that there is something about women which expresses an aspect of God that men alone cannot express, and vice versa for men. I will deal with these two understandings in reverse order.

As has been noted, DP argues that God's full experience of joy depends on a relationship with beings who have freely developed their potential to resemble God. An individual having fulfilled the first blessing (as DP holds Jesus to have done) becomes a "good object for the joy of God,"[24] since his or her mind/body unity becomes the substantial expression of the character and form of God. However, fulfillment of the second blessing allows for a more dynamic, creative expression of God. According to DP, men and women, having reached oneness with God individually, should then unite as representatives of God's masculinity and God's femininity. In Rev. Moon's words, "Within God there is a quality of a man's love and the quality of a woman's love. By having sons and daughters, God can expand in both directions; and by their coming together, they can become whole."[25]

Unification theology implies that a woman discovers and defines herself in relationship with God primarily, and then brings this version of a fulfilled humanity into a relation with a man. The same is true for a man. With the unity of man and woman, God's nature is more perfectly incarnated on the earth than it would be without such unity. As will be discussed in the section on restoration, the absence of a perfected woman (one on a par with Jesus) leaves the universe and God painfully lacking in completion.

The second significance of the Unification understanding of the male-female relationship pointed out by Dr. Kim is its potential for expressing love. Rev. Moon asks, "Why did God create man and woman to begin with? Their purpose was the consummation of love . . . God's blueprint for men and women came from his thinking about the ideal form of love."[26] He further elaborates on the creation of men and women in the following words:

Men were not made for the sake of power and domination but for women. When God undertook to create man he already had a blueprint for woman and tried to adapt his creation of man accordingly. In the same way, when God created woman he already had his blueprint of man in mind, and he created woman to match. It feels good to know that God had the love of our mates in mind when he created man and woman.[27]

Rev. Moon is most poetic when discussing conjugal love. Claiming that "God's ideal of creation is fulfilled in the relationship between perfected, unfallen men and women, in their love centered upon God,"[28] he often depicts a God who longs to experience the ecstasy of holy marital love. To illustrate:

When they are surrounded by that fireball of love, is it only the man and woman within, or is God also included inside? Yes, God is there with them. What would God feel? He wouldn't say, "I'm just bored." He would say, "I'm satisfied now!" When God is totally satisfied, he is like a drunk person.[29]

Men and women feel so intensely toward each other in their love and I want you to understand that God is just the same. When you are really enjoying the ecstasy of romantic love, God is enjoying that love too. God will be holding one hand of the husband and one hand of the wife, saying, "You two are mine forever, I will never release you."[30]

True to his teaching, however, Rev. Moon insists that conjugal love is not fulfilled in isolation. It expands horizontally:

The love between husband and wife is an example of universal, public love. When you love your husband, you are loving the entire male world, including the masculine attributes of God. When you love your wife, you are loving all the femininity of the universe, including God's feminine attributes.[31]

Most importantly, however, conjugal love requires a vertical dimension for its stability and productivity:

God desires the completion of the ideal of creation. What does that mean? It means the completion of the heavenly four-position foundation. The heavenly four positions are filled by God, the two parents, and the children. The line between God and the children is along the vertical line, while the parents' relation is necessary to provide the horizontal line.[32]

The harmonization of vertical and horizontal levels in the four-position foundation established by couples centered on God provides, according to Rev. Moon, the greatest latitude for multiple experiences of divine love:

> Three generations within a family make it whole, both vertically and horizontally. . . . Children who grow up in that kind of wholesome environment experience a balanced and harmonious life; they learn about the width and depth and all dimensions of loving relationships. Their families are a training ground for the balanced, global experience of all kinds of love.[33]

In sum, it can be said that Unification theology affirms the significance of the female-male relationship for the completion of God's hope for creation. This relationship has the potential to substantially incarnate God on earth, and to provide the opportunity to experience the multiple dimensions of God's love. However, Unification theology recognizes that this ideal has not really been manifest historically. Its discussion of the fall is an attempt to explain the problem of love.

Fall: Misdirected Love

The centrality of love in Unification teachings is carried over into its doctrine of sin. DP uses the Genesis story to express an understanding of the fallen condition which began in the love relationship of the original couple. While most Unificationists treat the doctrine as the revelation of an historic event, it is not necessary to do so in order to allow the impact of its paradigms to exercise profound psychological and spiritual effects on one who in some way takes the teachings seriously.

Before discussing the Unification doctrine of the fall specifically, I wish to comment on what seems to be a tendency in recent thought to avoid the male-female relationship as a focal point for understanding "society gone awry." To many, a focus on so small a unit as the heterosexual couple may seem a very unprogressive means of bringing about a transformation of society. Feminists aside, those Western theologians and philosophers of the last two centuries who have attempted to address the problem of human sinfulness by concentrating on institutional evil have tended to incorporate woman into man or into the family. Thus they have overlooked or underestimated the importance of the male-female relationship as a key to salvation or liberation.

For example, the late nineteenth-century American theologian, Walter Rauschenbusch (1861–1918), in his efforts to encourage an awareness of institutional evil, critiques interpretations of sin taken from the Genesis story. He claims that:

> . . . any interpretation of the nature of sin taken from Adam will be imperfect, because Adam's situation gave very limited opportunities for selfishness, which is the essence of sin. . . . The only persons with whom he could associate were God, Eve, and Satan. Consequently theology lacked all social details in describing his condition before and after the fall. It could only ascribe to him the virtues of knowing and loving God and of having no carnal concupiscence, and, by contrast, after the fall he lost the love and knowledge of God and acquired carnal desires. Thus a fatal turn toward an individualistic conception of sin was given to theology through the solitariness of Adam.[34]

Rauschenbusch's solution is to jump from the individual to the social, to move away from comparing ourselves with an original Adam to judging ourselves in light of the Kingdom of God as inaugurated by Jesus. Adam, despite the existence of God, Eve, and Satan, is still considered a solitary being. In light of the misogynist literature that has resulted from attention to the Genesis account of the fall, one might be relieved that Rauschenbusch overlooks the biblical Eve in his discussion of evil. Yet his own assumption that the significance of the Adam-Eve relationship would merely locate Adam's virtue or fallenness in terms of his carnality suggests that the view of women he has portrayed here has not substantially changed from expressedly patriarchal ones.[35]

Where Rauschenbusch subsumes the couple into the individual male, Marx transfers his discussion of the male-female relationship into an analysis of the family in the context of a larger economic and political analysis. In *The Holy Family,* he quotes the French Utopian socialist Charles Fourier's statement that "the degree of emancipation of women is the natural measure of general emancipation."[36] As Juliet Mitchell notes in *Woman's Estate,* women's situation becomes for Marx a symbol of general social advance, and the problem of specific male-female relations gets lost in a discussion of modes of production.[37] She offers a similar critique of Engels. Ultimately, by proceeding with such haste from the relationship between the sexes to one between classes, Marx and Engels fail to recognize a major problem with their theory, i.e., their inability to explain how sex-differentiation gets transformed into a hierarchical opposition between males who take the dominant position and females who are subordinated.[38]

Marx seems as anxious as any "idealist" to get beyond what he would consider the purely biological (ahistorical) realm of reproduction into the specifically human realm of production. This unmediated leap from biology to history, from the individual to the many, may be related, as Mary O'Brien argues in *The Politics of Reproduction,* to the male experience of paternity, which is essentially abstract. The relation between the male seed and the child is not mediated by the physical act of giving birth but is recognized in (uncertain) thought and mediated in social processes such as the male appropriation of the child through naming.[39]

This still does not explain why men have found it so important to deny female experience in order to legitimate their own. Psychoanalysis, while it rests on the unproven assumption of the natural superiority of the male and his symbols (e.g., *phallus*), at least teaches us to look at the developmental process of human beings, beginning from infancy, for clues to personality formation. Several scholars have utilized psychoanalytic insights to investigate the relationship between mother-dominated child-rearing and what Freud termed "the natural contempt of the male toward the female." It is not my intention here to delve into the variations on psychoanalytic theory proposed in recent times;[40] however, I would like to suggest that the associations found between the separation of the sexes, mother dominated child-rearing, low estimation of women, identity-conflict in male children, and "protest masculinity" (to name but a few elements which feed into the antagonism between the sexes) are quite compelling. At the very least, they encourage us to look back at the relationship which is necessary for the birth of each new generation: the heterosexual couple.

Feminist theologians look at the relationship between men and women and see in it the paradigm for other forms of oppression. Rosemary Radford Ruether writes:

> . . . a most basic expression of human community, the I-Thou relation as the relationship of men and women, has been distorted throughout all known history into an oppressive relationship that has victimized one half of the human race and turned the other half into tyrants. The primary alienation and distortion of human relationality is reflected in all dimensions of alienation: from one's self as body, from the other as different from oneself, from nonhuman nature, and from God/ess.[41]

The relation between the oppression of women and other forms of oppression has documented evidence in written law: for example, the laws which were devised for the treatment of the slaves brought to America during the seventeenth century was patterned on the laws pertaining to women and children.[42]

There is a basis in Unification theology for an agreement with the feminist claim that the "root of sin is sexism." That such is the case may seem astonishing, given that the basis for the discussion of the fall in DP is precisely that story which feminists have almost universally agreed is lethal to women: the Genesis 3 myth. The peculiar twist which DP gives the story, however, has allowed it to function in the minds of many Unificationists as quite liberating to women.[43] The twist has to do with the archangel's role in the fall and with the assertion that, in restoration history, men are in the position to restore the "archangelic nature."[44]

In Unification theology, the fall is described as the failure of the first parents to reach maturity in their love of God (fulfill the first blessing) before uniting with each other as spouses. DP states that an archangel was commissioned to assist the first parents in their growth process. As they grew in their love of God, the angel began to feel that God loved him less. He was attracted by the beauty which Eve reflected as a daughter loved by God, and eventually, instead of helping her grow in the direction God had intended, he took her love for himself. DP then states that Eve, realizing at that point that it was Adam and not the archangel who was to be her spouse, tempted Adam in order to "rid herself of the fear derived from the fall and stand before God by becoming, even then, one body with Adam."[45] The premature relationship between Adam and Eve substantialized the unprincipled one between Eve and Lucifer, initiating life on the foundation of immature and selfish love.

I do not wish to discuss here the plausibility of the story as such. I simply would like to point out that the Unification Church's working out of its doctrine of the fall suggests a fundamental agreement with the feminist association of sexism with the root of evil. By situating the fall at the beginning of human history, Unification theology asserts that we have never experienced a true female-male relationship. In the first fallen act, a male being (archangel) improperly dominated a female being (Eve), and in the second, a female repeated this failure to relate to the other in terms of God's purpose. According to Unification theology, the misuse of love, and the pain and resentment which follows from being either an active or a passive participant in the denigration of this highest of gifts, runs throughout human history.[46]

Restoration

Restoration, according to Unification thinking, takes place in the reverse order of the fall. Since the fallen nature was passed from the archangel to Eve and then to Adam, then the initiator of the restoration process would be a man in the position of Adam. All other men stand in the position of restoring the archangel, and all women stand in the position of restoring Eve.[47]

Unification theology follows in the Christian tradition in its affirmation of Jesus' messianic mission and describes him as having fulfilled the purpose of creation on an individual level. As such, he is said to have reached oneness with God, or to "possess deity." Through Jesus, then, God can be said to have experienced on earth the perfection of God's masculine nature, and it is this aspect of God which has predominated in Christian consciousness. In Rev. Moon's words: "Up to this time well-meaning Christians have been receiving father's love only, not mother's. They inherited father's flesh and blood only, not mother's, because Jesus alone could only be a father."[48]

Jesus' single status is seen as problematic by Unificationists. Because God's will cannot be completed without human response, according to DP, any providential moment must be analyzed in its twofold components of divine call and human response. Unificationists do not necessarily interpret all the events of Jesus' life as foreordained by God. According to Rev. Moon's revelation, Jesus was to have married a woman in the position of restored Eve but was unable to accomplish this family level of restoration because of the failure of the people of his time to unite with him. Because of this failure, he had no existential understanding of true marital love,[49] and Christian history evidences moments of great difficulty in regarding marital love to be as valuable as other forms of love.[50] Rev. Moon asks:

> Where is the Kindgom of Heaven? The Kingdom of Heaven begins when you become a man and a woman of perfection, and the man finds the perfect woman and the woman finds the perfect man. . . . For two thousand years Christianity had no way to clearly understand the meaning of this so they have interpreted it by saying that the bridegroom is the symbol of the Lord and the bride represents Christianity and mankind.[51]

DP does not, however, deny the value of what Jesus did accomplish through his willingness to live out the implications of his love, even to the point of the cross: "Did his sacrifice on the cross then come to naught? Not at all . . . if it had, Christian history could not have existed. We can never deny the magnitude of the grace of redemption by the cross. [But the cross] . . . has been unable to establish the Kindgom of Heaven on earth."[52] DP claims that Jesus' sacrifice accomplished "spiritual salvation," but that we still await "physical salvation."[53] Physical salvation, according to Unification teaching, requires the establishment, by the messianic couple, of a four-position foundation on the family level, providing the substantial base for the incarnation of God on earth. Because there was no woman in the position of spouse to Jesus, Unification theology would hold that God has never fully experienced God's femininity and that we have not witnessed the "deity" of the female.

In its insistence on a male-female couple as the locus of restoration, Unificationism is in agreement with the feminist rejection of an exclusively male Christ. Unificationists would argue that rebirth must take place through a man and a woman. Their only sacrament, that of marriage, carries out this view. Like the Christian baptism, it is believed to offer spiritual rebirth, but unlike Christian baptism, it must be administered by a couple, at this point, Rev. and Mrs. Moon, representing God's fatherhood and motherhood. In this ceremony, women stand in the position of restoring Eve and they take the "mother" position to their mates, who work out their restoration through them. The goal of this restoration process is the liberation of God and humanity through a reunion of all polarities centered on love.

As one might expect, an emphasis on the married relationship carries with it its own set of problems. We are still left with the task of restoring centuries of selfish love and of overcoming cultural patterns which have their basis in the domination of one being or group by another. The DP's use of subject-object language to describe the husband-wife relationship leaves the door open for continued male oppression of women (and oppression of men by women who expect men to live out their lives for them). DP's emphasis on the circular dynamics of giving and receiving between spouses is often forgotten, for the "archangelic mode" of domination is disregarded only with great effort.

Certain Unification teachings and practices help to counter the patriarchal tendency, however. Ideally, DP teaches, men and women should develop their personalities as God-centered individuals before uniting as couples. Such a view encourages the individual growth of women as daughters of God. Indeed, the activities of the Unification woman by and large cause her to grow beyond the experiences of her countryfolk. I think, for example, of my Japanese friend who left her fishing village in Japan to come to New York City. She once said to me, "I have tasted world vision. I cannot go back to my little fishing village and just worry about my own family." The attitude of Rev. Moon himself, as suggested in the following words, gives reason to believe the Unification Church will encourage the development of strong and capable women:

> I would really like to see you beautiful sisters become fishing captains and go out to sea, being so knowledgeable and dedicated that men won't mind taking orders from you. . . . You may look tiny and weak, but when men on the ship are scared to death, you women will take command and give orders to rectify the situation.[54]

Also significant is the role the woman plays in the working out of the restoration process within a Unification marriage. The "mother position" which the woman takes covers approximately three years. If this is taken seriously, men are given the opportunity to see their spouses in ways which otherwise may never have been apparent. The wife takes the "parental role" in the position of "restored Eve." This is important, because the fact remains that despite doctrinal changes which incorporate femininity into the Godhead, men are seldom inclined to expect God's direction coming from a woman. This "mother position" institutionalizes such a possibility. The fact that this position has a time limit is also noteworthy. The image of women as loving mothers has often enough been used to keep women subservient to the demands of the child/husband. By establishing a time period for this type of relationship, Unification practice may be fulfilling a psychological need on the part of the male while at the same time demanding that women and men grow beyond this type of relationship into a mutual one.

Interracial and international marriage is encouraged in the Unification movement as a means to restore relationships between historically conflicting groups of people. This aspect of the movement has a direct effect on the understanding of male-female roles. Once one starts comparing long-cherished concepts of femininity and masculinity on a cross-cultural basis, one begins to discover their foundation in social custom rather than in some preordained description of the way things are. Both men and women change as they try to work out relationships in this international environment.

Just what exactly a restored relationship would "look like" is still in the process of being discovered by Unificationists. One assumes that since there are all types of people, there will also be many variations in ways people choose to live out their marriages. Rev. Moon has certain views about how men and women should relate in marriage, and I would be misrepresenting him were I to say that he does not in some way accent the male's initiating role. However, he does not argue for a relationship of one-way obedience. In a Unification magazine, *Today's World,* a Unification man gives his testimony of his experience of Rev. Moon's talk at the time of this man's wedding:

> Then Father gave us the formula for happiness. "Wives, always say 'yes' to your husbands." And we men were looking forward to this, remembering what St. Paul had said about obedience. But then Father added something we had not heard before: "Husbands, always say 'yes' to your wives." We were crestfallen. It took me some time to realize that if each serves the other completely, only Satan will be miserable.[55]

Rev. Moon constantly stresses the theme that women were made for men and men for women. The repeated emphasis of this notion, and its working out in theory and practice, has the potential to correct the tremendous asymmetry which now exists between the sexes. To use traditional biblical language, the scenario of Adam and his "helpmate" must be transformed to one of Adam and Eve as equally significant people.[56]

In Unification life, both men and women are encouraged to help each other fulfill their marriage by extending beyond the marriage into the society, the nation, and the worldwide providence. A concrete application of the idea that femininity and masculinity refer equally to internal (character) and external (form) aspects of God and the created universe would be the insistence that both women and men concern themselves with all levels of life—the biological as well as the historical, the home-related as well as the polis-related.

If the Unification movement lives up to the promise of its philosophy, it has the potential to encourage both men and women to take responsibility for themselves and for the situation of the world. At this stage in the movement's history, there are numerous opportunities for women and men to challenge their limits beyond what would have been possible through ordinary activities of their pre-Unification lives. Unificationists are presently in a position to imagine and create new living situations, new modes of organizing the public and private dimensions of life. Whether this opportunity will be eagerly seized or grudgingly accepted as simply a factor of "restoration life" depends on the imagination and strength of the Unification members themselves.

NOTES

1. *Divine Principle* (Washington, DC: HSA-UWC, 1973) is the English translation of the text *Wol-li Kang-ron* [Discourse on the Principle] (Seoul, Korea: Segye Kidokyo Tongil Shillyong Hyophwe, 1966) which was written by Hyo Won Eu, an early disciple of Rev. Moon, as a result of direct conversations with him.
2. The majority of speeches available through HSA-UWC publications are transcribed versions of impromptu sermons delivered by Rev. Moon to Unificationists on Sundays and church holidays. To audiences who speak neither Korean nor Japanese, he usually speaks Korean and uses a translator. Translation difficulties, as well as the extemporaneous nature of these speeches, should therefore be kept in mind when making use of them.
3. San Hun Lee, *Explaining Unification Thought* (New York: Unification Thought Institute, 1981).
4. Young Oon Kim, *Unification Theology* (New York: HSA-UWC, 1980).
5. Chung Hwan Kwak, *Outline of the Principle, Level 4* (New York: HSA-UWC, 1980).
6. Sun Myung Moon, "The Center of Responsibility and Indemnity" (New York: HSA-UWC, January 30, 1983), p. 5.
7. By "patriarchal culture," I mean generally one built on male models of reality, supporting male privilege ideologically, often at the expense of individual males and always at the expense of women (although women may internalize oppression to the point of not recognizing it).
8. See Kari Elisabeth Børresen's *Subordination and Equivalence* (Washington, DC: University Press of America, 1981), for an analysis of Thomas Aquinas' and Augustine's understanding of Genesis in light of I Corinthians. For an example of the second way of watering down the Genesis implications, see Karl Barth's *Church Dogmatics,* III/1 (Edinburgh: T. & T. Clark, 1957), p. 196.

9. *Divine Principle,* p. 41.
10. Unification theology, however, is not dependent on Genesis 1:28 to such an extent that it would fall apart if exegetes were to prove that this passage allowed no such interpretation.
11. See the discussion of the four-position foundation in *Divine Principle,* pp. 31ff., and in Kwak, pp. 20–21.
12. Unification theology uses various metaphors to describe the relation between God and creation. Most commonly used are parent-child, mind-body, and artist-work of art.
13. In *Explaining Unification Thought,* Dr. Lee explains that the Korean words are retained in the English texts because the English translations "character" and "form" do not adequately convey the Korean meaning (Lee, p. 16).
14. *Ibid.* See also discussion of heart, p. 21, and in Kwak, p. 13.
15. Lee, p. 10.
16. *Ibid.,* p. 14. The refusal to separate *hyung sang* from *sung sang* in the realm of cause is significant from a feminist perspective. As feminist theologians have pointed out, "patriarchal" theologians have largely polarized reality into hierarchical dualisms and have defined as feminine those aspects of each reality which were deemed inferior. According to this way of thinking, males have identified themselves with God, spirit, and rationality and have granted themselves absolute authority to dominate women, nature, the body, and emotion. Thus those aspects of reality which were related to the more receptive pole of each duality were systematically devalued and divorced from classical notions of divinity. Even though *hyung sang* is valued, however, it is still improper and unhelpful to associate it with femininity alone, for such an association tends to deny women the possibility for self-transcendence and growth.
17. Discussed in *ibid.,* pp. 17–18; *Divine Principle,* pp. 20ff., and Kwak, pp. 11ff.
18. *Divine Principle,* pp. 24–25.
19. Lee, pp. 51–52.
20. In fairness to Dr. Lee, it must be mentioned that he does distinguish between women and femininity and men and masculinity, although he maintains that women have more feminine characteristics and men more masculine ones. *Ibid.,* pp. 101–103.
21. Kim, pp. 56–60.
22. *Ibid.,* p. 55.
23. *Ibid.,* p. 56.
24. *Divine Principle,* p. 43.
25. Sun Myung Moon, "Waiting to Live in the Kingdom of Heaven" (New York: HSA-UWC, December 20, 1981), p. 7.
26. Moon, "Happy Unification Church Members" (New York: HSA-UWC, May 22, 1977), p. 4.
27. *Ibid.*
28. Moon, "God's Day 1984" (New York: HSA-UWC, January 1, 1984), p. 4.

29. *Ibid.*
30. Moon, "Our Ideal Home, Part Three" (New York: HSA-UWC, September 11, 1983), p. 12.
31. Moon, "The Center of Responsibility and Indemnity" (New York: HSA-UWC, January 30, 1983), p. 8.
32. Moon, "The Present Situation, Centering Upon the Will of God" (New York: HSA-UWC, May 23, 1982), p. 6.
33. *Ibid.*, p. 7. See also *Divine Principle,* p. 49.
34. Walter Rauschenbusch, *A Theology for the Social Gospel* (Nashville: Abingdon, latest printing of 1917 text, 1981), p. 51.
35. Schleiermacher makes a similar move in *The Christian Faith* (Philadelphia: Fortress Press, English translation of the second German edition of 1830, 1976) where, on p. 253, he claims that "righteousness in the ordinary sense is concerned only with more extended social relations, such as a first human pair could not possibly have."
36. Quoted form Juliet Mitchell, *Woman's Estate* (New York: Vintage Books, 1973), p. 77.
37. *Ibid.*, pp. 76–80. For a similar critique of Engels, see Shulamith Firestone, *The Dialectic of Sex* (New York: Morrow Quill Paperbacks, 1970), pp. 4–6.
38. This point is brought up by Isaac D. Balbus, *Marxism and Domination* (New Jersey: Princeton University Press, 1982), pp. 80–83.
39. Mary O'Brien, *The Politics of Reproduction* (Boston, London, and Henley: Routledge & Kegan Paul, 1983), especially Chapter 5.
40. Some useful works on the subject are: Nancy Chodorow, *The Reproduction of Mothering* (Berkeley: University of California Press, 1978); Dorothy Dinnerstein, *The Mermaid and the Minotaur* (New York: Harper & Row, 1976); Juliet Mitchell, *Psychoanalysis and Feminism* (New York: Vintage Books, 1974); and Philip Slater, *The Glory of Hera* (Boston: Beacon Press, 1968).
41. Rosemary Radford Ruether, *Sexism and God-Talk: Toward a Feminist Theology* (Boston: Beacon Press, 1983), p. 161.
42. See Mary Ryan, *Womanhood in America* (New York: Watts, 1975), pp. 4–25.
43. See Sarah Petersen, "Sexism and Sin: Feminist Unification Possibilities," unpublished paper delivered at a conference on "Feminist Philosophy and Theology," sponsored by New ERA in Nassau, March, 1984.
44. Some distinction must be made, however, between being in the position to restore a particular nature, and always and at all times manifesting that nature. As examples of types of fallen nature, Adam, Eve and the archangel all represent ways of being "fallen" which both women and men have to deal with.
45. See discussion of the fall in *Divine Principle,* pp. 65ff.; and in Kwak, pp. 39ff.
46. *Divine Principle* recognizes that evil can expand beyond the proportions of its origins, taking on new dimensions in the process. Along with original sin, *Divine Principle* also refers to collective, hereditary, and individual sin (pp. 88–

89). Discussions of the social implications of Unification doctrine can be found in *Restoring the Kingdom,* ed. Deane William Ferm (New York: Paragon House, 1984).

47. The woman's role in the restoration process is less often discussed in Unification teachings than is the "Adamic" role. One reason for this is certainly historical: since *Divine Principle's* discussion of restoration history is derived largely from Old Testament sources, it is limited by the fact that the writers of these stories emphasized the "patriarchs." The concentration on the Adamic figure might also be grounded in the dynamics set up by the Unification idea that restoration takes place in reverse order of the fall, thus making the first concern of providential history the restoration of the "true Adam." Ultimately, however, full restoration requires a relationship between a perfected man and a perfected woman.

48. Moon, "How Can We Become One with God?" (unpublished speech, delivered January 15, 1972), p. 2. In other places, Rev. Moon has said that Jesus couldn't fully experience parental love, thus qualifying the manner in which we can even speak of Jesus as a father. It should be mentioned that *Divine Principle* speaks of the holy spirit's functioning as the spiritual bride of Jesus and as the spiritual mother of Christians (p. 213ff.). The exact nature of the holy spirit is never clearly defined, however. In Dr. Kim's *Unification Theology* (pp. 199–203) we get a picture of the holy spirit which goes beyond a feminine characterization. In a congratulatory address given by one of the church elders on the occasion of the marriage of In Jin Nim Moon (second daughter of Rev. and Mrs. Moon) we read: "Traditionally, in God there is the Father, the Son and the Holy Spirit. But we know that in God's nature there is True Father and Mother, and the Holy Son, and the Holy Spirit who is actually the Holy Daughter" (Young Whi Kim, quoted in *Today's World,* New York: HSA-UWC, March, 1984, p. 22).

    Basically, it is a Unification claim that however much the holy spirit may function as a mother, giving spiritual rebirth with Jesus to humankind, a living human female is necessary for the initiation of the process of complete rebirth.

49. Rev. Moon, in "God and the Building of the Kingdom of God," p. 11, says that "Jesus Christ cannot fully echo the words of God when he is talking about the love of husband and wife and the love of parents and children. Without his own experiences in that area, even Jesus cannot fully share the feelings of God."

50. Derrick S. Bailey provides a useful histoiy of this ambivalence in *Sexual Relation in Christian Thought* (New York: Harper & Brothers Publishers, 1959). There is a sense in which Unificationists would agree with the rightness of the ambivalence expressed toward marriage. According to Unification theology, because Jesus was unable to restore the marriage relationship substantially through his own marriage, marriage as the highest expression of divine love has not yet been made possible.

51. Moon, pp. 10–11.

52. *Divine Principle,* p. 142.

53. In his "Mission of Jesus" lecture delivered August, 1983, in Madeira, Portugal (available through the New ERA office), Anthony Guerra suggested a parallel between the Unification notions of physical and spiritual salvation and the traditional Christian notions of justification and sanctification, respectively. One might also speak of individual salvation as spiritual salvation, and family-level salvation as physical salvation.
54. Moon, "Our Newborn Selves" (New York: HSA-UWC, November 1, 1977).
55. John Kirkley, "The Blessing," in *Today's World* (September, 1983), p. 35. See also Moon, *New Hope: Twelve Talks by Sun Myung Moon* (New York: HSA-UWC, 1973), p. 53.
56. The restoration of symmetry is still wanting in the Unification movement as well. Despite quotations from Rev. Moon (such as that referred to in footnote 27) which argue for men and women being equally primordial in the mind of God, we occasionally hear statements such as, "the original individual image of man in the inner *hyung sang* of God (before the creation of the universe) was none other than the image of Adam himself . . . God then thought of another human, Eve, the helper for Adam, based on the image of Adam" (Lee, p. 69).

12

Earthly Love and Divine Love: A Secular Path to Mysticism in XIII Century Italy

GABRIELE ERASMI

Beauty, wherever it is seen, whether in humanity or in the vegetable or mineral world, is God's revelation of himself; He is the all-beautiful, those objects in which we perceive beauty being, as it were, so many mirrors in each of which some fraction of His essential self is revealed. By virtue of its Divine origin, the beauty thus perceived exercises a subtle influence over the beholder, waking in him the sense of love, whereby he is at last enabled to enter into communion with God himself. Thus God is the ultimate object of every lover's passion; but while this is as yet unrealized by the lover, while he still imagines that the earthly fair one is the true inspirer and final goal of his affection, his love is still in the 'typal stage', and he himself still on the 'allegoric bridge'![1] (Fazil, d. 1811. trans. E. J. W. Gibb)

In the second half of the thirteenth century, first at Bologna and then in Florence, a new school of poetry emerged which was to obliterate the notions of courtly love as traditionally expressed by the Provençal poets and their imitators. This new school took its name from a line in Dante's *Purgatorio,* where it was referred to as 'dolce stil novo' or 'the sweet new style.'[2] Indeed, it was so novel both in form and content that the founder of the school, the Bolognese Jurist Guido Guinizelli, was accused of "having changed the character of the pleasing utterances of Love."[3] This new character of love poetry first transpired in a song by Guinizelli which became the manifesto and the constant point of reference for the new poets.[4] If the contemporaries were at first struck by the difficult conceptual style of the song, a style that betrayed the atmosphere of learning of the University of Bologna, the real novelty of the poem consisted in two ideas. The notion of the 'gentle heart,' developed in the first four stanzas as a material and formal condition for the existence of love, which is thus equated with it, has usually been deemed to be the real point of departure for the new school. The other idea, that of 'the woman made an angel' which is presented in the last two stanzas of the poem, has been treated ambiguously. It has been noted that "while for the Provençals love meant paying faithful homage to the beauty and wisdom of a lady, who is implored respectfully for her favors and is deemed a source of virtue, the poets of *dolce stil novo* ennobled that idea and raised it to the threshold of Heaven."[5] For them "Love became a trepid adoration of a perfect being . . . an angel, in whom one finds happiness and comfort and from whose goodness and beauty radiates a higher spirituality."[6] It has been noted also that these poets are anything but consistent in adopting this idea, which is truly relevant only in Dante's *Vita Nuova* and will be fully explored only through the monumental effort of the *Divine Comedy.*

Even in Guinizelli's poems this notion is never developed and surfaces here and there only in fragmentary form. Were it not for the aforementioned song and for some scattered intuitions that we read today as anticipations of Dante, Guinizelli should be placed, as he was himself inclined to do, among the followers of Guittone, the main exponent of the Provençal tendency in Italy.[7] It is equally clear, however, that without this poem that exercised so much influence on the works of Dante and Guido Cavalcanti, the history of Italian and European poetry would have been quite different. To make it conceptually possible for Beatrice to open for Dante the mystical path to Empireum and become, thus, the symbolic bridge through which human love is transcended into divine love, it would not be enough to invoke the *Domina Philosophia* of Boethius,[8] nor the *Itinerarium mentis ad Deum* of St. Bonaventure,[9] nor the *De Causis* of Albertus Magnus,[10] nor, finally, the theories of love of Bernard of Clairvaux.[11] If Boethius could help in the transformation of Beatrice into an allegory of knowledge, if Bonaventure and Albertus could offer Dante the notion that the light of God revealed itself in the finite aspects of his creation, if Bernard could teach him the necessity of transcending love of self and of thy neighbour into divine love according to the indications of St. Augustine,[12] no one had ever asserted that earthly love for an earthly creature could open the way to the revelation of divine love. This revolutionary thesis, without precedent in Western thought, is presented for the first time in the two final stanzas of the Guinizelli song.[13]

In the first one of them, he introduces that same theory of light which Dante was to employ in this *Paradiso* and which originated in Bonaventure and Robert Grosseteste.[14] Illuminated by God, celestial intelligences turn freely to him through the heavenly spheres. Bonaventure had added that even man is illuminated by a spark of that divine light; therefore his destiny is to partake of the same happiness of heavenly intellects. By looking inside himself, within his own soul, and by looking out of himself to other created things, man will see a reflection of the light emanating from God and will be able to turn to it. Guinizelli re-elaborates these arguments in order to arrive, in the first four stanzas of the poem, at the postulation of the identity of love with the 'gentle heart.' Presupposing, therefore, the idea that divine light is reflected in the objects of creation, he concludes that through the reflected light that shines in the eyes of his beloved, man will be able to catch a glimpse of God, or, in other words, by loving a woman, he will love, by reflection, God. It is clear at this point that the theory of courtly love has been turned into a mystical path where a worldly conception of love coexists in dangerous balance with the traditions of Western mysticism.[15]

There is, indeed, a very serious risk of heresy for, as soon as we lose sight of the symbolic aspect of the mystical experience, we confuse the intuition of the concept with its ideal reality. In such an instance, the contemplation of the beloved would become the contemplation of God upon earth, and the resemblance of the creature with its creator would vanish into the potential identity of the creature with its creator. We would then have to replace the notion of the transcendence of God with the one of its immanence, and the "valley of tears" would itself become paradise. Starting from the mystical ideas of the Christian Bonaventure, we'll reach a conception completely foreign even to Platonism. Guinizelli is aware of this danger: in his last stanza he proceeds immediately to assert the impossibility of identifying earthly love with divine love. After death, when the poet will appear before God and face his eventual reproach, he will be able to say:

> An Angel she appeared to me
> of thine own kingdom;
> it was not my fault that I placed my love in her. (58–60)

The song ends with a mirthful smile and the sustained doctrine of the Bolognese Jurist resolves itself in poetry: love has been a vain conceit, but a beautiful one nonetheless. Its image was comforting, even though there was no reality to it.

We may understand better, at this point, the idea that Dante had of poetry as "a beautiful lie."[16] It has the same quality as the light emanating from the angelic woman. Says Beatrice in the *Paradiso:*

> Turn and listen;
> for not only in my eyes is paradise.[17]

The poetics of *dolce stil novo* is all here, in the platonic contemplation of beauty; such a contemplation becomes torment and passion and the soul dies when, as in Cavalcanti, it becomes conscious of the impossibility of the union between the creature and its creator, or it opens itself to the hope of grace when, as in Dante, love is purified by understanding and sustained by faith. These two attitudes are already implicit in Guinizelli. Critics have not paid sufficient attention to the conditional used in lines 47–50:

> Thus, woman in her beauty
> which shines in the eyes
> of her beloved, *should give*
> him such love for truth
> that he can never withdraw from her service.[18]

Because of it, the theory that divine intellect can be contemplated by man through the love that illuminates him could be interpreted as a mere possibility, an enticing analogy, which could be used to heighten the meaning of the experience of earthly love, or conversely, to stress its limitations, but which should not be taken too seriously for it could lead, as already noted, to doctrinal error and heresy. But there is another possibility: the conditional could be read as a conditional of opinion or hearsay, i.e., the poet would be merely reporting a notion, without necessarily assenting to it. Clearly, it is not his intention to present such a theory within the framework of formal Christian theology. Since poetry and love poetry are a secular activity, his goal is, instead, the renewal of the stale poetics of courtly love through the adaptation of its traditions to the new conditions of Italian society in the thirteenth century.

Such a society is characterized by a tension between a renewed religious spirit, oriented toward mysticism and the renunciation of the world, and an energetic assertion of secular values as a consequence of the rise of the bourgeoisie. The theory of the 'gentle heart,' which replaces the Provençal notion of aristocratic birth, revitalizes the poetics of courtly love by adapting it to the changing social conditions in Italy and, in addition, the theory of the angelic woman operates a successful compromise between the conflicting secular and mystical tendencies of this same society. The Franciscan movement, as one can infer from repeated formulae in the Cortona laudarium, had already defined the human aspirations to God as *fin amanza,* or *fin amour.*[19] If, as De Sanctis wrote, "knowledge was the mother of Italian poetry and its first inspiration came from the schools" and "a man of knowledge—read Guinizelli—was the father of Italian literature,"[20] we understand better how learning and mysticism could become fused into a new poetics, which, while continuing the Provençal tradition, differed from it for its social commitment and for its adherence to concrete existential conditions. Its novelty consists in allowing man to turn to God, the supreme aspiration of the age, without rejecting the world, which is the field of the endeavors of the new bourgeois society. The *Divine Comedy* is both the culminating achievement of *dolce stil novo* and the coherent synthesis of the Middle Ages. In it, political and social commitment go hand in hand with mystical aspirations and if, in the final analysis, it is the tale of a personal mystical experience, such experience is made possible by an initial commitment to an earthly love, which is progressively transcended.

As we have seen, this ideology, for it is ultimately far more than a poetics, emerged for the first time in the Guinizelli song, but its presuppositions cannot be found in, nor can they be derived from, contemporary theological notions. Just as the new fervor of political and economic life had to reconcile itself, somehow, to the renunciation of the world preached by Christian ideology, the idea of the angelic woman constitutes a doctrinally spurious, logically improbable, graft on the trunk of Christian asceticism. What continues to prevent us from realizing its alien quality and its important ideological significance is its inevitable link with the Provençal tradition. After the Albigensian Crusade, the last troubadors had moved toward a Platonic idealization of woman. This would argue in favour of the continuity between that tradition and the new Italian poetry. But while such a continuity exists, it is a mere literary continuity that fails to account for the relation between literary conceits and contemporary ideology and risks limiting the understanding of the different phases of courtly love as merely irrelevant fashions current in the upper classes.

Today, we can no longer doubt or ignore the complex link between Provençal culture and the superior Islamic civilization.[21] The increasing number of translations of Arabic poets from Spain shows that they had sung of woman and love in the same forms employed by the troubadors long before they did.[22] Yet we find it difficult to accept such a notion since our perception of the Arab woman remains that of an object of pleasure locked up in a harem, without other functions in a society completely dominated by males. We forget, however, that this abject condition of women never existed at the time of the great Islamic civilization, but was the progressive consequence of the successive Turkish conquest which led to the end of that civilization. We forget also, used as we are to the Romantic idealization of woman through seven centuries of European literature, that such a conception was, as S. Painter has shown, as foreign to the Medieval Germanic world as it was to the preceding Greco-Roman civilization.[23]

The question we must answer, and I do not think such an answer has been provided so far, is what were the conditions that created the premises for such an idealization of woman that also later found so much favor in the West? It is clear that only a partial answer could come from the study of the historical conditions of women in the Arab world.[24] Such conditions were probably not too different in the West, at least in some basic aspects. The answer is to be found rather, as always, in the relationship between literature and ideology.

The exaltation of earthly love among the Arab poets of Spain and the other provinces of the vast Islamic empire emerges and is developed within the context of the Muslim conception of life. If the latter admits to a paradise after death, Allah, the God creator, transcends completely its creation and reveals himself only through it. Mohammed is his prophet only insofar as he has perceived this truth. The created world is, thus, pervaded with the presence of God. He does not reveal himself in history as Christ does, he reveals himself all the time through his creation. God is everywhere in nature as well as in man. This pantheistic interpretation of reality, which Christianity has always rejected, leads to the important consequence that while man is painfully conscious of the transitory nature of things, he will not renounce the world in his aspiration to the eternal.

Ibn Hazm (994–1064) writes:

Were it not that this world below is a transitory abode of trial and tribulation, and paradise a home where virtue receives its reward, secure from all annoyances, I would have said that union with the beloved is that pure happiness which is without alloy, and gladness unsullied by sorrow the perfect realization of hopes and the complete fulfilment of one's dreams.[25]

In his search for the purest of pleasures, man will seek in nature that part in which divine aspects are most immediately manifest. Platonism, the constituent element of both Arab and Christian mysticism, is grafted onto this conception of the divine and causes the rise of Sufi mysticism.

Since God is the perfect form of being, man, who is separated from it, desires to become part of it. This desire is love, which is defined by Ibn Hazm as the reciprocal approach to the form in which being is completed. "Love is, therefore, a spiritual attachment, a fusion of souls." The cause of love, according to him, "is an externally beautiful form, because the soul is beautiful and yearns passionately for everything that is beautiful and inclines toward perfect images. If it sees an image similar to itself, it becomes fixed on it; and if it finds in it something of its own nature, it is irresistibly attracted to it and true love is produced. But if it fails to see beyond the image something of its own nature, its affection does not go beyond the form." In this search for the form that completes us, and we seek something similar to us, love for a concrete woman becomes inevitable. Ibn Hazm writes again: "I see a human form, but if I meditate more deeply, she appears to me as a body from the celestial spheres.[26] Guinizelli's angelic woman finds in this passage its clearest definition.

Awhadeddin Kermani defines the relationship between created forms and reality in even more explicit terms:

If my bodily eye gazes on created forms of beauty, that is because outward forms bear the impress of the inner meaning. We live in a world of forms and we cannot behold realities otherwise than through images and forms.[27]

We begin to realize that, for the Sufis, the beauty of the created form is an image of the divine beauty present in it, and is, therefore, a possible intermediary between man and God exactly as it was postulated in Guinizelli's lines 47–50 quoted earlier. As for the possibility of perceiving the ultimate form through the external beauty of forms, Al Ghazali (1059–1111), perhaps the greatest among the Sufis, has this to say:

As for the fourth reason (of love), it is to love every beautiful thing for its own beauty, and not for any satisfaction which can come from it. . . . Beauty can be external beauty, which is perceived with the eye of the head, or it may be internal beauty, which is perceived with the eye of the heart. . . . To perceive the second sort is the special property of men of heart, and none may share in it who know only the life of the lower world. All beauty is beloved by a perceiver of beauty, and if he perceives it with his heart, it becomes his heart's beloved. . . . So then, what is beautiful is to be loved, and the absolutely beautiful is the One who has no equal. . . . [28]

For Al Ghazali, as for Guinizelli, pure love is possible only for the man with a 'gentle heart.'

It remains to be seen to what extent human love, no matter how pure, can be transcended and become divine love. If we say that this is possible, man, through the sublimation of love, will identify himself with the beauty hidden in the created form, and will achieve, therefore, perfect harmony with the One. This possibility, already present in Indian mysticism, and expressed already in the Upanishads in the formula *tat tvam asi,* influences initially the Sufis and leads, thus, to the assertion that man is God.[29] Such a statement is unacceptable to both Christianity and Islam, and Guinizelli proceeds immediately to reject its implications:

When before God my soul shall stand, 'A mere woman,' he will ask, 'did you presume eternal? You crossed the heavens and up to me you came, all the while yourself deceiving in empty love. To me alone praise is due and to the queen of the eternal kingdom; cease then your vain fraud.' (51–57)

Al Hallaj (857–922) had dared hold this notion; he was deemed a heretic and was executed.[30] After this tragedy, the Sufis moved toward two antithetical positions. Among the judges who had indicted Al Hallaj, there was Ibn Dawud (d. 909), the author of the *Book of the Flower.* Maintaining a rigidly orthodox stance, he preached love, no matter how pure, can only be earthly love.[31] To reach God, we must first die, and Ibn Dawud died of love. In other words, man can only love God through his creation, can turn to God only with the words with which we express our love for a woman; to presume more than that would be a "fraud," a deceit of the imagination, a blasphemy.

Among the followers of Al Hallaj there were Ahmad Ghazali (d. 1126) and Ruzbehan Baqli of Shiraz (d. 1209). Avoiding the extremism of their teacher, they made a distinction between the apparent form of being and its hidden meaning. If, for Ibn Dawud, the hidden sense remained veiled, for Ahmad Ghazali and Ruzbehan it constituted the link, or bridge, between human and divine love. For Ruzbehan, divine love was not the transferring of love to a divine object, but the metamorphosis of the subject of human love.[32] As in St. Augustine, through the search for the objectivity of being we clarify its subjectivity within man. As long as man remains anchored to the notion of human love, he does not go beyond the allegorical level. Only when he will no longer distinguish the part from the whole, the external from the internal, and shall speak to God as if he spoke to a woman and shall speak to a woman as if he spoke to God, he will succeed in crossing 'the allegorical bridge' posited by Ruzbehan. As Jami (d. 1492) wrote later:

> When Beauty absolute beams all around, why linger finite beauties to embrace?[33]

Elsewhere he had also written:

> That heart which seems to love the fair ones of this world, loves Him alone.[34]

The homage of the Sufi mystic to the image of God, which is revealed to him through woman, becomes thus an homage to him whom she represents and symbolizes. At this point woman becomes, as in Ibn Arabi's *Futuhat* (1165–1240) and in Dante's *Divine Comedy,* a symbol of knowledge and man's guide to ultimate fulfillment.

Guinizelli does not go this far; with his witty ending he avoids taking a position and if, on one hand, when God scolds him, he appears to adumbrate the thesis of Ibn Dawud, on the other hand, in his answer to God he also leaves an opening for the thesis of Ruzbehan and Ibn Arabi. If it is now clear that it was in the Arab world that the ideological conditions for the idealization of woman were determined, it will be useful to add also that the Sufi conception of love was expressed in a symbolic and picturesque language, which is never far from poetry. In truth, the Sufis were poets, and their writings, which alternate prose and verse, could be considered the archetypal models for Dante's *Vita Nuova.*[35] The Sufis caused the rise of a varied erotic literature where, at times, eroticism was only the literal form of a poetry which concealed underneath it an allegorical significance. It is worth remembering that Ibn Arabi, like Dante, was compelled to write commentaries in order to show that his love poetry had actually a totally different meaning.[36] The love notions of the Sufis, bound as they are, to the joyful fruition of this world, could not be taken up by Christian theology, which connected life on earth with original sin, but they could address themselves to the concern of a new man who, first in Provence and then in the Italy of the Communes, was beginning the revaluation of life on earth. There, with St. Francis, the aspiration to the eternal was tempered by a serene acceptance of this world which is a divine creation; moreover, the rise of a new society with its universities and its contacts with the Arab world of Sicily and Spain,[37] allowed, inevitably, for an easier penetration of these ideas—especially since, on a different level, there were specific conditions and attitudes compatible with Sufi ideas. If for the Sufis, ours is a world of images of the divine, the Christian cult of the time filled its churches and cathedrals with frescoes and statues, whose purpose was the elevation of man's thoughts to God. And these images were considered sacred. Indeed, the Pseudo-Dionysius had written that "perceptible images lead us in great measure to divine speculation,"[38] and Basil the Great had similarly asserted that "The adoration of the icon passes to the prototype, that is to say, to the holy person represented."[39]

Sixty-four years ago, Miguel Asin Palacios revealed the profound resemblances between the works of Ibn Arabi and the *Divine Comedy.*[40] He showed also not only the possibility that Dante might have known the Arabic philosophical tradition, but that he had a great interest in it. His thesis was accepted by Islamists but continues to remain controversial among Italian scholars.[41] It is obvious that from the point of view of the latter, the *Divine Comedy* can only be understood as the final development of *dolce stil novo,* which Palacios substantially ignored. He limited himself to point out the Averroistic tendencies of Cavalcanti[42] and barely mentioned Guinizelli.[43] Similarly, he barely mentions Ibn Dawud[44] and seems to ignore Ruzbehan and Ahmad Ghazali, whose love theories are so close to the ones of *dolce stil novo.* Finally, he was inclined to see in some aspects of Sufism definite influences of Christian mysticism. Therefore, he tended to underestimate its ideological value and overestimated its external similarities. But if we succeeded in proving that the basic premises of *dolce stil novo,* the ideas of the 'gentle heart' and the 'angelic woman,'[45] can truly make sense only in connection with Sufi attitudes, and, therefore, that the path from Guinizelli to the *Divine Comedy* is a process of continuous analysis of those concepts, the remaining objections to the work of Palacios should subside.

The merit of Guinizelli who, as a professor at Bologna around 1270, might have had contacts with many of the translators from the courts of Frederick and Manfred, is in his ability to see, in these ideas from the Islamic world, the possibility of their adaptation to a society which was about to emerge from the Middle Ages, and which, even after Dante, through the mediation of Petrarch,[46] would continue for five more centuries to see in the love for a woman the supreme human experience.

NOTES

1. F. C. Happold, *Mysticism: A Study and an Anthology* (Penguin Books, 1970), p. 253.
2. Dante, *Purgatorio* XXIV, 57.
3. In a sonnet that begins with these lines: "Voi, ch'avete mutata la mainera/de li plagenti ditti de l'amore," its author, Bonagiunta Orbicciani from Lucca, who lived in the second part of the XIII century, scolded Guido Guinizelli for having introduced obscurity and learned language into poetry.
4. See Gustavo Adolfo Ceriello, *I Rimatori del Dolce Stil Novo* (Milano: Rizzoli [B.U.R.], 1950), pp. 20–23. This *canzone* is the fifth among 25 compositions by Guinizelli (pp. 13–41). A famous English translation is the one by Dante Gabriele Rossetti.
5. Giorgio Petrocchi, "Il Dolce Stil Novo," *Storia della Letteratura Italiana: Le origini e il Duecento,* Vol. 1 (Milano: Garzanti), p. 615.
6. *Ibid.,* p. 615 (my translation).
7. Guinizelli wrote a sonnet (XXIII), (see Ceriello, p. 37), addressed to Guittone d'Arezzo, where he called him father, praised his achievements, and submitted himself to his judgment.
8. Dante quotes or refers to Boethius a number of times: *Par.* X, 124–129; *Inf.,* V, 121–123; *Conv.* I, II, 13; II, XII, 2; II, XV, 1; I, XI, 8; II, VII, 4; II, X, 3; III, I, 10; III, II, 17; IV, XII, 4–7; IV, XIII, 12–14; *Mon.* I, IX, 3; II, VIII, 13; *Epist.* XIII, 89. Interesting for our purposes is *Conv.* II, XII, 2–8, where, under the stimulus of *De Consolatione Philosophiae,* where Boethius personified philosophy as a woman, Dante writes: " . . . giudicava bene che la filosofia, che era la donna di questi autori, di queste scienze e di questi libri fosse somma cosa. E immaginava lei fatta come una donna gentile, e non la poteva immaginare in atto alcuno, se non misericordioso. . . . "

9. While Dante refers to Bonaventure in *Par.* XII, he does not refer to the *Itinerarium,* that mystical work influenced by Avicenna (Ibn Sina) and Augustine, which many have considered an influence on the development of *Dolce Stil Novo.*

10. Dante refers to Albertus Magnus in *Par.* X, 97–99; he refers more specifically to *De Intellectu* in *Conv.* III, VII, 3 and there are additional references in *Conv.* II, XII, 21; IV, XXIII, 13; III, V, XII.

11. The mystical Bernard of Clairvaux is, of course, Dante's guide to Empireum (*Par.,* XXXII, 107; XXXI, 59–69, 94ff.–XXXIII, 50. In *Epist.* XIII, 80 Dante refers also to *De consideratione.*

12. Dante refers to St. Augustine fairly often; he knew the *Confessions* (*Conv.* I, II, 14), *De Civitate Dei* (*Mon.* III, IV, 7), *De Doctrina Christiana* (*Mon.* III, IV, 8), *De Quantitate Animae* (*Epist.,* III, 80).

13. For the text, see my translation of the two stanzas in question in the appendix.

14. The theory of light appears in the *Itinerarium, De Scientia Christi,* and in the *Commentary* to Peter Lombard; Robert Grosseteste presented his theory of light in *De inchoatione formarum* and *De Luce.* Both of them, while aspiring to a return to Augustinian Platonism, were influenced by the cosmology of Al-Farabi and Avicenna.

15. Western mystics never posit a concrete object of love as a possible intermediary between man and God. Their language is always abstract. When Thomas Aquinas speaks of spiritual love as the result of contemplating spiritual beauty and goodness, "Contemplatio spiritualis pulchritudinis vel bonitatis est principium amoris spiritualis" (Summa theol. I, II, quaestio 27, art. 2), he obviously implies that the mystic must transcend the concrete and the material, which cannot, therefore, be the object of spiritual love.

16. Dante, *Convivio,* II, 1, 4.

17. Dante, *Paradiso,* XVII, 20–21; see also XV, 32–36.

18. The text is particularly difficult; what I translated as "for truth" is, for some, the adverbial "in truth"; Rossetti, while translating differently, interpreted as I do. There are also other problems of interpretation, for which see again Petrocchi, pp. 624.

19. Cortona, *Laudarium* 93. A selection of these poems, set to music, is in the Nonesuch Records Series.

20. Francesco De Sanctis, *Storia della Letteratura Italiana* (Milano: Barion, 1937), p. 29 (Chapter 2: "I Toscani").

21. See in general, for this question, Robert Briffault, *The Troubadors,* edited by Lawrence F. Koons (Bloomington: Indiana University Press, 1965), particularly Ch. 2; and Sydney Painter, *French Chivalry* (Ithaca, N.Y.: Cornell University Press, 1957), p. 110.

22. For the forms see again Briffault, pp. 24–79 and, for additional texts see A. J. Arberry, *Aspects of Islamic Civilization* (Ann Arbor: The University of Michigan Press, 1967), pp. 256–278.

23. Painter, pp. 95–106; see also Bede Jarret, *Social Theories of the Middle Ages* (Boston, 1926), pp. 70–73.

24. See Gustave E. von Gurnebaum, *Medieval Islam* (Chicago: University of Chicago Press, 1969), pp. 170–220.

25. James Kritzeck, *Anthology of Islamic Literature* (Penguin Books, 1964), pp. 147–148. The complete text of Ibn Hazm's *The Dove's Necklace* has been edited by A. R. Nykl, in *A Book Containing the Risala Known as "the Dove's Neck-Ring" about Love and Lovers* (Paris, 1932).

26. This and the immediately preceding texts are quoted in Henry Corbin, *Histoire de la philosophie Islamique* (Paris: Gallimard, 1964). (Italian Transl. by Vanna Calasso as *Storia della Filosofia Islamica* [Milano: Adelphi, 1973], pp. 227–231.)

27. Quoted by Cyprian Rice, *The Persian Sufis* (London: G. Allen, 1964), p. 102.

28. See John Alden Williams, *Islam* (New York: Washington Square Press, 1961), p. 187. Note that Dante refers to Al Ghazali on substance in *Conv.* II, XIII, 5 and on the nature of the soul in IV, XXI, 2.

29. I am not too sure of the extent to which the Sufis may have been influenced by Indian philosophy; I am told that there is quite a bibliography on the subject. In any case, given the general contacts at different levels between India and the Arab world, it is not unlikely that Buddhism, on the one hand, and Tantric practices on the other may have also exercised some indirect influence on the Sufis. But the most important influence must have come from Advaita Vedanta. According to its monistic doctrines, as exemplified by the teachings of Sankara, the world as we know it is a projection of Brahman, but it is *Māyā,* the effect of magic or illusion, and has no reality. The only reality is Brahman, with which the individual soul is identical. If the soul can learn to ignore the illusion and concentrate on itself, it will achieve union with the Brahman. This process of meditation is the path that leads to salvation. This doctrine presents clear analogies with the attitudes assumed by Al Hallaj. For Sankara and *Advaita Vedānta,* see Karl H. Potter, *Presupposition of India's Philosophies* (Englewood Cliffs: Prentice-Hall, 1963), pp. 164–167. See also A. L. Basham, *The Wonder that Was India* (New York: Grove Press, 1959), pp. 327–328.

30. L. Massignon, *La Passion d'al-Hallaj* (Paris, 1922); see also, Claud Field, *Mystics and Saints of Islam* (London, 1910), pp. 68–78.

31. For an account of Ibn Dawud see Corbin, pp. 202–203.

32. See Corbin, pp. 202–205. Corbin has also translated and edited the work of Ruzbehan as *Le Jasmin des Fidèles d'amour* (Paris: Adrien-Maisonneuve, 1958). Helmut Ritter has edited the *Intuitions of the Faithful of Love,* and there is now an English translation in the Gibb Memorial Series.

33. Happold, p. 252.

34. See John Alden Williams, p. 153.

35. We should keep in mind, however, that Boethius' *De consolatione philosophiae,* so often alluded to in Dante (see Note 8), must have been, with its alternation of prose and verse, the more immediate model that Dante could imitate.

36. Alfred Guillame, *Islam* (Baltimore: Penguin Books, 1969), p. 150.

37. See Bernard Lewis, *The Arabs in History* (New York: Harper & Row, 1966), pp. 115–130 and 164–165.
38. Quoted by Grabar Chatzidakis, *Byzantine and Early Medieval Painting* (New York: Viking Press, 1965), p. 4.
39. *Ibid.,* p. 4.
40. Miguel Asin Palacios, *La escatologia musulmana en la Divina Comedia* (Madrid, 1919; Tercera Edicion: Madrid, 1961). English translation by Harold Sutherland, as *Islam and the Divine Comedy* (London: Cass, 1968).
41. See, however, a more recent book by Enrico Cerulli, *Il "Libro della Scala" e la questione delle fonti Arabo-Spagnole della "Divina Commedia"* (Citta del Vaticano, 1949), for a more favourable attitude.
42. See the English translation, pp. 255n, 271.
43. *Ibid.,* p. 64, 271.
44. *Ibid.,* p. 273: "Ibn Daud of Ispahan, in his *Book of Venus* of the ninth century, analyses and defends Romantic Love."
45. It has been pointed out that the notion of 'donna angelicata' may have been present already in the followers of Guittone. Petrocchi (p. 621f.) refers specifically to Inghilfredi, Guittone himself, and Guilhelm de Saint Gregory. But the uneasiness of the Guittonians *vis-à-vis* Guinizelli's poetry is in itself evidence of a radical transformation of the ideals of courtly love and of a doctrinal depth not evident in their work. Secondly, their vague references to the angelic qualities of the woman are reduced to similes and metaphors of popular origin, derived in turn from the iconography of angels in painting and sculpture. It is well known that these representations imitated the image of the winged victory of the Greeks, and this changed the ephebic *angelos* of the Gospels into a feminine image. Thus, in consideration of the complex notions in Guinizelli, the popular references to women as angels cannot constitute a conceptual precedent, especially when such references occur in such contexts as the following:

    L'altra sera, ben mio, vinni al tuo letto
    Un angelo del cielo me parivi

    (The other night, my dear, I approached your bed and you looked like an angel from heaven.) See again Petrocchi, *ibid.,* p. 621f.
46. Petrarch's love poetry, while derived initially from the conceits of 'dolce stil novo,' moves progressively to a more secular vision of woman, increasingly represented as an entirely earthly but sublime creature, whose love can inspire man to fulfil himself on earth and could console man for his mortality. Petrarch is, thus, the necessary link between 'dolce stil novo' and Romanticism.

APPENDIX

Guido Guinizelli, Canzone 5, (last two stanzas) lines 41–60

"In Heavenly Spirits
God the Creator reflects himself
more than does the sun in our eyes resplend;
that Spirit who his nature conceives
to be above the Spheres, as to Heaven he aspires,
naturally obeys Him
and, thus, quickly achieves the sweet fulfillment
of God's just will.
Likewise, woman in her beauty
should the truth reveal
which shines forth from her eyes,
to him who in her love
never deflects from her service due.

When before God, my soul shall stand,
'A mere woman', he will ask, 'did you presume
eternal?
You crossed the heavens and up to me you came
all the while yourself deceiving
in empty love.
To me alone the praise is due
and to the queen of the eternal kingdom;
cease thus your vain deceit.'
I will then say: 'An angel she appeared to me
of thine own kingdom,
it was not with fault that I fell in love with her.'"
(trans. G. Erasmi)

Bibliography

Bandopadhyaya, M., *Kāmāyanī* (New Delhi: Ankur Publishing House, 1978).

Basu, A., "Kāshmir Śaivism," *The Cultural Heritage of India,* Vol. IV (Calcutta: The Ramakrishna Mission Institute of Culture, 1956).

Beck, Lois, and Kiddie, Nikki, eds., *Women in the Muslim World* (Cambridge, Mass.: Harvard University Press, 1978).

Bharati, A., *The Tantric Tradition* (London: Rider and Company, 1969).

Bharati, Sushila (trans. and ed.), *Kāmāyanī* (Hyderabad: Milinda Prakasan, 1966).

Bhattacharyya, N. N., *History of the Tantric Religion* (New Delhi: Manohar Publishers, 1982).

Carmody, Denise L., *Feminism and Christianity: A Two-Way Reflection* (Nashville: Abingdon Press, 1982).

Chakravarty, C., *The Tantras: Studies on Their Religion and Literature* (Calcutta: Punthi Pustak, 1963).

Chatterjee, J. C., *Kāshmir Śaivism* (Srinagar: Kashmir Series of Texts and Studies, 1911).

Christ, Carol P., and Plaskow, Judith, *Woman Spirit Rising: A Feminist Reader in Religion* (San Francisco: Harper & Row, 1979).

Collins, Sheila D., *A Different Heaven and Earth* (Valley Forge, Pa.: Judson Press, 1974).

Cowell, E. B., and A. E. Gough (trans. and ed.), *Sarvadarśana-saṁgraha* (London: Kegan Paul, Trench, Trubner and Co., Ltd., 1904).

Daly, Mary, *Beyond God the Father* (Boston: Beacon Press, 1973).

Daly, Mary, *Gyn/Ecology* (Boston: Beacon Press, 1978).

De Sales, Francis, *Introduction to the Devout Life* (New York: Image Books, 1972).

Falk, Nancy, and Gross, Rita M., *Unspoken Worlds: Women's Lives in Non-Western Cultures* (New York: Harper & Row, 1980).

Fernea, Elizabeth W., and Bezirgan, Basima Q., ed., *Middle Eastern Women Speak* (Austin: University of Texas Press, 1977).

Gross, Rita M., ed., *Beyond Androcentrism* (Missoula, Mont.: Scholars Press, 1977).

Grou, Jean, *Manual for Interior Souls* (London: Burns Oates & Washbourne Ltd., 1892).

Gupta, R. K., *Kāmāyanī para Kashmiri Śaiva darśana kā prabhāva* (Delhi: Rakesh Prakasan, 1976).

Harper, Steve, *John Wesley's Message for Today* (Michigan: Zondervan Corporation, 1983).

Hughson, S. C., *Spiritual Guidance* (New York: Holy Cross Press, 1948).

James, Janet Wilson, ed., *Women in American Religion* (Pennsylvania: University of Pennsylvania Press, 1976).

Jash, P., *History of Śaivism* (Calcutta: Roy and Chandhury, 1974).

Jones, Rufus M., *Pathways to the Reality of God* (New York: The Macmillan Company, 1931).

Kaw, R. K., *The Doctrine of Recognition* (Hosiarpur: Vishveshvaranand Institute, 1967).

Kelly, Thomas R., *A Testament of Devotion* (London: Harper & Brothers Pub., 1941).

Leidecker, K. R., (trans.), *Pratyabhijñāhrdaryam* (Madras: The Adyar Library, 1938).

Maimonides, Moses, *The Guide for the Perplexed* (New York: Dover Publications, Inc., 1956).

McNamara, William, *The Art of Being Human* (New York: The Bruce Publishing Company, 1962).

Plaskow, Judith and Romero, Joan A., eds., *Women and Religion* (Missoula, Mont.: Scholars Press, 1974).

Prasad, Jayashankar, *Kāmāyanī* (Allahabad: Bharati Bhandara, 1964–65).

Rosaldo, Michaelle, and Lamphere, Louise, eds., *Woman, Culture and Society* (Stanford: Stanford University Press, 1974).

Ruether, Rosemary, *New Woman, New Earth* (New York: Seabury Press, 1975).

Ruether, Rosemary, ed., *Religion and Sexism: Images of Women in the Jewish and Christian Traditions* (New York: Simon and Schuster, 1974).

Sadani, J. K., (trans.), *Kāmāyanī* (Calcutta: Rupa and Co., 1975).

St. John of the Cross, *The Collected Works of St. John of the Cross,* trans. Kieran Kavanaugh and Otilio Rodriguez (Washington, D.C.: ICS Publications, 1979).

Sanders, E. K., *Sainte Chantal* (London: Society for Promoting Christian Knowledge, 1928).

Shah, R. C., *Jaishankar Prasad* (New Delhi: Sahitya Adademi, 1978).

Singh, J. D. (trans. and ed.), *Introduction to Śiva Sūtras: The Yoga of Supreme Identity* (Delhi: Motilal Banarsidass, 1979).

Spretnak, Charlene, ed., *The Politics of Women's Spirituality* (Garden City, New York: Anchor Press, 1982).

Stagg, Evelyn, and Stagg, Frank, *Women in the World of Jesus* (Philadelphia: Westminster Press, 1978).

Stopp, Elisabeth, *Madame de Chantal, Portrait of a Saint* (London: Faber and Faber, 1962).

The Book of Discipline of the United Methodist Church 1980 (Tennessee: The United Methodist Publishing House, 1980).

Thompson, Francis, *Poetical Works* (London: Oxford University Press, 1969).

Underhill, Evelyn, *Mysticism* (New York: The World Publishing Company, 1967).

Vanderwall, Francis W., *Spiritual Direction: An Invitation to Abundant Life*, Foreward by Henri J. M. Nouwen (New York: Paulist Press, 1981).

Washbourn, Penelope, *Becoming Woman: The Quest for Spiritual Wholeness in Female Experience* (New York: Harper & Row, 1979).

Werblowsky, R. J. Zwi, "Women . . . And Other . . . Beasts" (A Review Article) *Numen* XXIX, fasc. 1 (July, 1982), pp. 123–131.

Wesley, John, *Selections from the Letters of John Wesley,* Living Selections from Great Devotional Classics, ed. J. Manning Potts (Tennessee: The Upper Room, 1951).

Wesley, John and Charles, *John and Charles Wesley, Selected Writings and Hymns,* The Classics of Western Spirituality, ed. Frank Whaling (New York: Paulist Press, 1981).

Wilson-Kastner, Patricia, *Faith, Feminism, and The Christ* (Philadelphia: Fortress, 1983).

Wilson-Kastner, Patricia, "The Once and Future Church: Women's Ordination in England," *The Christian Century* 100, no. 7 (Mar. 9, 1983), pp. 214–216.

Woodroffe, Sir J. G., *Shakti and Māyā* (Bombay: Oxford University Press, 1917).

Woodroffe, Sir J. G., *Shakti and Shakta* (New York: Dover Publications, Inc., 1978).

Zikmund, Barbara Brown, "Women in Ministry Face the '80's," *The Christian Century* 99, no. 4 (Feb. 3–10, 1982), pp. 113–115.

Contributors

RUTH TIFFANY BARNHOUSE, Professor of Psychiatry and Pastoral Care, Southern Methodist University, Dallas, Texas.

PASCALINE COFF, O.S.B., Executive Secretary, A.I.M. North American Board for East-West Dialogue, Sand Springs, Oklahoma.

EWERT H. COUSINS, Professor, Department of Theology, Fordham University, New York, New York.

GABRIELE ERASMI, Associate Professor, McMaster University, Canada.

PATRICIA E. GLEASON, Th. D. Candidate, Harvard Divinity School, Cambridge, Massachusetts.

BINA GUPTA, Associate Professor of Philosophy, Director, South Asia Language and Area Center, University of Missouri, Columbia, Missouri.

CHRISTOPHER J. LUCAS, Professor, Department of Higher and Adult Education, Director, Center for International Programs and Studies, University of Missouri, Columbia, Missouri.

EVELYN S. NEWMAN, Director, Chapel Ministries Inc., Protestant Chaplain, State University of New York at Stony Brook, Stony Brook, New York.

RICHARD PAYNE, President and Publisher, Amity House Publications, Inc., Editor in Chief, The Classics of Western Spirituality, Warwick, New York.

KRISHNA SIVARAMAN, Professor of Religious Studies, McMaster University, Canada.

THAIYAR M. SRINIVASAN, Visiting Professor, McMaster University, Canada.

HENRY O. THOMPSON, Associate Professor of Religion and Society, Unification Theological Seminary, Barrytown, New York.

Index

The index is of persons and major themes in the book, including those in references and footnotes. A number in brackets [ ] behind a page number refers to a footnote on that page. The numbers in **bold face** refer to pages written by the person indexed.

Nouwen, Henri J. M. 145, 154 [13], 225
Nykl, A. R. 219 [25]

O'Brien, Mary 196, 204 [39]
O'Connor, John 137 [16]
O'Connor, M. 181 [12]
O'Flaherty, Wendy 15 [6], 16 [8]
Ochshorn, Judith 185 [40]
Odell-Scott, David W. 174, 184 [34]
Orbicciani, Bonagiunta 217 [3]
Ornstein, Robert E. 111, 114 [6]
Orr, William F. 183 [27], 184 [33]
Otwell, H. 182 [20]

Painter, Sidney 218 [21], 219 [23]
Palacios, Miquel Asin 216, 217, 220 [40]
Parvati 4
Patanjali 107
patriarchal society 23–24
patriarchy, the Trinity and 38–39
Paul 21, 27, 89, 142, 148
Paul, Diana Mary 185 [39]
Paul, Diana Y. 35 [22]
Payne, Richard 12, **51–70,** 226
Pendleton, William 167
Peterson, Sarah 204 [43]
Petrarch 217, 220 [46]
Petrocchi, Giorgio 217 [5], 218 [18], 220 [45]
Pfeiffer, Franz 50 [6]
philosophy, Hindu 87–103
Phipps, William E. 183 [24], 184 [37]
Piaget, Jean 180 [6]
Plaskow, Judith 222, 224
Plato 93
polar principles in yoga and tantra 106–114
polarity
  brain functioning and 111–112
  merging and 110–111
Potter, Karl 219 [29]
Potts, J. Manning 225
Prakasan, Milinda 86 [10]
Prasad, Jayashankar 79, 82–85, 86 [6], 224
psychobiology of yoga 106–108
psychology, love and 18–19
Pundit, M. P. 114 [3]

Quinn, Archbishop 36 [35, 37]
Quint, Joseph 50 [6]

Rahner, Karl 36 [35]
Ramakantha 75, 76
Ramakrishna 62
Rao, K. L. Seshagiri 185 [39]
Rasputin 59
Rauschenbusch, Walter 194, 195, 204 [34]
reality, ultimate 73–74
reason 178–179
receptivity, feminine quality of 20–23
Reed, Bruce 36 [34]
Reed, William L. 180 [2]
relationship, man-woman 116–202
religion 24–27
Rest, James R. 186 [43]
restoration, Unification theology of 198–202
Rice, Cyprian 219 [27]
Richard of St. Victor 44
Ricoeur, Paul 180 [2]
Ritter, Helmut 219 [32]
Robbins, Jerry K. 181 [7], 182 [15]
Robinson, H. Wheeler 183 [30]
Rodriguez, Otilio 154 [11], 224
Romero, Joan A. 224
Rosaldo, Michaelle 224
Rousseau, Richard W. 185 [40]
Ruether, Rosemary Radford 24, 35 [20, 28], 175, 180 [5], 184 [37, 38], 196, 204 [41], 224
Rumi, Persian poet 176–177
Ruprecht 50 [6]
Russell, Letty M. 184 [36]
Ruzbehan 216, 219 [32]
Ryan, Mary 204 [42]

Sadani, Jikishandas 86 [11], 224
Sahi, Jyoti 36 [38]
sakti and siva 75–85
Sanders, E. K. 154 [29–31, 37, 38], 183 [30], 224
Sariputra 25
Schaupp, Joan 35 [25]
Schillebeekx, Edward 180 [5], 182 [16]
Schleiermacher, Friedrich 204 [35]

Scholem Gershom 70 [7]
Schopenhauer, Arthur 84
Schram, Abner 185 [39]
Scroggs, Robin 170, 174, 181 [6], 183 [28], 184 [33, 36]
secular path to mysticism 207–217
sex
as sacrament 67–70
as sacred 63–67
sexuality in marriage 51–70
Shah, R. C. 224
Shaw, Anna Howard 186 [41]
Shuster, Nancy 35 [23]
Singh, J. D. 224
Siva 4
Sivaraman, Krishna 11, **87–103,** 226
Skanda 4
Slater, Philip 204 [40]
Smith, Amanda Berry 186 [41]
Smith, Jane I. 185 [39]
Smith, Michael A. 184 [38]
Socrates 182 [15]
speculation, Christian 116–136
Speiser, Ephraim 180 [5]
spiritual director, the role of the 139–153
spiritual formation 146–153
Spretnak, Charlene 224
Srinivasan, Thaiyar M. 10, 11, **106–114,** 115 [7], 226
Stagg, Evelyn 224
Stagg, Frank 224
Stanford, John 35 [8]
Steere, Douglas 22, 35 [13]
Stern, Karl 34 [1]
Stopp, Elizabeth 149, 159 [19, 21, 32–36, 39] 224
Storr, Anthony 137 [21]
Suchoki, Marjorie 180 [5]
Suso, Rhineland mystic 62
Sutherland, Harold 220 [40]
Swedenborg, Emanuel 167
Swidler, Arlene 185 [38]
Swidler, Leonard 182 [20], 183 [32], 185 [38, 39]
symbolism
Hindu 71–85
in Kāmāyanī 71–85
in Kāshmir Śaivism 71–85
masculine-feminine 71–85
sexual 59–63
symbols 33–34
Szikszai, Stephen 183 [31]
tantra and yoga 106–114
Tappen, Ruth M. 157, 180 [2]
Tavard, George 185 [38]
Teresa of Avila 125, 146, 149, 176
Tertullian 123, 175
Thales 182 [15]
Thiselton, Anthony 183 [29]
Thistlewaite, Susan Brocks 169, 183 [25]
Thomas, Hilah F. 184 [35]
Thompson, Francis 6, 155 [42], 183 [29], 186 [40], 224
Thompson, Henry O. **154–179,** 186 [43], 226
Thompson, Joyce E. 186 [43]
Tolbert, Mary Ann 182 [20]
tradition 175–177
Judeo-Christian 63–67
transformation 28
Trible, Phyllis 181 [6, 9, 10, 13] 182 [15, 20], 183 [23]
Trinity, the 37–49
Christian mysticism and 39–42
patriarchy and 38–39
Trobridge, George 182 [21]
Tzu, Lao 23, 35 [14]

Ulanov, Ann 18, 34 [5, 7], 35 [9]
Underhill, Evelyn 149, 154 [22, 23, 28], 225
Unification perspective on male-female relationship 187–202
unitary and bi-polar 73–74
United Methodism, sources of authority and 177
Upaniṣad, Bṛhadāraṇyaka 21
Uppsala 183 [31]

Vandenhoeck 50 [6]
Vanderwall, Francis W. 154 [13], 225
Vedanta, Advaita 90, 219 [29]
Victoria, Queen 158, 163
Vivekananda, Swami 114 [1]
Von Hugel, Baron 149
Von Rad, Gerhard 180 [3, 4, 5], 181 [7]
Vos, C. J. 182 [20]

Wahlberg, Rachel Conrad 184 [32]
Walker, William O. Jr. 184 [33]
Walther, James A. 183 [27], 184 [33]
Washbourn, Penelope 225
Wellhausen, Julius 180 [4]
Wesley, Charles 153 [2, 5], 154 [20], 225
Wesley, John 139–141, 143, 146, 153 [2, 5, 6, 8], 154 [20], 174, 177, 178, 184 [35], 223, 225
Whaling, Frank 140, 153 [2], 225
White, Alma 186 [41]
White, John 115 [8]
White, Mollie Alma Bridwell 177
wholeness 28
Widengren, George 183 [31]
Wiebke, Walther 185 [39]
Wigner, Eugene 114
William, Deane 205 [46]
William, John Alden 219 [28, 34]
Williams, James G. 182 [20]
Williams, R. J. 182 [16]
Wilson-Kastner, Patricia 225
Woodroffe, J. G. 225
Woodward, Kenneth 34 [7]
Wright, G. Ernest 180 [2], 183 [26]

yang and yin 17–18
yoga and tantra 106–114

Zaehner, R. C. 89
Zerner, Ruth 183 [29]
Zikmund, Barbara Brown 225
Zimmerli, Walther 183 [30]
Zolla, Elemire 20, 35 [8]